Frames of Justice

Frames of Justice

Implications for Social Policy

Leroy H. Pelton

Transaction Publishers
New Brunswick (U.S.A.) and London (U.K.)

Copyright © 2005 by Transaction Publishers, New Brunswick, New Jersey.

All rights reserved under International and Pan-American Copyright Conventions. No part of this book may be reproduced or transmitted in any form or by any means, electronic or mechanical, including photocopy, recording, or any information storage and retrieval system, without prior permission in writing from the publisher. All inquiries should be addressed to Transaction Publishers, Rutgers—The State University, 35 Berrue Circle, Piscataway, New Jersey 08854-8042. www.transactionpub.com

This book is printed on acid-free paper that meets the American National Standard for Permanence of Paper for Printed Library Materials.

Library of Congress Catalog Number: 2004062103
ISBN: 0-7658-0296-1
Printed in the United States of America

Library of Congress Cataloging-in-Publication Data

Pelton, Leroy H.
    Frames of justice : implications for social policy / Leroy H. Pelton.
      p. cm.
    Includes bibliographical references and index.
    ISBN 0-7658-0296-1 (cloth : alk. paper)
     1. Social justice. 2. Social policy. 3. Religion and sociology. I. Title.

HM671.P45   2005
303.3'72—dc22   2004062103

To my dear sister,

Marjorie

Contents

Preface	ix
1. Biblical Justice	1
2. Nonviolence and Liberal Philosophy	25
3. Principle and Sentiment	43
4. Social Science and Public Policy	59
5. Need, Desert, and Nondiscrimination	73
6. Justice and Social Policy	99
7. Frame Politics	137
8. Faith and Reason	169
References	207
Name Index	215
Subject Index	219

Preface

This book is about justice and social policy. I begin by examining the Bible to ascertain the fundamental ways in which human beings construe justice. I find three major frames of justice reflected there: group justice, individual desert, and life affirmation. Each of the frames has its distinct implications for social policy, and all contemporary social policies reflect one or more of the three frames. These frames of justice, in turn, have their origins in a universal sense of justice.

This book is devoted to analyzing these frames and their implications for social policy. I compare and contrast the philosophies of nonviolence and liberalism for the purpose of elucidating the differences between the desert and life-affirmation frames. I attempt to unravel the complex relationships between principle, sentiment, reason, justice and its frames, and social policy.

Since social science research is widely used to inform public policy, I examine its problematic relationship to justice and its frames in policymaking. Social policy scholars have focused far more on the effectiveness of policies—and this largely in terms of statistical outcomes reflecting aggregate data analyses—than they have on their justice. This book is an attempt to redirect the attention of the social policy literature to the question of justice and social policy, and to the examination of the relation of outcomes and their conceptualizations to matters of justice.

I explore how all three frames of justice, for better or worse, give direction to current social policy, and devote particular attention to the social policy implications of the life-affirmation frame. I also discuss political strategies in relation to the frames, since it is politically possible, at certain times, to shift the frames from which policies will flow.

There is demonstrable evidence, all too abundant, that human beings are capable of enormous and unlimited evil. Much of it is done in the name of desert, rationalized in terms of desert, and even driven by justice construed as desert. The notion of desert, in religion, philosophy, and social policy, is scrutinized throughout this book. It is contrasted with the principle of life affirmation and is examined in the context of the moral question of the relationship between means and ends.

A special note concerning my use of the Bible, and later the Koran, is necessary here. Although I know that I started this project by wanting to identify the fundamental conceptions of justice that inform and shape social policy, I recall less clearly what led to my decision to seek these frames of justice, or policy frames, in the Bible. But while writing my previous book, *Doing Justice*, in which my focus was on examining group constructs reflected in social policy, I developed an increasing fascination, even obsession, with the plea for justice that Abraham makes to God concerning the fate of the inhabitants of Sodom and Gomorrah. I was also aware, since the time of writing my first book, *The Psychology of Nonviolence*, that Mohandas Gandhi was influenced by the Sermon on the Mount in his development of the philosophy of nonviolence. Moreover, a strong influence on my deep concern with justice has been my own group heritage. The roots of this influence lie in the Holocaust, but also in the focus on the affirmation of life and pursuit of justice found in so many parts of Jewish tradition.

Some biblical scholars may resent my intrusion into their territory. They may point out that I have no credentials specific to their field, or that I am not familiar with the many alternative methods with which biblical scholars approach their work. Scholars of the Koran may argue that this text loses much in its translation from the Arabic (presumably more so than the Jewish Bible in its translation from the Hebrew, or the New Testament in its translation from the Greek), and that many of its statements are subject to multiple translations, as well as interpretations.

My study of this literature is quite limited and narrow of purpose: to determine the frames of justice that might be reflected there. Moreover, while the commentary about the Bible is vast, the Bible itself (as well as the Koran) is quite circumscribed and accessible. I agree with the scholars who insist that everyone has the right to read and interpret the Bible directly, without the intercession of others' interpretations. Alan Dershowitz provides a particularly eloquent defense of this position in his book, *The Genesis of Justice* (2000, pp. 9-11, 18-20). Leo Tolstoy (1885), in fact, recommended this as the best way to proceed. My personal view is that the Bible is a marvelous reflection of, or window into, the human mind, particularly in regard to the human mind's constructions concerning justice, ethics, community, and the meaning and purpose of human existence. Since the Bible is one place where individuals have concerned themselves with such questions, it is a source of abundant data regarding the conceptual structures of justice that arise through the human mind's interaction with the world. It did, in fact, prove to be a good starting point for my analysis of human conceptions of justice and their policy implications, and for not only identifying, but also illustrating through quotation from its wondrous stories and prose, the three major frames of justice reflected there.

Scholars contend that different parts of the Bible originated at different times, that it is the work of many authors and redactors, and even that different parts of the same statements, such as those attributed to Jesus, may have been written at different times and by different authors. But in analyzing the Bible for frames of justice, my concern is less with what Jesus himself, for example, might have said or meant, than with the principles themselves that the statements suggest, and the implications of such principles for social policy development.

The conclusions I draw within the first chapter are certainly open to challenge. But I have presented my case, and the burden shifts to those who would dispute my claims to present support for their own specific challenges. My central conclusion in chapter 1 is that three distinct frames of justice, which I describe, are documented in the Bible. Later in the book, I conclude that these same three frames are documented in the Koran. Given the evidence that I present, I believe that these conclusions would be extremely difficult to deny. In chapter 1, I also assert that there is no evidence of a genesis or development from one frame to another in the Bible. The gaps in our knowledge concerning the genesis of the Bible itself, noted above, present a problem not for this verdict of "not proven," but for those who might be inclined to dispute it. Moreover, I present some evidence to support my assertions that these frames have their origins in a universal sense of justice that, together with the three frames, have existed in human minds from time immemorial. All three frames continue to coexist within the human mind, and are manifested in both inter- and intragroup relations. The salience of one policy frame over another at particular times and in particular places is influenced by a variety of factors, but open to human choice.

I borrow the notion of policy frames from Donald Schön and Martin Rein in their book, *Frame Reflection* (1994), although I impart different meaning to the term, as frames of justice. Chapter 1, "Biblical Justice," was originally published, under the same title, in the *Journal of the American Academy of Religion*, December 2003, Vol. 71, No. 4, pp. 737-765. Chapter 4, "Social Science and Public Policy," was originally published under the title of "Misinforming Public Policy: The Illiberal Uses of Social Science," in *Society*, July/August 2000, Vol. 37, No. 5, pp. 61-69. Both are reprinted here with permission and with changes only in punctuation and in the manner of citing references. Portions of the last subsection (on foreign policy) of chapter 6 are taken from my book, *Doing Justice* (State University of New York Press, 1999), and are reprinted with the publisher's permission. I am grateful to the University of Nevada, Las Vegas for awarding me a faculty development leave for the spring semester of 2003, during which time I completed a significant portion of this book.

All references in this book to the writings that are contained in the Tanakh (the Hebrew or Jewish Bible) are to the Jewish Publication Society (1985). All references to the New Testament are to *The Holy Bible: King James Version* (1991). All references to the Koran are to Dawood (1999).

1

Biblical Justice

In biblical times, we are told, Samuel relayed the Lord's command to Saul, king of Israel: "I am exacting the penalty for what Amalek did to Israel, for the assault he made upon them on the road, on their way up from Egypt. Now go, attack Amalek, and proscribe [put to death] all that belongs to him. Spare no one, but kill alike men and women, infants and sucklings, oxen and sheep, camels and asses!" (I Samuel 15:1-2; translated in Jewish Publication Society, 1985). Hence Saul enlisted an army of more than 200,000 men and destroyed the city of Amalek, putting all the people to the sword. But he spared King Agag, and the best of the sheep and oxen (I Samuel 15:4-9). Therefore the Lord said to Samuel: "I regret that I made Saul king, for he has turned away from Me and has not carried out My commands" (I Samuel 15:10-11). Two centuries earlier, at the time of the Amalekites' offending deed, God had said to Moses: "Inscribe this in a document as a reminder, and read it aloud to Joshua: I will utterly blot out the memory of Amalek from under heaven!" (Exodus 17:14) Thus, we may say, the sins of the parents were to be visited even upon generations yet unborn, and they were.

Group Justice and Individual Justice

This, of course, was not the first instance of group justice in the Tanakh (the Jewish Bible, or Old Testament, which includes the Torah, or Five Books of Moses [Pentateuch]), nor would it be the last. Early on, God decided to destroy by flood all of animal and humankind, except for Noah and his family and the animals he was instructed to take on board his ark, because "God saw how corrupt the earth was, for all flesh had corrupted its ways on earth" (Genesis 6:12). In delivering the Israelites from slavery in Egypt, God visited plagues upon Egyptians without differentiation among them, culminating in the slaying of all of the Egyptian first-born, "from the first-born of Pharaoh who sat on the throne to the first-born of the captive who was in the dungeon" (Exodus 12:29).

In Deuteronomy, it is said: "When the Lord your God brings you to the land that you are about to enter and possess, and He dislodges many nations before you—the Hittites, Girgashites, Amorites, Canaanites, Perizzites, Hivites, and Jebusites, seven nations much larger than you—and the Lord your God delivers them to you and you defeat them, you must doom them to destruction: grant them no terms and give them no quarter" (7:1-2). And it is said further, in regard to them, "...you shall not let a soul remain alive" (20:16). God will "wipe out" (9:3) the Anakites, and it is "because of the wickedness" of all of these nations that God is dispossessing them (9:4).

When Joshua led his troops in the attack on Jericho, they "exterminated everything in the city with the sword: man and woman, young and old, ox and sheep and ass" (Joshua 6:21). They took no prisoners at Ai; all the inhabitants of that city were exterminated (Joshua 8:26). Joshua continued in this manner, until they conquered most of the country (Joshua 10-11). David, in his time, fought countless battles and slew tens of thousands: "When David attacked a region, he would leave no man or woman alive" (I Samuel 27:9). Yet, as king, we are told, "David executed true justice among all his people" (II Samuel 8:15).

Indeed, we are to assume that the justice that David executed "among all his people" must have been of an individual form. In fact, in the Tanakh there are numerous clearly stated precepts regarding individual justice and prohibiting the violation of individuals, and these statements constitute quite an elaborate policy network of justice. The famous Ten Commandments prohibit murder, stealing, bearing false witness against another person, and even so much as coveting another person's possessions (Exodus 20:13-14). Later in Exodus it is said that a stranger (within the community) must not be wronged or oppressed (22:20). One must not convey false rumors (23:1). One must not go along with the mighty (or multitude) to do wrong, or pervert one's testimony in favor of the mighty in a dispute, or "show deference to a poor man in his dispute" (23:2-3). The rights of the needy in their disputes must not be subverted (23:6).

When a man reaps the harvest of his field, he "shall not reap all the way to the edges of the field, or gather the gleanings" of his harvest (Leviticus 19:9). Neither shall he pick his vineyard bare or gather the fallen fruit of his vineyard, for "you shall leave them for the poor and the stranger" (19:10). "You shall not defraud your fellow," commit robbery, "insult the deaf, or place a stumbling block before the blind," render an unfair decision, favor the poor or show deference to the rich, "deal basely with your countrymen," "hate your kinsfolk in your heart," or "take vengeance or bear a grudge against your countrymen" (19:13-18). One must use an honest balance and weights, and not falsify measures (19:35-36).

Moreover, it is written: "If...there is a needy person among you...do not harden your heart and shut your hand against your needy kinsman. Rather, you must open your hand and lend him sufficient for whatever he needs...open your hand to the poor and needy kinsman in your land" (Deuteronomy 15:7-8, 11). Deuteronomy also says: "You shall not judge unfairly: you shall show no partiality; you shall not take bribes... Justice, justice shall you pursue..." (16:19-20). Procedural safeguards are established, for example: "A single witness may not validate against a person any guilt or blame for any offense that may be committed; a case can be valid only on the testimony of two witnesses or more" (19:15). It is also written: "When you make a loan of any sort to your countryman, you must not enter his house to seize his pledge. You must remain outside, while the man to whom you made the loan brings the pledge out to you" (24:10-11). In fact, if the debtor is a poor man and has given you as security a garment he wears to protect him while he sleeps, then you must return this pledge when the sun goes down (24:12-13). Furthermore: "You shall not abuse a needy and destitute laborer, whether a fellow countryman or a stranger in one of the communities of your land," and you "must pay him his wages on the same day, before the sun sets..." (24:14-15).

Yet this individual justice is the justice of desert, violations of which, in other words, have consequences. Already to Noah God had confided that He would "require a reckoning for human life, of every man for that of his fellow man" (Genesis 9:5) and that "Whoever sheds the blood of man, by man shall his blood be shed" (Genesis 9:6). In Exodus it is said: "He who fatally strikes a man shall be put to death" (21:12), unless he did not do so by design (21:13). He who strikes his father or mother, or even insults one of them, shall be put to death (21:15, 17). He who kidnaps a man shall be put to death (21:16). Also: "When a man steals an ox or a sheep, and slaughters it or sells it, he shall pay five oxen for the ox, and four sheep for the sheep" (21:37). A thief "must make restitution; if he lacks the means, he shall be sold for his theft" (22:2). But if the animal he stole is found alive in his possession, then he shall pay double, meaning that he must return the animal and give an additional one as a fine (22:3; Hertz, 1972, p. 311). He who starts a fire that destroys another's property must make restitution (22:5).

In Deuteronomy, it is said: A "wayward and defiant son" who does not obey his parents and who is "a glutton and a drunkard" shall be brought to the attention of the community by his parents and put to death (21:18-21). If it is found that a man, after marrying a woman, has falsely accused her of not having been a virgin, then he shall be flogged, shall be fined a 100 shekels of silver to be given to the girl's father, and lose the right ever to divorce her (22:13-19). However, if the charge proves true, then the girl shall be stoned to death (22:20-21). When a dispute between men is decided in a court of law, then if the guilty one is to be flogged, he shall be given lashes "by count, as his guilt warrants," up to but not more than forty lashes (25:1-3).

The law of the "talion" regarding individual desert is first stated in Exodus this way: "When men fight, and one of them pushes a pregnant woman and a miscarriage results, but no other damage ensues, the one responsible shall be fined.... But if other damage ensues, the penalty shall be life for life, eye for eye, tooth for tooth, hand for hand, foot for foot, burn for burn, wound for wound, bruise for bruise" (21:22-24). Many scholars have pointed out that the "eye for an eye" principle was meant to reduce the severe disproportionality of punishment and that there is little evidence that even such precise tit for tat was ever actually carried out under law in the Israelite community except in regard to punishment for murder. The important point for our purposes is that this principle in any case involves the justice of desert.

It would be tempting to conclude that group justice is reserved for outside groups (save for the stranger within the community), whereas the justice of individual desert is applied to relations within the group and community. This, however, would be an incomplete picture. The famous story of Job expresses the timeless human longing for or belief in a just world, in which people get what they deserve and deserve what they get. Job insists that he did nothing to deserve the disasters and tragedies visited upon him, while to onlookers, the very fact of these calamities proves that Job has not been as righteous as he claims to be. One of them insists that God "pays a man according to his actions, and provides for him according to his conduct" (Job 34:11). Job's riches are finally restored to him. But what is often overlooked in this story is that his previous children, all of whom were destroyed, are not brought back to life and did not get what *they* deserved. Indeed, they merely were enlisted as props in an object lesson. Collective punishment is presumably carried out with no regard for the lives of the others in the collectivity except as vehicles for the deepening of the punishment or suffering to be felt by the prime subject.

Already in the Ten Commandments it is said that "I the Lord your God am an impassioned God, visiting the guilt of the parents upon the children, upon the third and upon the fourth generations of those who reject Me, but showing kindness to the thousandth generation of those who love Me and keep My commandments" (Exodus 20:5-6). Thus, punishment as well as benefits would accrue to future generations on the basis of the blameworthiness or praiseworthiness of their ancestors—a form of group justice.

It is true that later in the Torah it is written, "...do not bring death on those who are innocent and in the right..." (Exodus 23:7) and "Parents shall not be put to death for children, nor children be put to death for parents: a person shall be put to death only for his own crime" (Deuteronomy 24:16). Yet much later in the Tanakh, when Jeroboam became king of Israel and made two golden calves for the people to worship (I Kings 12:28), God vowed: "I will sweep away the House of Jeroboam utterly, as dung is swept away" (I Kings 14:10). Then, because King Baasha of Israel (who was the instrument through which God destroyed the House of Jeroboam, not sparing "a single soul") "followed the ways of Jeroboam," God vowed to sweep away his house also, and this was carried out by Zimri, who killed him and "did not leave a single male of his, nor any kinsman or friend...in accordance with the word that the Lord had spoken" (I Kings 15:29-34; 16:1-13). But because King Ahab of Israel repented for crimes that he had committed, God decided not to destroy his house in his lifetime; rather, "I will bring the disaster upon his house in his son's time" (I Kings 21).

Even so, God says through the prophet Jeremiah that "every one shall die for his own sins" and again through the prophet Ezekiel: "The person who sins, only he shall die" (Jeremiah 31:30; Ezekiel 18:4). Here (in Ezekiel 18) God gets very emphatic and specific about this and goes on to speak of repentance—even the wicked one will not die if he repents of all his sins and does what is right and just from thereon. God gets defensive about His laws: "Yet you say, 'The way of the Lord is unfair.' Listen, O House of Israel: Is My way unfair? It is your ways that are unfair!" (Ezekiel 18:25) Bewilderingly, only a few pages later, God is claimed to say: "I will wipe out from you both the righteous and the wicked" (Ezekiel 21:8).

In Numbers 16, Korah, Dathan, and Abiram "rise up" against Moses, together with 250 "chieftains of the community," protesting his leadership (16:1-3). When Korah "gathered the whole community" against Moses and Aaron, God said to Moses and Aaron: "Stand back from this community that I may annihilate them in an instant" (16:21). But they said, "When one man sins, will You be wrathful with the whole community?" (16:22). So God told Moses to instruct the community to withdraw from around the abodes of Korath, Dathan, and Abiram, and Moses said to the community: "Move away from the tents of these wicked men...lest you be wiped out for all their sins" (16:26). It is written: "Now Dathan and Abiram had come out and they stood at the entrance of their tents, with their wives, their children, and their little ones" (16:27). Suddenly, "the ground under them burst asunder, and the earth opened its mouth and swallowed them up with their households, all Korah's people and all their possessions" (16:31-32).

In Numbers 17, "the whole Israelite community railed against Moses and Aaron, saying, 'You two have brought death upon the Lord's people!'" (17:6) God once again threatens to annihilate the entire community "in an instant." Then Aaron "ran to the midst of the congregation, where the plague had begun amongst the people" and he "put on the incense and made expiation for the people; he stood between the dead and the living until the plague was checked," but 14,700 had already died (17:8-14).

Earlier, when the Israelites built a golden calf to worship at Mount Sinai, God said to Moses: "Now, let Me be, that My anger may blaze forth against them and that I may destroy them, and make of you a great nation" (Exodus 32:10). Moses pleaded with God: "Turn from Your blazing anger, and renounce the plan to punish Your people" (32:12). And Moses' plea was successful, for God renounced the punishment He had planned (32:14). Yet this is not the end of the matter. When Moses came down from the mountain and saw the calf for himself, he became enraged, and he ordered the Levites to "go back and forth from gate to gate throughout the camp, and slay brother, neighbor, and kin" (32:27). Some 3,000 were killed. God then said to Moses: "He who has sinned against Me, him only will I erase from My record" (32:33). But: "Then the Lord sent a plague upon the people" (32:35). Are we to assume that the plague distinguished between those who sinned and those who did not? The Torah is silent on this point.

There are many other passages to indicate that group justice was to be applied to the Israelites themselves and not only to other groups: "If you hear it said, of one of the towns that the Lord your God is giving you to dwell in, that some scoundrels from among you have gone and subverted the inhabitants of their town, saying, 'Come let us worship other gods'...you shall investigate and inquire and interrogate thoroughly" (Deuteronomy 13:13-15). And if the fact can be established, "put the inhabitants of that town to the sword... Doom it and all that is in it to destruction..." (Deuteronomy 13:16). When, and because, King David "sinned" by ordering a census to be taken of the people, God sent a pestilence upon Israel, and 70,000 people died prior to David's plea of the obvious, that he alone was guilty (II Samuel 24).

Finally, there is little doubt that the elaborate and strangely eloquent blessings and curses in the Torah refer to consequences that God will impose on the Israelites as a group. In Leviticus it is said: "If you follow My laws and faithfully observe My commandments, I will grant your rains in their season, so that the earth shall yield its produce and the trees of the field their fruit...you shall eat your fill of bread and dwell securely in your land.... But...if you reject My laws and spurn My rules...I in turn will do this to you: I will wreak misery upon you...you shall be routed by your enemies, and your foes shall dominate you.... I will loose wild beasts against you, and they shall bereave you of your children and wipe out your cattle...and if you withdraw into your cities, I will send pestilence among you, and you shall be delivered into enemy hands.... You shall eat the flesh of your sons and the flesh of your daughters.... I will lay your cities in ruin...I will make the land desolate, so that your enemies who settle in it shall be appalled by it. And you I will scatter among the nations, and I will unsheath the sword against you" (26:3-33).

Again in Deuteronomy, God's blessings (7:12-24; 11:22-25; 28:1-14) and curses (11:17; 28:15-68) are enumerated (by Moses) as the desert of obedience or disobedience to God. But again, they are group oriented. If the Israelites obey God and faithfully observe all His commandments (and these concern not only ethics, but also rituals and obedience to God), then they shall be granted abounding prosperity (28:1-14). But if they do not heed the Lord, they shall be cursed in the city and in the country, and in their comings and goings. The Lord will let loose against them "calamity, panic, and frustration in all the enterprises you undertake, so that you shall soon be utterly wiped out." The Lord will strike them with "consumption, fever, and inflammation, with scorching heat and drought, with blight and mildew," and put them to rout before their enemies: "Though you take much seed out to the field, you shall gather in little, for the locust shall consume it.... Though you beget sons and daughters, they shall not remain with you, for they shall go into captivity.... The Lord will bring a nation against you from afar...a ruthless nation, that will show the old no regard and the young no mercy.... [T]he Lord will inflict extraordinary plagues upon you and your offspring... You shall be left a scant few... The Lord will scatter you among all the peoples... Yet even among those nations you shall find no peace..." (28:15-65).

However, after all of this, if "you return to the Lord your God," then He "will restore your fortunes and take you back in love... He will bring you together again from all the peoples where the Lord your God has scattered you" (Deuteronomy 30:1-3). And Moses concluded: "I have put before you life and death, blessing and curse. Choose life..." (Deuteronomy 30:19).

A Sense of Justice

Yet all of this is preceded—on the order of centuries, if we are to take the Bible literally—by one of the most incredible verbal exchanges between God and man concerning justice in all of the Bible: that pertaining to the fate of Sodom and Gomorrah (although much later, as we have seen, Moses and Aaron were also willing to argue with God over the nature of justice). God begins by saying to Himself: "Shall I hide from Abraham what I am about to do... For I have singled him out, that he may instruct his children and his posterity to keep the way of the Lord by doing what is just and right..." (Genesis 18:17-19). He then says: "The outrage of Sodom and Gomorrah is so great, and their sin so grave!" (18:20). Abraham comes forward and says: "Will You sweep away the innocent [or righteous] along with the guilty [or wicked]? What if there should be fifty innocent within the city; will You then wipe out the place and not forgive it for the sake of the innocent fifty who are in it? Far be it from You to do such a thing, to bring death upon the innocent as well as the guilty, so that innocent and guilty fare alike. Far be it from You! Shall not the Judge of all the earth deal justly?" (18:23-25)

God responds by conceding that if He finds fifty innocent ones within the city of Sodom, then He "will forgive the whole place for their sake" (Genesis 18:26). Abraham then proceeds to bargain Him down to forty-five, then to forty, then to thirty, then to twenty, and finally to ten. Each time, God concedes that He will "not destroy" the whole city for the sake of the proposed number of innocents (18:27-32). It has been debated why Abraham did not attempt to bargain all the way to one, as individual justice would require. But it is reasonable to assume that when faced with the awesome power of an angry God, a man who knows himself to be "but dust and ashes" (18:27) might be inclined to press his luck only so far. The gist and trend of Abraham's argument indicates that he possessed what we might call a "sense of justice" and that this sense of justice recognized that justice is an individual matter, that justice must pertain to individuals. Moreover, Abraham must have assumed that God has a similar sense of justice, proof of which is that he attempted to appeal to it. And God verifies this assumption by responding positively to each of Abraham's pleas. Yet even earlier, in Noah's time, after the Flood, God reveals His sense of justice by vowing "never again" to "doom the earth because of man," or to "ever again destroy every living being, as I have done" (Genesis 8:21).

At the outset of this startling verbal exchange between God and Abraham, as we have seen, God wonders whether or not He should tell Abraham what He is about to do. Perhaps He hesitates not out of belief that what He is about to do is just (in which case there would be no reason to "hide" it from Abraham), but rather, because He knows it to be unjust. Alternatively, we can view His willingness to enter into a debate with Abraham as a preconceived effort to help Abraham to develop and refine his own grasp of justice so that he may be better able to instruct his offspring in keeping "the way of the Lord by doing what is just and right." In the end, however, God does destroy Sodom and Gomorrah and "all the inhabitants" (Genesis 19:23-25). Because it is reasonable to assume that at the least—even if we were to grant that all of the adults were "wicked"—there must have been babies living within the cities, we must believe that God pushed ahead with group justice despite Abraham's pleas and even despite His own sense of individual justice. It seems that His passion overcame his sense of justice, and determined His actions. This should not surprise us, for these same struggles between principle and sentiment go on in human minds, such as those that created the Bible.

The argument that Abraham formulates is one that opposes group justice, but no argument is made against the destruction of the guilty individuals. Will You sweep away the righteous *along with* the wicked? Abraham asks. We cannot know from his words whether he believes in capital punishment or even in the more general justice of desert (should people, in turn, be violated for their crimes?) or whether he has simply decided to put forth the most expedient argument, believing that God holds to the justice of desert.

A sense of justice is revealed within the region even prior to the Ten Commandments and outside of the Torah. One example is the Hammurabi Code (circa 1750 BCE). But this code, as does the Torah, reveals the value it places on life by prohibiting murder, on the one hand, and prescribing the penalty of death, on the other (Article 153, in Edwards, 1904/1971). The law of the talion is also clearly expressed here in the literal form of an eye for an eye (Article 196) and a tooth for a tooth (Article 200: "If a man has knocked out the teeth of a man of the same rank, his own teeth shall be knocked out"). In this code, a man who has killed someone else's daughter faces the penalty of his own daughter being put to death (Articles 209-210), a form of group justice. But, in addition, the penalty of death may apply to theft and home invasion (Articles 8-10, 21).

Most interestingly, the Hammurabi Code concludes with a form of the group-oriented blessings and curses evident in the Torah. If any successor of Hammurabi, "the king of justice," does not heed his words, then may the gods allot him "years of famine...the dispersion of his people..." May the gods "devastate his land...annihilate his people...obstruct his rivers at their sources, and prevent the growth of corn, the life of men, in his land." May the gods "take away from him the rains of heaven, and dry up the outflow of springs...waste his territory with want and famine...burn up his people like a wisp of rushes...curse him with deadly curses, his reign, his land, his officers, his people, and his soldiers" (in Edwards, 1904/1971, pp. 75-80).

Thus, in the Hammurabi Code, as sometimes in the Torah, the value placed on the nonviolation of human life is revealed in the very edicts prescribing severe forms of desert and group justice, and the value to be protected or upheld is contradictorily violated in the consequences prescribed.

The Principle of Life Affirmation

This reverence for human life, *but without condition, judgment, or exception*, arguably has been most eloquently expressed in the words attributed to Jesus Christ in the Sermon on the Mount (*The Holy Bible: King James Version*, 1991; Matthew 5-7; Luke 6:17-49) and other parts of the New Testament. Here I will refer to it as the principle of life affirmation. This perspective can be construed as nonjudgmental from such statements as "Judge not..." (Matthew 7:1), and "He that is without sin...let him cast a stone" (John 8:7). It can be construed as unconditional, and therefore contrary to a desert perspective, from such statements as: "Ye have heard that it hath been said, An eye for an eye, and a tooth for a tooth: But I say unto you, That ye resist not evil: but whoever shall smite thee on thy right cheek, turn to him the other also" (Matthew 5:38-39). Finally, it can be construed as exceptionless from such statements as: "Love your enemies, bless them that curse you, do good to them that hate you, and pray for them which despitefully use you, and persecute you..." (Matthew 5:43-44).

Although these words attributed to Jesus have often been regarded as constituting a radical, even revolutionary, departure from the Tanakh, many modern biblical commentators have argued that most if not all of the precepts expressed there have specific roots in the Tanakh (Allison, 1999, pp. xi, 94, 100; Worth, 1997). They have done so by identifying parallel quotations with similar probable meanings in scattered Tanakh verses. For instance, in Exodus it is said that if one encounters his enemy's ox or ass wandering, then he must take it back to him (23:4). In fact: "When you see the ass of your enemy lying under its burden and would refrain from raising it, you must nevertheless raise it with him" (Exodus 23:5). In Isaiah it is said: "I offered my back to the floggers, and my cheeks to those who tore out my hair. I did not hide my face from insult and spittle" (50:6). In Psalms the speaker notes that "malicious witnesses repay me evil for good," yet when they were ill, the speaker mourned, fasted, and was saddened as though the inflicted were the speaker's friend, brother, or mother

(35:11-14). In Proverbs it is said: "If your enemy is hungry, give him bread to eat; if he is thirsty, give him water to drink" (25:21). Indeed, it can be said that these precepts are reflected more generally in the "Love your fellow as yourself" statements in the Tanakh (e.g., Leviticus 19:18), and in "You shall love [the stranger who resides with you in your land] as yourself" (Leviticus 19:34).

Yet these plausible antecedents often stand in contradiction to other passages in the Tanakh. Furthermore, given a context consisting of other Tanakh statements already alluded to above, it is possible that "enemy" in the so-called parallel statements is meant to refer to one's individual enemies within the community and not to enemies without. One can argue that Jesus' statements are derivable from, but not explicit in, statements in the Old Testament. However, some biblical scholars have interpreted even Jesus' statements to apply only to personal enemies (according to Allison, 1999, p. 103; e.g., Worth, 1997, p. 117). Indeed, many Christian scholars have gone to great lengths to narrow the possible meaning and implications of the Sermon on the Mount, claiming that Jesus meant one or another statement to apply only to the courts, or only to personal affairs, or otherwise construing such statements as "turn the other cheek" and "judge not" within the narrowest possible contexts (see, e.g., Worth, 1997, pp. 117, 235-246; Carson, 1999, p. 54; Fox, 1989, p. 76). Leo Tolstoy, in his book, *What I Believe* (1885), takes to task the scholars of his time for reading into and distorting the sermon, thereby trivializing its meaning, rather than taking the words at their face value. In turn, some modern scholars have criticized Tolstoy for believing that the sermon has, and was meant to have, political implications. They point with condemnation especially to Tolstoy's conclusions from the sermon that the state should disband its army and abolish its courts (see, e.g., Allison, 1999, pp. 2, 8; Fox, 1989, p. 11).

In any event, no matter how much we can debate the extent to which Jesus' statements have parallels or roots in the Tanakh, expressions of the fundamental principle of reverence for human life without exception can be found in sources outside of the Tanakh, and even prior to it. In a Babylonian text that might have been composed as early as the 1600s BCE (see Klassen, 1984, p. 34), it is said: "Do not return evil to your adversary; Requite with kindness the one who does evil to you, Maintain justice for your enemy, Be friendly to your enemy" (in Pritchard, 1969, p. 595). However, this again may be meant to apply to individual enemies in personal disputes.

Yet the fundamental principle of reverence for life without exception, and not only human life, is expressed by the Jain religion of India in its central tenet of *ahimsa* (noninjury). Written articulation of *ahimsa* is evidenced in the Hindu text, *Mahabharata*, composed possibly as early as 300 BCE (Smart, 1993, p. 52): "Abstention from injury, by act, thought, and word, in respect of all creatures, compassion, and gift (charity), constitute behavior that is worthy of praise" (in Radhakrishnan and Moore, 1957, p. 164). This text also states: "One should never do that to another which one regards as injurious to one's own self....

Ahimsa is...the highest truth from which all *dharma* [righteousness] proceeds.... *Ahimsa* is the highest *dharma*...the highest teaching" (in Chapple, 1993, pp. 16-17). There are some indications, not in writing, but in images depicted in the seals of the ancient Indus Valley civilization, that the origins of Jainism and its practice of *ahimsa* may go back as far as 3000 BCE (Chapple, 1993, pp. 5-9), 1,000 years before even Abraham is thought to have lived. One of the most revered teachers of Jainism and *ahimsa*, Mahavira, is believed to have been born no later than 540 BCE and, according to Jain tradition, to have had a long line of predecessors (Chapple, 1993, pp. 9-10).

Three Major Policy Frames

I conclude that three major policy frames are reflected in the Bible: those of group justice, the justice of individual desert, and the principle of life affirmation. The group-justice frame distinguishes among groups, in social policy, and applies the notion of desert not only to groups rather than individuals but even across generations yet unborn within a group. The justice-as-individual-desert frame posits that in a just world people get what they deserve and deserve what they get. But furthermore, this frame implies that if people do not get what they deserve, then it is up to society to ensure that they do. This latter position is illustrated, in its negative form, in the familiar "eye for an eye" law of the talion. The principle-of-life-affirmation frame refers to intrinsically moral action based on unconditional reverence for human life, and is perhaps most famously illustrated in statements attributed to Jesus that allude to loving your enemy, returning good for evil, not resisting evil, judging not, forgiving, and going beyond what is asked.

As I have illustrated throughout, there is abundant evidence and documentation of the existence of each of these frames in the Bible. These frames seem to "fit" the "data" provided in the Bible. The terminology, of course, might raise objections. I refer to "policy frames" because each frame has its own social policy implications, for both intragroup and international (or intergroup) relations. Alternatively, they can be called frames of justice, because they govern the presumably rightful conduct of a community (or nation) toward the individuals within it, and toward the communities (or nations) outside of it. The name of the first policy frame, "group justice," might appear to many to be an oxymoron, especially if we focus upon the nature of the most prevalent illustrations of this frame that are provided in the Bible. These concrete illustrations, indeed, seem to violate our sense of justice, as reflected in Abraham's argument with God over justice. Yet, as I shall discuss later, the abstract essence of this frame as manifested in seemingly more benign policies (along with a continuance of its more horrific manifestations) is abundantly evident in modern times, and is apparently considered as justice by many, although it continues to bother our sense of justice.

These frames, of course, are not without previous recognition. There certainly are scholars who have acknowledged, in their own way, a distinction between the second and third frames presented here (e.g., see Worth, 1997, p. 122, who also points out that these two frames coexist both in the Tanakh and the New Testament), although many have done so in the process of wishing to make the case for a sharp departure from the Tanakh by Jesus and the New Testament, with the implication of a greater nobility of Christian morality and practices over those of Judaism. Conscious recognition of the first frame is already seen within the Tanakh itself in words attributed to both God and Abraham. Though it is conceivable that some could argue that the three frames I have identified are not "accurate" in some way, the more likely argument concerns the possible existence of additional frames, which the claimant would then have the responsibility to identify. One plausible candidate is a frame of restitution, which I have debatably subsumed under the desert frame, as a form of desert. The only justifications I offer for not addressing it in separate and more extensive discussion here, as a fourth frame, is that in the most serious types of human conduct, such as killing or maiming, restitution in the sense of restoring is not realistically possible. Furthermore, if the one responsible for less serious behavior, such as theft, refuses to make restitution, then we are thrown back to one or another of the first three frames. Thus I argue, although admittedly tenuously, that I have sought to identify the major policy frames, and that restitution does not qualify as one of them. Surely, however, it is possible that other major frames may reasonably be proposed. Moreover, it may be possible to derive some hybrid frames from the three identified here.

A Genesis of Justice?

I also conclude that although it is tempting to cast the three frames of justice (group justice, individual desert, and life affirmation) as having evolved sequentially in human thought and action, representing progress toward higher concepts of justice, the truth is far more complicated. I contend that these three frames do not form a progressive sequence in the Bible, each previous one being forsaken for the next, but rather, all three are reflected and interwoven throughout the Tanakh and, as I shall discuss below, the New Testament.

There is no indication in the Bible of a genesis of justice, or development of the sense of justice, on the part of either God or man. God has administered group justice ever since the time of the Flood. He does so to cities harboring many "wicked" individuals. He does so to the Egyptians in the process of freeing the Israelites, to the nations that attack or even fail to help the Israelites in their subsequent wanderings, and to the nations to be dispossessed from the Promised Land. But God also administers group justice among the Israelites themselves, at the time of their wanderings in the desert wilderness, during their established residence in the Promised Land, and in their dispersal from that land. God even visits group justice upon those who were not yet born at the time of the iniquities of their ancestors, and He does so among the Israelites as well as other nations. Moreover, the group justice that is administered involves not only punishment for iniquities, but also reward for virtuous conduct, although one cannot read the Bible without gaining the impression that God is more concerned with obedience to Himself than, more narrowly, with man's adherence to moral principles embodied in divine law, and that He administers reward and punishment accordingly (even if of a group nature).

Yet before, during, and after these countless instances of group justice, a sense of justice regarding individual human life has always been manifest. As far back as when Cain killed his brother Abel, God said to Cain: "What have you done? Hark, your brother's blood cries out to Me from the ground!" (Genesis 4:10) Indeed, group justice itself was often administered as a response to some individuals' violations of other individual human lives. However, after the Flood, God vows never again to destroy everyone. The Ten Commandments, given to the Israelites after leaving Egypt, prohibit murder and other violations of individuals, although even here there is also a statement of group (intergenerational) justice. Also at the time of Moses, additional principles concerning nonviolation of individuals—such as those safeguarding procedural justice for individuals so that they may not be wrongfully judged, those concerning the care and treatment of the poor and the needy, and those concerning the evenhanded and fair treatment of others—are established, and it is made clear that all such principles, including those expressed in several of the Ten Commandments, are to be applied to all within the community, including strangers. That the principles in actuality were not applied to people of other groups not residing among the Israelites (or passing through) is evident in the histories of group conflict recorded in the Tanakh. Yet it is clear that they were applied within the community, despite the fact that evidence of group justice even within the community can be found. But even the mere formulation of the principles *qua* principles establishes the fact that a sense of justice regarding individuals resided in the minds of human beings at that time.

In addition, it is misleading to say that the principles articulated by or attributed to Jesus have their *roots* in other articulations found in the Tanakh because here "roots" imply causes and historical development, when the roots may actually be the nature of the human mind itself. I argue that the three frames do not even originate in the Bible but rather, have their origins in a universal "sense of justice" whose manifestations are evidenced in other parts of the region in which the biblical saga is set and in other parts of the world, possibly even before the time of Abraham. Where the human mind exists, there is a sense of justice, and this sense of justice can yield articulation into principles reflecting one or another of the three frames at any time. (What might determine that time will be discussed below.)

It is possible that the sense of justice existed even prior to its articulation in the spoken or written word. Yet only in the word can it find expression in particularities. These expressions may vary, and the many articulations of individual justice represented in the Bible can be regarded as real achievements. Nonetheless, the point can be made that there is no evidence to contradict the proposition that human beings had a sense of justice based on a reverence for or valuing of human life from time immemorial, or as soon as the human mind became capable of abstract thought. Moreover, all three frames have existed along with that sense of justice, and they exist in thought as well as action within our world today. All three frames are even manifested within the legal codes and social policies of modern liberal democracies.

The Three Frames in the New Testament

Much as there are contradictions to the life-affirmation frame in the Tanakh (in the form of the group and individual-desert frames) at the same time that there are manifestations of it there too, there are also contradictions to it in the New Testament. The very precepts of the life-affirmation frame are couched in desert terms by Jesus himself: Whosoever so much as angrily insults his brother "shall be in danger of hell fire" (Matthew 5:22). "Love your enemies... For if ye love them which love you, what reward have ye?" (Matthew 5:44-46) "For if ye forgive men their trespasses, your heavenly father will also forgive you..." (Matthew 6:14). "Judge not, that ye be not judged. For with what judgment ye judge, ye shall be judged; and with what measure ye mete, it shall be measured to you again" (Matthew 7:1-2). The latter statement is strangely consonant with "an eye for an eye," which Jesus claims to reject, or is it only God who will do the judging and the meting, or only others who play by those rules? To those who are persecuted for righteousness' sake and for the sake of Jesus, he says, "great is your reward in heaven" (Matthew 5:10-12). Jesus says that at the end of the world, "the angels shall come forth, and sever the wicked from among the just, And shall cast them into the furnace of fire..." (Matthew 13:49-50). In the vision of Revelation, the dead "were judged every man according to their works" (20:13).

Even the group-justice frame is abundantly evident in the New Testament. Sending his disciples among the Israelite cities, Jesus says: "And whosoever shall not receive you, nor hear your words, when ye depart out of that house or city, shake off the dust of your feet. Verily, I say unto you, It shall be more tolerable for the land of Sodom and Gomorrha in the day of judgment, than for that city" (Matthew 10:14-15). He proceeds "to upbraid the cities wherein most of his mighty works were done, because they repented not," repeating his threat, for example, to the city of Capernaum (Matthew 11:20-24).

The strangest form of group justice, however, is on the positive side of the coin, so to speak. Christ, we are told, offered himself as a sacrifice to bear the sins of many (Hebrews 9:11-28); "Christ died for us...we shall be saved by his life" (Romans 5:8-10); "through the grace of the Lord Jesus Christ we shall be saved..." (Acts 15:11). He "washed us from our sins in his own blood" (Revelation 1:5). Here we have a kind of reversal or opposite of collective guilt in the form of collective salvation, although only those who believe in Jesus will be saved (John 3:13-18, 36; 2 Thessalonians 1:7-9; Hebrews 9:28). (This form of group justice represented by the idea of Jesus dying for the salvation of others has parallels in the Tanakh. There, as already mentioned, God says that He shows kindness "to the thousandth generation of those who love Me and keep My commandments" [Exodus 20:6]).

Not only is the group-justice frame thus continued in the New Testament, but an ominous new guideline for group formation is proffered by Jesus himself: one must believe in God's "only begotten Son" in order to have eternal life or otherwise be condemned to suffer the wrath of God (John 3:13-18, 36). Further, John portrays "the Jews" as the enemies of Jesus throughout his book. Peter addresses "ye men of Israel," "all the house of Israel," and "all the people of Israel" as the killers of Jesus (Acts 2:22-23, 36; 3:12-15; 4:10), and asks them to repent and be baptized in the name of Jesus, so that their "sins may be blotted out" (Acts 2:38; 3:19). We are told that the Lord Jesus will, "in flaming fire," take vengeance "on them that know not God, and that obey not the gospel of our Lord Jesus Christ." They "shall be punished with everlasting destruction from the presence of the Lord..." (2 Thessalonians 1:7-9).

Indeed, greater emphasis seems to be placed on getting people to believe in Jesus as the son of God, and in his resurrection, than on the teaching of moral principles (see, e.g., Acts 13:33-39; Romans 9:31-32; 10:1-10; Galatians 2:16; 3:2-25). This has its parallel in the Tanakh in the greater emphasis placed there on obedience to God relative to moral principles. True, as in the Tanakh there is the implicit claim that by obeying God one will be righteous, the implicit claim in the New Testament is that one will be "saved" by being righteous. But we have learned that God, at least as portrayed in the Bible, is not always moral in His conduct. Thus it cannot be said unequivocally that obedience to God, or holding to the belief that Jesus is the son of God and was resurrected, corresponds to righteous behavior.

Continuing Manifestations of the Three Frames

The obsession with person and faith over principle with progression to the point of calling Jesus God (Hebrews 1:8-10), when combined with the group accusation that "the Jews" killed Jesus (1 Thessalonians 2:14-15), set the stage of history, as we know now in retrospect, for horrible manifestations of the group frame to be applied to Jews. There is compelling evidence that not only groups of Christians, but organized Christianity in the form of the Church and its leaders, including popes, fostered prejudice against, and hatred and persecution of Jews through much of European post-New Testament history (Carroll, 2001; Kertzer, 2001), hypocritically violating any conceivable interpretation of Jesus' teachings and the Sermon on the Mount. To what extent this long history of Jew hatred and systemic lethal discrimination against Jews contributed, ultimately, to the advent of the Holocaust is still debated, as is the degree of the modern Catholic Church's direct complicity in the Holocaust itself (Carroll, 2001; Kertzer, 2001).

Manifestations of the group frame in intergroup relations, of course, have not been limited to Christian persecution of Jews. In the last decade of the twentieth century alone, modern activation of the group frame in the form of mass slaughter was abundantly evident in many parts of the world and mostly in conflicts that have pitted ethnic groups against each other. In these wars, which can be more accurately described as series of massacres, the targets of violence have been determined by ethnic group identity, with any member of the other ethnic group being deemed fair game. Serbian political leaders inspired the indiscriminate Serbian slaughter of Albanian Muslims in Kosovo by stirring up "memories" of the Serbian defeat there at the hands of the Muslims' supposed ancestors (the Turkish Ottomans) 400 years prior. Ethnic hatred fueled the war in Bosnia, in which Serbs visited indiscriminate atrocities upon Croats (partly inspired by the massacres of Serbs led by the Nazi-sponsored Croatian government more than four decades earlier), and upon Muslims (including the systematic rape of Muslim women and girls), and all sides committed extreme acts of group cruelty. The breakup of the Soviet Union was followed by several wars within former Soviet territories between ethnic groups, including Christians and Muslims. Elsewhere in Asia, Iraq warred against its Kurds, and deadly conflicts between Muslims and Hindus in India, Sinhalese (mostly Buddhist) and Tamils (mostly Hindu) in Sri Lanka, and Israelis and Palestinians are ongoing. In Africa, Hutus massacred hundreds of thousands of Tutsis in Rwanda, and Tutsis massacred Hutus in Burundi. By 1995, 1.5 million people had died in the civil war in Sudan (going back to the 1980s), and hundreds of thousands had died in the civil war in Somalia, few of them soldiers (Sivard, 1996, p. 19). Of course, war itself is the practice of the group frame in its most deadly form, in that the enemy is defined solely in terms of being a member of the other group or nation.

That, reminiscent of the Israelites in biblical times, the individual-desert frame continues as the dominant policy frame governing relations within the group and community throughout modern times, even in the legal codes and social policies of modern liberal democracies, hardly needs documentation here, so pervasive are its manifestations. Indeed, the idea of people getting what they deserve is commonly identified as synonymous with justice itself. The criminal justice systems of modern liberal democracies, if not of virtually all of the nations of the world, are premised on the notion that those who commit crimes must be punished for them. In the United States, the continuing practice of capital punishment for murder exemplifies the "eye for an eye" principle. Although the motives expressed for punishment occasionally include deterrence, rehabilitation, and incapacitation, punishment for the sake of retribution remains central to the system.

However, the application of the individual-desert frame to the construction of social welfare policies has been more problematic. In attempts to provide people with what they presumably deserve, the modern welfare state has often constructed policies containing eligibility requirements that inevitably distinguish between its "deserving" and "undeserving" citizens along highly contestable lines. In the United States, many policies are built upon group stereotypes concerning, for example, old age and disability. The provision of old-age Social Security benefits is based on questionable generalizations about the poverty, low income, loss of income, and frailty of "the elderly." "Universal" medical insurance exists (Medicare), but it is mostly limited to those over a certain arbitrarily designated age. Under the Temporary Assistance for Needy Families program (TANF), largely designed for poor single mothers and their children, in some states a child born to a mother while she is on TANF will be denied benefits granted to the child born before the mother went on TANF. In effect, children similarly situated in regard to need will be treated differently. In all states, if the mother has ever been convicted of a drug-related felony offense, then the TANF benefits her family can receive will be reduced. Again, children similarly situated with regard to need will be treated differently, and thus, punishments for the "sins" of the mother are visited upon the children. Other social policies, too, presume to distinguish between the "deserving" and "undeserving" along group lines. Much-debated affirmative action policies determine who shall receive certain benefits, credits, or deficits, in areas ranging from college admissions to employment candidacy, based on racial, ethnic, and gender group distinctions.

My point is that such policies—and there are many of them—attempt to "reward" deserving people by, in effect, constructing groups on the basis of generalizations that presumably distinguish the deserving from the undeserving in terms of factors relevant to the types of provisions to be offered. Because they do not in fact differentiate between all individuals in this relevant manner (e.g., need or merit), we are brought back to the group frame of "justice." Ironically, then, attempts made ostensibly to develop policies based on the policy frame of individual desert often result in group-based policies. Other policies do not even attempt to address desert but, in effect, divide the citizenry into the favored and unfavored anyway. In some American policies, the geographical area in which one resides will determine the level of benefits in an arbitrary manner. TANF benefits very greatly in size from one state to another. Children residing in impoverished localities will be provided less adequately funded public education than other children. In the United States, federal income tax policies are riddled with group distinctions. For example, hefty tax breaks are awarded to people who own their own homes and have mortgages, whereas they are denied to those who rent their living quarters. Thus the acceptance of the group and/or the individual-desert frame for the development of social policy opens the door wide to the specter of interest groups clamoring for special treatment—creating all manner of creative justifications for why they, as opposed to others, are deserving of a particular treatment—and politicians pandering to group interests while losing sight of individual justice.

Hence, just as we were compelled to conclude that not only the individual-desert frame but also the group frame was applied to relations *within* the ancient Israelite community, we must also conclude that the group frame is pervasively manifested in the policies governing the internal affairs of modern democratic nations, despite these nations' emphasis on individual rights. One might argue that such policies are a long way in a benign direction from the cruelty and human destruction of the examples of group frame applications we began with. Therefore, I must reiterate that my concern here has been with the most fundamental and abstract core of justice formulation—abstract principles, if you will—that I call policy frames, which indeed may yield a wide range of manifestations in various policies. Moreover, the domestic group-based policies just alluded to here have substantial impact on individuals, and can lead to the factionalization of a community into group conflict and even violence.

As for the life-affirmation frame, at first glance we might be tempted to say that we find little sign of it in the policies of modern states and that, indeed, throughout history it has been honored, when at all, more in rhetoric, or in its breach, than in its application. Certainly, if we were to look for its manifestations only in the abolishment of armies and courts, then we would not find it. For starters, we can say that the abolition of capital punishment in some countries is in itself an expression of the principle of life affirmation, as are attempts in some countries to provide humane treatment for criminals while they are in prison. As I mentioned before, the rules of procedural justice established in ancient Israel as well as in many modern nations, in that they respect individuals regardless of what they may have been accused, can be viewed as an expression of this frame. Social welfare policies established by many nations to address poverty and need (as flawed as they are) can be construed as manifestations of this frame. Universal health care policies established by a number of modern nations to include all of their citizens are certainly consistent with the principle of life affirmation. The existence of foreign economic aid policies represent at least an intent to extend the application of the principle of life affirmation to people beyond one's borders. Moreover, even attempts to develop weapons for "precision bombing" and to limit destruction, as much as possible, to inanimate military targets and infrastructure during warfare are an expression, however feeble, of respect for the individuals of enemy nations. We can conclude, however, that the implications of the life-affirmation frame have been less developed and given less serious thought than either of the other frames, and that surely the mere development of the possible implications of this frame in the form of alternative policy proposals is a worthwhile task and wide open field for scholars and others in the future.

Choosing Frames

A few concerns about the sense of justice and the evolution of justice remain to be addressed. If both the sense of justice and all three frames of justice were present from the beginning of human history, then in what sense, if any (aside from verbal elaboration, explication, and derivation), can we speak of the evolution of justice? To answer this question, we must first note that justice frequently, though not always, serves practical purposes, and also that new circumstances sometimes promote the feasibility of new expressions of the sense of justice without the cost that previously would have been entailed.

Much of the Bible seems to be an effort at providing explanations for events that had already happened. When the story is told that the king of Assyria captured the land of the Israelites and deported them to Assyria for settlement (II Kings 17:1-6), we are then told: "This happened because the Israelites sinned against the Lord..." in that they worshiped other gods, committed wicked acts, spurned God's laws, followed the customs of the nations around them, and made molten idols (II Kings 17:7-18). In this view, the events in the Tanakh are not indicative of a vengeful God but rather, of the fact that the Israelites, as a group, suffered many calamities, did what they thought they had to do, and then attributed it all—natural disasters, plagues, battle victories and losses—to God.

Assuming with Miles (1996, p. 166) that the Tanakh is a mixture of history, myth, and fiction, it is reasonable to suppose that the body of legends, religious beliefs, rituals, customs, and ethical precepts that we call the Jewish religion arose out of the necessity of leaders to mobilize and discipline a group of people for the purpose of establishing a viable society and securing a land to live in after coming out of Egypt. The leaders decided to head northeast to a land that flowed with milk and honey, which was the reason why that land was already so heavily populated. This effort would require a cohesive group and a well-disciplined army, for the purpose of winning battles and wars, and of conquest. Such discipline and social organization would be further necessary for maintaining national stability even after conquest, and while inevitably mingling with the people of other groups in a crowded land, and having hostile nations on one's borders. These necessities determined the shape of the religion and the rise of laws of justice. The establishment and enforcement, in intragroup relations, of ethical codes of conduct, fair treatment of all individuals, courts of law, procedural justice, impartial judgment, and concern for the poor might greatly increase individuals' allegiance to the group, and the strength of this group cohesion might form the basis on which a well-disciplined and dedicated army could be developed. Justice, although emanating from a sense of justice, also has its practical uses. In Deuteronomy, Moses says to his people: "Keep, therefore, all the Instruction that I enjoin upon you today, so that you may have the strength to enter and take possession of the land that you are about to cross into and possess, and that you may long endure upon the soil..." (11:8-9).

Yet, as we know all too well from modern history, a passion for order can override a passion for justice. Prescriptions in the Torah against cross-dressing (Deuteronomy 22:5), for the disproportionality of punishment (e.g., death for insulting parents [Exodus 21:17]), and for capital punishment for homosexual acts, bestiality, and adultery (Exodus 22:18; Leviticus 20) may be construed as overzealous attempts to maintain social order that overlook the extent to which such edicts might be violating individuals. Cross-dressing and homosexual behavior—much as today for some—perhaps were viewed as representations or manifestations of disorder.

Moreover, as much in biblical times as is evident in today's world, there was competition among the three frames of justice in human minds. In the zeal to maintain order and discipline, the group frame occasionally trumped individual justice even as applied within the Israelite group (with the group justice actions usually attributed to God), as we have already seen. But the group frame predominated in regard to members of the enemy group, even to the point of group annihilation, despite some indications of respect for individuals even in the sphere of warfare (such as Israelite rules governing interaction with captive women). The Israelites "justified" their own actions in terms of the wayward influence that members of other groups might have on Israelites, potentially undermining their allegiance to God and to their own group's traditions and legal code of justice. Because such a scenario would result in the breakdown of the very same group discipline and cohesion that would ensure the survival of the group, the justification thus offered takes the form of "necessity."

To be sure, we have seen many attempts at group annihilation that continue in modern times. But even as we condemn this extreme, we do commonly apply the group frame to members of the enemy group in warfare (although it is not only in warfare but, indeed, in many aspects of international relations that we apply the group frame, valuing the lives of members of our own group above those of others). Conscious of our use of the group frame in warfare, we justify it in terms of necessity. It is difficult to wage war without killing indiscriminately. Ultimately, it can be said that if we had devised means other than warfare for dealing with severe conflict and achieving our objectives, then we would have employed them. This was the lifelong quest of Mohandas Gandhi in his development of the philosophy and strategies of nonviolence—to find alternatives to violence, based on the principle of life affirmation, as means for resolving severe group conflict. Indeed, he acknowledged being influenced by Jain philosophy, as well as by the Sermon on the Mount, and the writings of Tolstoy.

It is not enough to say that the institution of slavery, for example, pervasive in biblical times, was simply the "norm" of the times or reflected the attitudes of the times, for we can ask: What did the attitudes of the time reflect? That the frames of individual justice were salient even in regard to deliberation about slaves is evidenced in Israelite precepts in the Tanakh concerning their humane and respectful treatment, albeit within the larger context of oppression (Exodus 21:2-11, 26-27; Deuteronomy 23:16-17). Perhaps these humane regulations regarding slaves—as well as the substitution of animal sacrifice for human sacrifice in religious rituals—were in fact Israelite innovations that stood in contrast to the practices of surrounding groups at the time. If so, then they might have been instituted to serve the very same purposes of other measures noted above, namely, to increase allegiance to the group, thereby strengthening it. Yet the institution of slavery itself and even the subjugation of women may have been perceived by the Israelite group no less than by surrounding groups as necessities of economic survival or prosperity, or merely advantageous in other ways.

The point is that while the sense of justice and its competing cognitive expressions in the form of the three frames have always been part of the human mind, what we perceive as advances in justice (from the group to individual frames) are facilitated by the declining necessity, profitability, or desirability of previous arrangements, and the increased feasibility of new ones. These transitions, in turn, are spurred by new physical and social circumstances in the form of physical inventions and technological innovations (even social inventions), the discovery of new resources, and the development of new knowledge. In the economic sphere, mechanization may reduce the advantages of slavery, for example. In recent decades, the development of the contraceptive pill facilitated women's liberation. Gandhi's social invention of nonviolent strategy expanded the possibilities of waging conflict without need to resort to violence.

We can see such dynamics currently in progress in regard to the harming and killing of animals. In the Torah, even amid elaborate prescriptions pertaining to animal sacrifice rituals and laws concerning the slaughter of animals and which animals may be eaten, there are indications of guilt that reflect, in however meager ways, that the human sense of justice and principle of life affirmation extend to animal life. In regard to eating animals, for example, the following limitation is attributed to God's command: "You shall not partake of the blood of any flesh, for the life of all flesh is its blood" (Leviticus 17:14). The Torah requires that the ox not be muzzled while it is threshing (Deuteronomy 25:4), for it would be cruel to incite an animal's desire for food while at the same time denying the food to it (Hertz, 1972, pp. 854-855). Elsewhere in the Tanakh it is written: "A righteous man knows the needs of his beast" (Proverbs 12:10). Moreover, the rabbinical regulations concerning the method of the slaughter of animals for food are, in part, meant to reduce the suffering of animals at the time of death (Hertz, 1972, pp. 854-855). Yet the desire to eat meat has trumped vegetarianism and its manifestation of the sense of justice in most human communities to the present time. However, it is conceivable that new knowledge about the health disadvantages of meat and the health advantages of vegetarianism, and about how to obtain within a vegetarian diet whatever advantages exist in the eating of meat, might tip the scales toward more widespread vegetarianism in the future.

To be sure, there are other types of influence on the choice of operative frames. As we have already seen in the Bible, passion can win acceptance of the group frame over the individual-desert frame, and even of the latter over the life-affirmation frame. On the other hand, persuasive appeals to one's sense of justice can sometimes win acceptance of the individual-desert frame and even the life-affirmation frame.

However, the concept of individual desert seems to be such a central and enduring part of the sense of justice that we have cause to wonder whether a policy network built solely on the life-affirmation frame could ever come to pass or indeed be viable. Social psychological studies have indicated that we may have a strong need to believe that people get what they deserve and deserve what they get (Lerner, 1980). We have a sense that people *should* get what they deserve, in the form of punishment, reward, or compensation. The achievement of such balance is often defined as justice itself. When justice so defined is pursued on an individual basis, it can indeed be achieved in some instances: in courts of law, individuals are prosecuted for intentionally and seriously violating others and, if found guilty, are punished through imprisonment, fines, or other means. Individuals, corporations, and even governments can be sued for intentionally or negligently causing loss or damage to others, and in some cases they are forced to pay some manner of restitution to the particular individuals who suffered the damage or loss. And in the American-led war on terrorism (the terrorism itself being among the most abominable expressions of the group frame) at the start of the twenty-first century, there seems to be no compunction about killing the individual terrorists themselves, based on an individual-desert frame, although other loss of life is regretted and attempts are made to avoid it.

Yet, when attempts are made to apply the individual-desert frame to classes of people based on common factors tenuously related to individual loss, damage, or blameworthy or praiseworthy behavior itself, the individual-desert frame itself is, in fact, violated. I have argued that this is the case in war itself, and in many of the group-based social policies that have been propagated in the name of individual desert. In fact, American social welfare policies are laced with group distinctions that violate the principle of individual desert in the very (or ostensible) attempts to address individual desert. Yet even in countries in which group-based social welfare policies are as plentiful as they are in the United States, such as in many western European countries, some truly universal policies, for example, in the area of health care insurance, are in place, which is indicative of the fact that they can win broad public support. Such policies can be said to stem from the individual-desert frame of justice only in the sense that all individuals are construed as deserving of the benefits to be provided. But at this point of universality the individual-desert frame disappears into the life-affirmation frame, in that all individuals are deemed equally worthy of having their lives supported through health care merely because they are human beings. It follows that, in the United States, well-conceptualized advocacy based upon the life-affirmation frame would have the potential to succeed in replacing current health care insurance policies, which cover the aged and the poor, with truly universal health care insurance.

Not even in regard to criminal justice policy is reformulation based on the life-affirmation frame out of the question. As already mentioned, the abolition of capital punishment in some countries, attempts to treat criminal prisoners humanely, and rules of procedural justice can be viewed as expressions of this frame. But punishment for the sake of retribution remains central to the system. It is possible, however, to develop a criminal justice system focused on taking whatever steps may be necessary to prevent the recurrence of severe crimes, rather than on retribution (Pelton, 1999a, pp. 125-163). Because such steps may include imprisonment, even if for purposes other than retribution, it may satisfy the human desire for retribution (which cannot be distinguished from revenge) anyway. Because we already have a hybrid system, influenced by the life-affirmation frame to some extent, as well as by the individual-desert frame, it may be possible to move to a system based on the same frames but focused on prevention and tinged with retribution rather than the other way around. Perhaps only if and when the public becomes convinced of the *practicality* of such a reoriented system in terms of reducing severe crime would such a shift to greater centeredness on the life-affirmation frame become politically feasible.

In the Bible itself, God, like humans, often acts out of passion rather than justice, and humans have to stay the passion of God, as God has to stay the passion of humans. God formulates principles of justice, perhaps as much to guide Himself as to guide human beings, but often "forgets" those principles when He acts, and applies the group frame. Then, too, God was just as puzzled as humans in devising ways to do justice, particularly in regard to intergroup or international conflicts and relations. Even when we attempt to establish a justice of desert, we open the door to the proven capaciousness of human imagination to rationalize or "justify" all manner of violative and murderous acts in the name of desert. The judgmentalism necessary for justice as desert founders on the shoals of who will do the judging.

As I have argued throughout, the sense of justice and the three frames of justice are part of the structure of the human mind, thus preceding practical considerations rather than being based on them. However, the choice of frame to be acted upon may be influenced by practical considerations. By creating a system that benefits everyone individually, without discrimination, justice may have the effect of peace, thus additionally benefiting those within the community, in that the poor may be less likely to rise up against the rich, subgroup against subgroup, and family against family. The establishment of justice may bear its own deserts for the community that establishes it, whether that community is a narrow group or the world. But such a peaceful justice most feasibly may be built on the life-affirmation frame, for the capacity of the human mind to make individual judgments of just desert is deeply flawed, and can only lead to selection and division. To the extent that all life is interdependent, and increasingly so because of modern technology, the good of the individual will be contained in the good of all, and justice will converge with practicality. Yet individual instances of people not getting what they deserve will continue to exist (whether they are caused by genetic disease, accident, or whatever), and the notion that individual deserts fashioned by human beings will do justice for everyone will continue to be an illusion.

The historical cycles of group violence did not begin with the persecution of the Israelites in Egypt, nor will they end with current wars. Yet there are choices. For example, the tragic long-standing Israeli-Palestinian conflict has its roots in a complex European prehistory of hatred, group prejudice, discrimination, and violent oppression going back thousands of years and culminating in the Holocaust. But history cannot be undone, and the question becomes, What will promote or constitute justice? Mutual application of the group frame perpetuates destruction. Even the individual-desert frame is counterproductive, for who is to interpret and determine who is "deserving" of what? The only reasonable frame to apply is that of life affirmation, putting aside all differing versions of Israeli-Palestinian group history and even the notion of desert. Application of the life-affirmation frame demands policies that promote the well-being of every individual within the region, regardless of group identity, group history, or notions of desert. Justice for each individual requires that Palestinians and Israelis, both cooperatively and unilaterally, focus on what can be done to enhance the lives of all of the individuals in both groups from here on out.

Ultimately, we are attracted to the life-affirmation frame not because of its possible convergence with practicality, but because it goes to the core of what our sense of justice is, which is that life should not be violated. In broader conclusion, we must agree with Dershowitz (2000) that it is precisely the many instances of injustice to be found in the Bible that provoke and refine our thinking about the nature and meaning of justice itself.

2

Nonviolence and Liberal Philosophy

In his development of the philosophy and strategies of nonviolence, Mohandas Gandhi acknowledged the influence of the principle of reverence for life without exception embodied in the ancient Jain philosophy and religion of India—expressed there as *ahimsa*, or noninjury—as well as its manifestations in the Sermon on the Mount in regard to *human* life, to the extent of loving one's enemies and returning good for evil. This principle of life affirmation, without condition, judgment, or exception, dictates the ethic of means and ends so much associated with nonviolence—that the means must be consistent with the ends, and hence no matter how lofty are the visions of the just and peaceful state of affairs to be attained, no individual should be violated in the process. It is because the individual must not be violated in any way that he or she must not be used as a means to an end, but is in fact the end. Such is the logic of any principle of justice derived from an absolute value of the sanctity of human life.

The focus of classical liberalism, too, is the individual, and it frames this emphasis in the form of rights that denote certain spheres of inviolability in regard to the individual, no matter what other ends are to be achieved. In fact, it can be argued that the high regard in liberal philosophy for individual rights, individual freedom, and even equality of opportunity, is merely derivative from the core liberal value of respect for the individual human life. The priority in liberal philosophy is that of the individual over any vision of the "common good." Thus, like nonviolence, liberal philosophy respects process, for it proclaims that individuals are not to be violated within the process. Liberalism's means orientation is reflected in its valuing and constructing of such procedural rights as freedom of speech and assembly, due process in criminal justice proceedings, and nondiscrimination.

The wisdom of a philosophy of means (since other types of philosophies also claim to have human welfare at heart) stems from the fact that individuals are often violated within the means. When such violations occur or are intended, myriad rationalizations, theories of intended ends, interpretations of history, and judgments are offered by way of justification, but the victims are no less dead or otherwise violated. The reality is in the means, which are actions that are concrete and in the here and now, while the justifications and intended future ends are in the realm of speculation. Values that pertain to means and to individuals as ends are safeguards against the known and dangerous human capacity for limitless justification.

It is in Immanuel Kant's formula of humanity that we see most starkly the apparent common ground that classical liberal philosophy holds with that of nonviolence: "So act that you use humanity, whether in your own person or in the person of any other, always at the same time as an end, never merely as a means" (1785/1998, 4:429).[1]

Yet Gandhi formulated his philosophy and strategies of nonviolence as a means of waging social conflict, often against governmental policies, while liberal philosophy evolved to address the form and functions that government should take. Their differences, in part, are due to these different challenges that they were devised to address. My purpose here is to explore the differences in the two philosophies, as well as in the forms of social policy that the frames of justice embedded in them may suggest.

Universality

According to Kant's universal principle of right (1797/1996, 6:229-231), any action is right, or not contrary to justice, "if it can coexist with everyone's freedom in accordance with a universal law" (i.e., a law that we would be willing to have everyone live by). But he further states that coercion that is opposed to any hindrance of such freedom (which is itself coercion) is right, or not unjust, in that it is consistent with such freedom. "Hence there is connected with right by the principle of contradiction an authorization to coerce someone who infringes upon it" (6:231).

Now it is clear that every governed society employs coercion, and that liberal democratic societies employ and legitimize their use of coercion in the name of justice and the protection of liberty. Indeed, Kant's classical liberal view is that the function of the state is to protect its citizens' freedom, through coercion if necessary (Ladd, 1999, p. xxxvi; Sullivan, 1996, p. xx). This coercion may extend to its most extreme form, violence, although Kant chooses to call only the "illegitimate" use of coercion by the name of violence (Ladd, p. xxxv). Be that as it may, there is an internal consistency, or logic, within Kant's formulation of freedom and coercion. The problem is the question of the consistency of this formulation with that of the means-ends principle.

Either we pose that individuals exist as ends in themselves, and therefore have "absolute worth," not merely worth "for *us*," and exist as ends "such that no other end, to which they would serve *merely* as means," can be put in their place, since their worth is not "conditional" and "contingent" (Kant, 1785/1998, 4:428; italics in original); or we pose that individuals may be coerced and violated to protect our own freedom or that of others—that is, our own interests or that of others—and thus in effect, be used merely as means for an end other than themselves under some circumstances.

It would seem that the first formulation is implicit in the means-ends principle, namely that human beings are *never* to be used merely as means, and Kant reinforces this interpretation with his implication that human worth is not conditional and contingent (1785/1998, 4:428). Yet the meaning of universality implied in this formulation, namely the application of a maxim to everyone at all times, without exception, condition, or exclusion (with regard to treatment of its object), differs from Kant's meaning when he refers to a maxim that we would be willing to have everyone live by (even though both forms can be described as the "universality of application"). It is the latter meaning that is embodied in Kant's formula of universal law, "act only in accordance with that maxim through which you can at the same time will that it become a universal law" (4:421), as revealed in the examples Kant used to illustrate this imperative (4:421-423). In fact, Kant's freedom-coercion formulation itself makes it clear that universality in the sense of a maxim applying to everyone, without exception, condition, or exclusion, must be distinguished from Kant's usage here, as a maxim that we would be willing to have everyone live by.

The difference is important because many of us would be willing to have everyone live by, for example, the maxim that we should not treat individuals merely as means except if they attempt to interfere with our own freedom. The maxim would be universal in the sense of the formula of universal law, but in allowing exceptions for when individuals may be treated merely as means, it would be nonuniversal in regard to the professed intrinsic value of individuals as ends in themselves. Indeed, Kant's formula of universal law is quite unspecific in its implications, since many alternative and even contradictory maxims can fit its prescription. Even though we might be willing to have everyone live by the freedom-coercion formulation, it would still be in violation of the means-ends principle. In fact, it would raise a contradiction, because if the means-ends principle declares that individuals are ends in themselves, then there is inconsistency in saying that some individuals at some times are not ends in themselves. The latter is an abrogation of the moral principle of means and ends as a universal moral principle without exception. Yet both the means-ends and freedom-coercion formulations are compatible with Kant's formula of universal law.

While the means-ends principle refers to right conduct (the nonviolation of the individual) within the means and for its own sake, and therefore universality in the sense of nonexception, some philosophers have claimed that Kant's formula of universal law rests directly upon our presumed interests. I cannot will a universal law of lying, according to Kant, because then no one would believe me, and would pay me back in the same coin. Likewise, under a universal law of uncharitableness, if cases occurred in which I needed the charity of others, I would be robbed of all hope of assistance for myself (Kant, 1785/1998, 4:422-423). These examples, that Kant used to show that there are maxims that are not acceptable under the formula of universal law because we could not reasonably will them to become universal laws, spurred Arthur Schopenhauer (1839/1995, pp. 88-91) to argue that under Kant's formula of universal law, moral obligation rests only on assumed reciprocity, and therefore egoism. John Stuart Mill (in his essay on "Utilitarianism") says of Kant's formula of universal law: "To give any meaning to Kant's principle, the sense put upon it must be, that we ought to shape our conduct by a rule which all rational beings might adopt *with benefit to their collective interest*" (1863/1990, p. 470; italics in original). While Mill does not intend this as a criticism, and asserts (in his essay "On Liberty") that he regards "utility as the ultimate appeal on all ethical questions" (1859/1990, p. 272), he also asserts that in benefiting some individuals, one must assure himself that he is not violating the rights of anyone else (1863/1990, p. 453).

John Rawls (1971, p. 11) claimed that principles of justice are those that "free and rational persons concerned to further their own interests would accept in an initial position of equality." His theory, as he said, is based on the concept of the social contract found in Kant as well as in Locke and Rousseau. In fact, his "original position," which can be construed as a position in which individuals are merely looking out for their own interests as known to them at the time—in ignorance of what status they will hold, what abilities they will be endowed with, and what circumstances they will encounter in life—seems to be a refinement of Kant's formula of universal law. But Rawls (1971, p. 3) also stated that each person "possesses an inviolability founded on justice that even the welfare of society as a whole cannot override." Yet he also said, intriguingly, that "one conception of justice is preferable to another when its broader consequences are more desirable" (1971, p. 6).

Now one's appreciation of the value or intrinsic worth of the individual might ultimately stem from sentiment toward oneself, or self-interest (contrary to Kant's position on this, but that is another story), but it is the commitment to the universality of nonexception that takes the value beyond mere interest and transforms it into a moral principle to be applied for its own sake without regard or reference to interest. Kant does speak of duty, but it is lost to presumed interest in his freedom-coercion formulation. It is hence Kant's formula of universal law, which accommodates his freedom-coercion formulation, that opens the door to the consequentialist reasoning which has sometimes been attributed to him.

Many just arrangements and distributions agreed to within a democratic society may be said to be contractual, but the inviolability of the individual is not merely a matter of contract—according to nonviolence and at times to liberalism—but of morality and justice. An implicit social contract there may be, but moral obligation goes beyond contracts to right conduct for its own sake, and not in fulfillment of any contract or any expectation of reciprocity.

If everyone at all times were to treat others as ends and not merely as means, we would be in fine shape, but we live in a world in which that is not the case. Now what? We may presume that it is in our interests to take coercive and even violent actions we think are necessary to protect our interests, and we might even call it justice, but the universality of nonexception seemingly expressed in the means-ends principle is then a casualty. To treat individuals as ends without exception would not seem to be in our interests without exception, yet it best reflects the nonviolent ethic and the intrinsic moral value of the sanctity of (or reverence for) human life.

At best, we can say that liberal philosophy, throughout the course of its development, has shown an ambivalent commitment to the absolute and universal value of the individual as an end itself, that is, to the nonviolation of the individual without exception and even within the means, as an intrinsic moral value that refers to nothing beyond the individual and is abided by simply for its own sake. Its ambivalence arose in the course of addressing the difficult task of envisioning the form and functions of a just government, which can hardly be imagined to exist in the complete absence of coercion. The philosophy of nonviolence, on the other hand, in the course of its own development, and facing a different difficult task—that of successfully waging social conflict and doing so in a just manner—has expressed deeper and stronger commitment to nonviolation of the individual, to the means-ends principle in its unconditional form, and to noninjury or to *action based on the refusal to do harm* (as Bondurant [1967, p. 23] construes what she calls the full force of *ahimsa*). Yet it is likewise difficult to imagine a mode of waging severe social conflict—one in which perhaps the clash of seemingly diametrically opposed interests have not proven to be susceptible to reason, persuasion, negotiation, or protest, which are in fact the first stages of nonviolent strategies—without coercion or injury to individuals.

Freedom and Coercion

The liberal philosopher Isaiah Berlin (1969, p. 137) said that "there is no value higher than the individual" and thus to use individuals for my ends is "a contradiction of what I know men to be, namely ends in themselves." While it is clear that Kant emphasized the intrinsic worth of the individual person as the anchor of his philosophy, he also reasoned from the necessity of a well-ordered society for the benefit and protection of the individual. Likewise, although nonviolent philosophy holds to the intrinsic worth of the individual, it additionally reasons from the practical necessity of waging social conflict successfully, that is, of achieving just arrangements that serve our interests as well as others'.

Berlin said that coercion "implies the deliberate interference of other human beings within the area in which I could otherwise act" (1969, p. 122). In this sense, he continued, one lacks freedom if "prevented from attaining a goal by human beings" (1969, p. 122). Now the withdrawal of our cooperation does seem to fit this bill. Yet noncooperation is a crucial "weapon" in the arsenal of nonviolent strategy (see, e.g., Pelton, 1974, pp. 149-190, for an account of the role of noncooperation as a concept and instrument in the philosophy and strategies of nonviolence). In the course of waging social conflict, reason, persuasion, negotiation, and protest may need to be supplemented by noncooperation, not only as a moral obligation to resist evil, but in order to achieve successful conflict resolution. Gandhi realized that while the noncooperation of one person may be moral, the organized noncooperation of many people is politically powerful as well. He often said that no government, even the most despotic, could exist without the cooperation of the people (Gandhi, 1961, pp. 14, 116, 157; Shridharani, 1939, p. 29).

Nonviolent noncooperation may be characterized as a unique form of coercion, but coercion nonetheless. In taking such forms as social and economic boycotts and strikes, nonpayment of taxes, and mass resignation from government positions, noncooperation interferes with the activities of other people and prevents them from obtaining their goals, but it does so through withdrawal of cooperation with social and economic institutions. (In those instances in which noncooperation happens to break the law, it can be referred to as civil disobedience.) To the extent that our cooperation was necessary for the continuance of the institutions, we have inconvenienced and discomforted others who have benefited from them. Such assertion of power may force our adversaries to reconsider their positions and decide to begin or resume negotiations with us, but in any event, the institutions that required our participation for their existence will cease to exist. During the renowned Montgomery Bus Boycott, the segregated front-back ridership pattern ceased to exist because black people had withdrawn their participation in it, and the economic viability of the bus system itself was threatened. An unjust system requires for its existence the "cooperation" (even if coerced) of the oppressed as well as the oppressors. Noncooperation has a coercive influence on others to the extent that they depend upon and have come to expect our compliance with their own actions.

If our adversaries resort to threats and violence to gain our withdrawn support, then we can maintain our own freedom of action to the extent that we are willing to suffer for it. As Gandhi (1961, p. 67) said: "He who has not the capacity of suffering cannot non-co-operate." Our ability and willingness to suffer allows us to maintain our autonomy and self-control and to continue our refusal to comply with injustice even in the face of coercion. Noncooperation is a concept at the heart of nonviolent philosophy in that it implies the autonomy, freedom, and responsibility of the individual to resist participation in injustice or unjust systems.

The source of coercion in nonviolent noncooperation is the assertion of individual freedom in its most fundamental sense: the retention of the autonomy (some would say "right") not to be used by others for their own ends, and to maintain the refusal to participate in—or lend one's own mind, body, and actions to—such use. Indeed, Berlin maintained that the "whole of the Kantian morality" and the "mysterious phrase about men being 'ends in themselves'" lies in the assumption that every human being possesses "the capacity to choose what to do, and what to be, however narrow the limits within which his choice may lie, however hemmed in by circumstances beyond his control" and "rests on the view that it is a marvelous thing in itself when a man pits himself against the world, and sacrifices himself to an ideal without reckoning the consequences" (Berlin, 1951, p. 337). Yet Kant, so intent on maintaining societal order, held that there is no right to resistance to or rebellion against the state, and that the people have a duty to put up with even "an unbearable abuse of supreme authority" (1797/1996, 6:320). Even John Rawls, in referring to civil disobedience, worried that if many groups "were all to act in this way, serious disorder would follow" (1971, p. 374).

Rawls speaks of the limits in which one has a "right" to civil disobedience. But from the perspective of nonviolent philosophy, the freedom not to participate in enterprises that one considers to be evil or unjust, even if legal, is not a right granted by others, but a moral duty carried out with a willingness to exercise that freedom even under the prospect of suffering at the hands of others as a consequence. Rawls' worry is reminiscent of Kant's test of universality: What if everyone were to do that? The answer of a votary of nonviolence would be that the injustice would fall. However, the votary of nonviolence does in fact impose upon his or her consideration and enactment of civil disobedience other general limits proposed by Rawls (1971, pp. 371-377), that is, to limit it to instances of substantial injustice in which less drastic means have been exhausted, and to instances in which it is not likely to contribute to a general and chaotic societal disorder.

Perhaps Kant thought of rebellion and resistance only in terms of violence and coercion. Perhaps, too, this is what Jesus had in mind when he said "resist not evil" (Matthew 5:39). But Gandhi sought to resist evil, and his challenge was to seek and find viable alternatives to violence in every mode of social conflict, whereas Kant merely assumed that coercion to the point of violence on the part of the state may sometimes be necessary in order to protect human freedom. The conscious striving toward the ideal of nonviolence obliges us to be concerned about the nature of our means far more than is present in Kant's philosophy or liberalism. It cannot be taken as a given that coercion beyond noncooperation, nor violence, may sometimes be necessary in order to defend freedom and reverence for human life; nor that means cannot be found to reduce harm to the adversary and others even while implementing noncooperation. A consistency between freedom and the means used to protect and assert freedom cannot be declared by fiat, but must be sought through the creation and discovery of superior means. Such is the focus of nonviolent philosophy.

Desert and Noncooperation

Apparently, Kant's principle of treating persons as ends, and not merely as means, did not prevent him from favoring the death penalty for murder (1797/1996, 6:333). Now many of us would be willing to live by the principle of capital punishment for murder. It cannot be said to be inconsistent with Kant's formula of universal law. It can even be argued that there is no inconsistency in inferring the death principle from his unique formulation of the means-ends principle. Kant favored punishment for its own sake, with the death penalty as a form of retribution or just desert (6:331-333). He was opposed to using punishment merely for the purpose of deterring others by way of making an example of the person to be punished, because in the latter case it could be said that the person is used as means to an end. "He must previously have been found *punishable* before any thought can be given to drawing from his punishment something of use for himself or his fellow citizens" (6:331; italics in original). With the death penalty instituted as retribution, it can be said that the person, as the perpetrator of the crime, is being treated as an end and is being punished as such, for his or her own deed—and it can even be said, with the granting of respect to him or her as a person.

Yet advocacy of the death penalty seems to circumvent the reason *why* the means-ends principle is formulated, namely, because the individual has absolute worth. Ironically, at the same time that the death penalty prescription for murder reveals the value a society places on human life, it also contradictorily violates that value. In other words, from the perspective of the life-affirmation principle, to support life through life-destroying acts is itself a contradiction. This principle of life affirmation, as universal without condition, judgment, or exception, dictates the ethic of means and ends so much associated with nonviolence. If killing is wrong, then it is always wrong. It is *because* the individual must not be violated in any way that he or she must not be used as a means to an end, or harmed in the *process*. The means must be *consistent* with the end, so that if the end is to affirm life, the means must also affirm life within itself. From the nonviolent perspective, Kant's acceptance of capital punishment for murder in order to affirm life is indeed approval of the treatment of a person merely as means, and not as an end.

Similarly, Kant's logic that any coercion opposed to any hindrance of freedom is consistent with freedom is not acceptable to nonviolence. Surely, there are degrees of violation of another's freedom, and killing is the ultimate violation, whether performed by the murderer or by the governmental agent of retribution. Nonviolent noncooperation, on the other hand, strives to minimize violation of others' personal freedom. In its quest for noninjury, at least, nonviolence, consistent with the universality of nonexception, makes no distinction between innocent person and criminal, or friend and adversary, and thus strives for an undifferentiating reverence for human life, even within the means.

But Kant's insistence on retribution (whosoever has committed murder "must *die*" [1797/1996, 6:333; italics in original]) differs from the logic of his freedom-coercion principle because it is not, by definition, something used to counter any present or future hindrance to freedom. Hence his endorsement of violent coercion is not only for the protection of freedom, but also for deserved punishment. It is clear that even this justice of desert is consistent with Kant's formula of universal law, as much as is the principle of life affirmation.

Although we have focused here on capital punishment, the more general issue of desert is raised. While liberalism, historically, has been comfortable with the concept of desert, nonviolence is not. Surely, there are many liberals who are against capital punishment (even though they may subscribe to desert in other matters), and their position on this is consistent with the principle of life affirmation. Yet one of the crucial differences between nonviolence and liberalism might lie in the concept of desert. While only the life-affirmation frame of justice is reflected in nonviolent philosophy, a mixture of two frames of justice, those of life affirmation and justice as individual desert, is reflected in liberal philosophy.

A votary of nonviolence, according to Gandhi (1961, p. 77), "will always try to overcome evil by good, anger by love, untruth by truth, *himsa* by *ahimsa*." (Yet good should be done for its own sake.) Reminiscent of the entreaties in the Sermon on the Mount to "love your enemies, bless them that curse you, do good to them that hate you" (Matthew 5:43-44), this perspective of returning good for evil stands directly contrary to the reward/punishment perspective of desert. It precludes promises of reward as well as threats of punishment. To be sure, reward and punishment often can be viewed as merely two sides of the same coin. If, only contingent upon certain behavior, we promise to provide to the other something that he or she wants or desperately needs, then we at the same time threaten to withhold it if that behavior is not forthcoming. In this case, aside from the rhetoric that may be employed, use of the presumed power of reward is indistinguishable from that of punishment. While it is true, as mentioned before, that noncooperation has a coercive influence on others to the extent that they depend on and have come to expect our compliance with their own actions, the nonviolent perspective allows for returning good for evil while the desert perspective does not. From the latter perspective, people "deserve" certain rewards or punishments for their past deeds, and it is right to threaten punishment or promise reward for the sake of eliciting desired behaviors in the future. Conversely, it is wrong to "reward" bad behavior—and not practical, since that behavior will thereby be "reinforced."

When nonviolence takes the form of noncooperation, "it is not non-cooperation with the evil-doer but with his evil deed. This is an important distinction. The (votary of nonviolence) co-operates with the evil-doer in what is good..." (Kumarappa, 1961, p. iv). Noncooperation with the evil deed but not with the evildoer, while cooperating with him or her in what is good, can be viewed as an attempt to focus on the issues without prejudice to persons. This ideal cannot be perfectly attained, of course, because actions directed toward issues affect the people involved in those issues. Our noncooperation may certainly be viewed by those who want our cooperation as punishment, and our cooperation as reward. Yet the concept of cooperation/noncooperation is distinctly different from that of reward/punishment. For one thing, we administer rewards and punishments to others on the basis of our judgment of their past deeds and of them, while we cooperate or noncooperate on the basis of our judgment of the current issues and of our own participation in them. We administer reward/punishment as retribution or approbation for past deeds, and/or as a deterrent or incentive, and/or for purposes of rehabilitation (i.e., to change the person him- or herself). Reward and punishment look backward and forward, while cooperation and noncooperation focus upon the present.

It is true that Gandhi sought to change the attitudes of his adversaries, to convert them, to win their hearts and minds, with the aid of nonviolent noncooperation. But noncooperation is launched for its own sake, to withdraw one's participation in and contribution to the immediate and ongoing matter of injustice and evil. We do not act on a notion of desert, unless it is on our judgment that the current enterprise or social system is deserving or undeserving of our participation. "Non-cooperation in the sense used by me," said Gandhi, "must be non-violent and, therefore, neither punitive nor vindictive nor based on malice, ill-will or hatred" (1961, pp. 161-162).

Since nonviolent noncooperation (not all strikes, boycotts, etc., accord with nonviolent philosophy) is with unjust and oppressive systems, and with evil itself, the nonviolent activist strives to distinguish between issues and systems on the one hand, and people on the other. Thus, even during campaigns of noncooperation, nonviolent action is characterized by a constant willingness to seek out opportunities to cooperate with others, even the adversary, in constructive activity, and includes an active concern for their welfare. Not only is physical injury to the adversary forbidden, but also "the primary necessities of the opponent's life" must be left unscathed (Shridharani, 1939, p. 294). In some cases, the prospect of harm to others is not really present at all. The organized refusal of Indians in South Africa, under Gandhi's leadership, to register as "Asiatics" as ordered by a discriminatory law, could not have harmed government officials or brought suffering to people other than those who had noncooperated. Yet the Indian boycott of foreign cloth, led by Gandhi in India, left jobless a large number of workers in England's textile industry. Alas, noncooperation has its coercive aspects, and the referent for coercion is necessarily people, not issues.

Yet from the nonviolent perspective, noninjury must be of paramount concern, and we must strive to express reverence for human life universally, without condition, judgment, or exception. Whenever desert conflicts with these purposes, it must be excluded. But beyond this, desert is precluded because it distinguishes between deserving and undeserving people, and fails to distinguish between people and their deeds. It judges people for their past deeds, and thereby often condones means that are inconsistent with the ends of life affirmation.

How Shall Justice Be Construed?

In contrast to the nonviolent perspective, John Stuart Mill certainly held to justice as desert. He claimed (in his essay on "Utilitarianism") that "it is universally considered just that each person should obtain that (whether good or evil) which he *deserves*; and unjust that he should obtain a good, or be made to undergo an evil, which he does not deserve" (1863/1990, p. 466; italics in original). He further stated that the "precept of returning good for evil has never been regarded as a case of the fulfillment of justice, but as one in which the claims of justice are waived, in obedience to other considerations" (Mill, 1863/1990, p. 466) that he does not specify. Later in the same essay, he claimed that "retribution, or evil for evil" is "closely connected with the sentiment of justice, and is universally included in the idea" (1863/1990, p. 474).

Yet elsewhere (in his essay on "Representative Government") he claimed there to be a "vast interval" between the morality of the Pentateuch and that of the Prophecies, and between the latter and that of the Gospels (1861/1990, p. 341). He speaks of this as progress, and speaks of it in the context of discussing government. Now since this "progression" has often been considered to have gone from justice as desert and loving one's neighbor to returning good for evil and loving even one's enemy (although erroneously, according to many modern scholars, as discussed in chapter 1, since the elements of the Gospels alluded to here were already present in the Tanakh), it is unclear whether Mill thought that Jesus did not mean that the principles he espoused should be applied to government or, like many Christians, Mill admired the principles in the abstract but considered their application to real life to be impractical.

Yet there is also the matter here of whether the "precept of returning good for evil" can be considered a principle of justice, a principle contrary to justice, or something else again. Mill asked, in this same essay on utilitarianism, what the distinguishing character of justice might be. He concluded that the distinguishing character of morality, which he claimed encompasses justice, is that we consider any conduct to be wrong, "according as we think that the person ought, or ought not, to be punished for it" (1863/1990, p. 468). Thus Mill defines morality (and hence justice) in terms of desert. Justice is to be further distinguished from the wider sphere of morality, according to Mill, in that it involves the idea of a personal right; injustice involves violating other persons' rights. This feature, he also claimed, "constitutes the specific difference between justice, and generosity or beneficence" (1863/1990, p. 469). "No one has a moral right to our generosity or beneficence, because we are not morally bound to practise those virtues towards any given individual" (1863/1990, p. 469). Thus, whether or not the precepts contained, for example, in the Sermon on the Mount, can be considered moral obligations, or further, obligations of justice, depends upon whether or not anyone "has a moral right to our generosity or beneficence." It seems to me that the philosophy of nonviolence, and the core value of reverence for human life, posit that they do, and in that case, what Mill might have had in mind when referring to "generosity and benevolence" may be called obligations of justice. Moreover, it may not be the "sentiment of justice," as Mill would have it, "to punish a person who has done harm" (1863/1990, p. 469), but the sentiment of revenge, which, nonviolence must hold, has no place in justice.

Definitions, of course, are arbitrary, and are set by implicit common agreement. The concept of justice, however, has always had an ineffable or particularly intangible quality, although we all have a *sense* of justice. One dictionary definition construes justice in terms of desert, another as impartiality or fairness (all definitions cited here are from *Webster's New World Dictionary*, 1994). In that yet another definition is rectitude, and one definition of the latter term is "conduct according to moral principles," it is at least allowable within the vagueness of the grounds of common agreement to posit that justice refers to those actions that respect, support, and enhance (human) life without exception.

It is possible to construe life affirmation as justice because, from the perspective of the life-affirmation frame, violation of life is injustice. It is so unconditionally and without exception. Hence we have a *principle* of life affirmation. From that, it is a short step to say that not to *affirm* life is injustice. We have seen this already in Kumarappa's statement about cooperating with the evildoer in what is good, and Gandhi's agreement with the concept of returning good for evil. "I accept the interpretation of *ahimsa*, namely, that it is not merely a negative state of harmlessness but it is a positive state of love, of doing good even to the evil-doer" (Gandhi, 1961, p. 161). Even Kant (1785/1998, 4:423) implied that a principle that entailed merely passively not violating others, and not actively helping others too, cannot be willed as a universal moral principle. Thus Schopenhauer (1839/1995, p. 92) reduces Kant's intended moral principle to: "Injure no one; on the contrary, help everyone as much as you can." In any event, nonviolence, grounded solely in a life-affirmation frame of justice, can be seen to eschew justice as desert. The notion of returning good for evil is diametrically opposed to the desert concept. This is evident in Gandhi's concept of constructive program, or constructive work, to be discussed below, which also clearly moves us from noninjury, if viewed in any narrow sense, to affirmation.

Constructive Program and Modern Liberalism

An integral part of Gandhi's nonviolent campaigns was constructive work, even in the midst of conflict. During a campaign on behalf of peasants working on indigo plantations, he initiated constructive work in the form of development of primary schools for children, sanitary work, instruction in hygiene, and treatment of skin disease (see Sharp, 1960, pp. 34-37). Although he believed that constructive work should be done for its own sake (Gandhi, 1961, p. 101), he also believed that for exploitation of the peasants to cease, not only the redress of immediate grievances was necessary, but also the uplift of the peasants through education, improved living conditions, increased social awareness, and increased self-respect. This was the path to freedom. Gandhi's constructive program designed for Indian independence included communal (Hindu-Muslim) unity, the elimination of untouchability, the domestic production of cloth, village sanitation, basic and adult education, women's liberation, education in health and hygiene, and economic equality (Gandhi, 1941). By economic equality, however, he did not mean everyone's possession of equal material wealth, but rather sufficient food, clothing, and shelter for everyone (Bondurant, 1967, p. 153).

Constructive work also included development of parallel structures. In calling for the boycott of British courts, schools, legislative councils, and cloth, Gandhi also called for the establishment of parallel schools, arbitration boards, and public service organizations (Nanda, 1958, p. 204; Bondurant, 1967, p. 184). Constructive work is what makes nonviolence positive, life affirming, and constructive throughout. Although the foregoing examples of it concerned Gandhi's own people, its extension to the adversary is consistent with nonviolent philosophy. Indeed, as mentioned earlier, votaries of nonviolence will constantly seek out opportunities to cooperate with others in constructive activity. As we have already seen, "cooperation with good" includes an active concern for the welfare of others, including the adversary.

Although classical liberalism reacts to the fear of government tyranny over the individual, and has therefore placed much emphasis on the establishment of individual rights against the encroachment of government, what can be called modern liberalism is concerned not only with rights protection, but the active promotion of welfare and well-being. Yet the right to "life, liberty, and the pursuit of happiness" proclaimed in the American Declaration of Independence can be interpreted as at least a right to (equal) opportunity. Thus we can derive modern liberalism from classical liberalism: the purpose of just government is not only to protect individual freedom from outside encroachment, but also to promote (equal) opportunity for all.

There is a difference between using coercion to protect liberty, and devising social policies in which only issues of resource distribution are involved. As we have seen, the violence of the death penalty cannot be defended through Kant's freedom-coercion formulation, but only through some concept of desert. Liberalism has employed the concept of desert to also shape and justify its social distributional policies. Gandhi's constructive program, of course, was not a government program, and in some aspects was meant to replace government by building parallel structures, or parallel government. But we can ask how, if we were to be guided by its spirit of the constructive support of human life and development, and not at all by desert, the ensuing social policies might differ from those often propagated by liberalism.

Implications for Forms of Social Policy

For nonviolence, the means-ends principle proceeds from the moral value of the sanctity of human life. Liberalism can be generated from this single moral value also, but more often it has been conceptualized as stemming from a social contract, or from the reasoning present in Kant's formula of universal law—which can accommodate the means-ends principle as construed in nonviolence, but also maxims contradictory to it. It can be said, in a sense, that the difference between what morality would oblige and justice would oblige is narrower in the philosophy of nonviolence than in Kant's philosophy, unless we were to declare that whatever is practical is also moral.

Because the social contract, Kant's formula of universal law, and Rawls' original position formulation can accommodate contradictory maxims, they are vague and contradictory in their policy implications, which include, for example, both the acceptance and nonacceptance of capital punishment. From the perspective of nonviolence, justice is derived from reverence for human life, and not from implicit social contracts, or the choices that one would make or the arrangements that one would endorse in Rawls' original position. Both Kant and Rawls would place reverence for the individual human life at the center of their philosophies of justice, yet they did not reason (even within pure theory) from that value alone. Hence, arguably, they did not oblige themselves to apply rationality to the problem of developing alternative means to violence and coercion as intently as Gandhi did.

Therefore, if we inquire into the policy implications that nonviolence might hold for liberalism, it can be said that one challenge that it poses is to find the means to narrow the spheres of state coercion and violence as much as possible. It has often been pointed out, of course, that governmental tax collection, for the purpose of operating government, is itself coercive. Although I will propose in chapter 5 that the taxing of citizens is not "theft," as some libertarians would describe it, it must be concluded nonetheless that the very act itself of collecting taxes is coercive. We should at least be concerned about minimizing the coerciveness of the tax system itself, or the extent of the violation of persons that we threaten. Imprisonment for tax evasion, for example, should not be necessary because the taxes owed could be collected through confiscation of property or garnisheeing future wages.

The vexing problem of taxation notwithstanding, we should at least strive to narrow the uses of state coercion to the obstruction of acts that are severely violative of others, and their forms to those that are least injurious to others, all the while seeking alternatives to coercion altogether. Thus, capital punishment would be abolished. Imprisonment would not be used for the sake of retribution, but only as is necessary to restrain the guilty from severe violation of others.

Government policies would not be used as vehicles for "social engineering," as they often are today. Thus they would not take the form of providing incentives or disincentives (which are, in effect, projected reward and punishment justified on grounds of desert) for presumably desirable or undesirable behaviors. Social engineering includes the coercive prohibition of behaviors that are not in themselves violative of others' lives (often in search of the supposed "common good"). It must be said that even Gandhi was not immune to its temptations. He proclaimed: "Prohibition of intoxicating liquors and drugs and boycott of foreign cloth have ultimately to be by law.... Drink and drugs sap the moral well-being of those who are given to the habit" (Gandhi, 1961, p. 326). He took "prohibition of drink and intoxicating drugs and of gambling" to be part of his constructive program (Gandhi, 1961, pp. 100-101). Perhaps in greater consistency with the basic tenets of nonviolence, Berlin (1969, p. 137) said that "to manipulate men, to propel them towards goals which you—the social reformer—see, but they may not, is to deny their human essence, to treat them as objects without wills of their own, and therefore to degrade them."

It is difficult to say where to draw a line between Gandhi's philosophy of nonviolence and the wider sphere of his political, economic, and other views. Some of these views might be said to be Gandhi's own derivations from the philosophy, but are we to equate them with the philosophy itself? Bondurant (1967), in her excellent analysis, treats both the essential elements of the philosophy of nonviolence and his political, religious, and economic views. Certainly, Martin Luther King, Jr. faithfully represented and executed, in large part, the philosophy of nonviolence in the mid-twentieth-century American civil rights struggle, without necessarily adhering to or supporting Gandhi's many positions taken on social, political, and economic structures and issues. In this analysis comparing nonviolence and liberalism, I refer only to the core precepts and strategies of nonviolence as already described above.

If we were to be guided by the nonviolent precepts of reverence for human life, noncooperation, "cooperation with good," and constructive work in the formation of social policies, then basic human needs would be addressed without reference to desert and without condition. As Bondurant (1967, p. 19) points out, "concern for human needs lies at the core of Gandhian teaching." Welfare benefits would be distributed in order to address dire need, and not to control the behaviors of the needy. Hence, in the United States, public assistance to mothers with children would not be reduced or eliminated on the basis of time limits, conviction for a drug offense, or, as in some states, the children's school attendance records, or the birth of a new child. Policies designed to address financial need would do so in a universal manner, and so there would not be separate policies, each with their own eligibility requirements, for financial aid to the elderly, women with children, disabled people, veterans, and victims of disaster. Homeless people would be provided housing, without condition. If health care insurance is to be provided to some, such as the elderly, then it would be provided to all.

The question for a liberal society is not only how much government intervention there should be, but to what extent that intervention should be coercive. Programs and services meant to prevent injury and promote people's well-being should be offered in abundance, but on a noncoercive basis. Thus, child welfare services would not be forced upon impoverished parents under threat of child removal, as they are in today's child welfare system in the United States and elsewhere. Only the continuance of injurious behavior and conditions that cannot be addressed or remedied in other ways, and not the refusal to accept services, would then make one liable to coercive intervention. The aim of coercive systems within a liberal democratic society is to limit harm to others in situations in which noncoercive means are not viable or cannot be found. In order to limit the domain of coercion as much as possible, and contribute to its contraction, we must consider whether we can achieve the same goals of limiting harm by establishing and expanding noncoercive, voluntary-acceptance preventive programs and services.

The approach suggested here expands the role of intervention in services offered to individuals on a voluntary-acceptance basis and narrows the scope of coercive intervention, and, hopefully, the need for coercive intervention. The objective is to increase the facilitative capacities of government to protect and promote the well-being of all individuals within the society, while limiting the presumed need of its coercive capacities to do the same, for the former is consistent with the nonviolation of the individual, while the latter is not. The process ideal to aspire to is to limit the domain of coercion as much as possible by increasing individual opportunity for growth and development as much as possible.

Implicit in all that has been said here is that since government is the instrument of community, and because the community is composed of individuals, then the community has moral obligations similar to those of individuals, and it is thus obliged to act through government to fulfill them. These moral obligations are beyond or aside from the requirements of any implicit social contract, and may trump what individuals might have agreed to in Rawls' original position. Even if viewed as contractual obligations, the contractual formulation of liberalism would limit them to members of the community. But from the nonviolent perspective of justice—as well as from the perspective of liberalism when construed as stemming solely from the moral value of the sanctity of human life—such moral obligations would extend to all individuals, even beyond the community in which any implicit social contract may be said to exist, and even to adversaries outside of the community. Foreign policy would be predicated upon the central value of the sanctity of human life, and we would strive to uphold this value within the processes and means of policy implementation. We would strive to avoid the use of violence by developing viable alternatives for conducting foreign policy and waging conflict, and withdraw our complicity in actions that contribute to violence and the destruction of human life. We would foster and join in support of constructive and life-supporting enterprises even in adversary nations, under the principle of cooperating with good while noncooperating with evil.

Social Utility

There remains the question of whether social utility is most successfully promoted through the justice of desert or through justice as life affirmation in accordance with the philosophy of nonviolence. After all, the social engineering practiced by liberal democratic societies is meant to serve some purposes of social utility. At the same time, it is true that Gandhi and King believed in the ultimate superior utility of nonviolence over violence in terms of the collective interest of humankind. But the arguments made with especial eloquence in the sermons and writings of King, in regard to the convergence of nonviolence with the practical interests of humankind, are arguments made after the fact of the acceptance of nonviolence on moral grounds alone. To argue that such acceptance might ultimately prove to be in our mutual interest is quite different from arriving at the acceptance of moral principles by way of reasoning from social utility. Indeed, only moral principles accepted for their own sake, given our limited rationality and our uncertain knowledge of our future, may be powerful enough to guide us toward a higher rationality and fulfillment of our mutual interests.

According to Rawls (1971, p. 30): "All ethical doctrines worth our attention take consequences into account in judging rightness. One which did not would simply be irrational, crazy." But the primary consequence that the ethical doctrine of nonviolence takes into account is not apart from the means, but within them. It concerns how each and every individual is treated. Hence the question of consequences becomes a question of the means themselves: Do the means, regardless of other intended ends, violate the individual? The consequence of cooperation with good and constructive work is within the means, as much as is that of violence, coercion, and violation. Hence nonviolence does not look forward or backward, but focuses upon the justice or injustice of actions, or inactions, in the present. Therein lies its social utility.

Gandhi once said: "In our *ignorance* we must kill rabid dogs even as we might have to kill a man found in the act of killing people" (in Erikson, 1969, p. 422; italics added). He also said: "I do believe that where there is *only* a choice between cowardice and violence I would advise violence" (Gandhi, 1961, p. 132; italics added). He viewed resort to violence as a necessity due only to our current ignorance, but no less morally regrettable and inconsistent with justice for that. For Kant, on the other hand, coercion in the cause of protection of freedom is "right." What is the practical difference, one might argue, between claiming that an action is immoral and thus morally regrettable, even if necessary in our current state of ignorance, and declaring that because it is necessary, it is right or moral or just in itself? We might answer with another question: If we do not regard violence as morally wrong in an absolute sense, then who is to judge whose violence is immoral and whose is "moral"? If violence were not morally regrettable, then it would not stand in need of the justifications we usually rush to bring to our own use of violence. If we were not to consider violence to be morally regrettable, then we would not be motivated to search for other means to protect our lives and interests, since each set of means could be regarded as the moral equivalent of the other.

The social utility of nonviolent philosophy includes the fact that it presses us, far more than philosophies that assume that violent coercion will always be needed as an option in defending liberty and that revere the notion of desert, to seek to minimize coercion and to develop alternative means to violence. It can be said that Kant's freedom-coercion formulation violates the means-ends principle for the sake of presumed social utility. On the other hand, nonviolent thinking pushes the envelope, as it were, by trying to resolve the contradiction by rationally seeking nonviolent alternatives.

Ultimately, Gandhi claimed, we "are helpless mortals caught in the conflagration of *himsa*." He said that "man cannot be wholly free from *himsa*. So long as he continues to be a social being, he cannot but participate in the *himsa* that the very existence of society involves..." (Gandhi, 1954, pp. 427-428). Yet he had faith in human reason to create and discover new ways of affirming life within the means, and further constraining the domain of *himsa*, even if never perfectly achieving the ideal of nonviolence, much as we will never perfectly achieve the ideal of liberal democracy.

Note

1. In references to Kant, the first number after the date of the edition consulted refers to the volume number of the standard German edition of Kant's works, and the second number refers to the pagination of that edition. The page numbers are given in the margins of most translations, at the point at which the page begins in the standard edition.

3

Principle and Sentiment

In the Torah it is written: "When you reap the harvest of your land, you shall not reap all the way to the edges of your field, or gather the gleanings of your harvest. You shall not pick your vineyard bare, or gather the fallen fruit of your vineyard; you shall leave them for the *poor* and the *stranger*" (Leviticus 19:9-10; see also Leviticus 23:22; italics added). The principle seems clear: need must be addressed. Perhaps it was assumed in those days that all strangers, not having brought their wealth with them, were always in need of support from the community, in terms of food and lodging. Specific mention of them was for the purpose of inclusion of people who might otherwise have been thought to be excluded from the application of the principle addressing need.

Yet it is also written: "When you reap the harvest in your field and overlook a sheaf in the field, do not turn back to get it; it shall go to the stranger, the *fatherless*, and the *widow*... When you beat down the fruit of your olive trees, do not go over them again; that shall go to the stranger, the *fatherless* and the *widow*. When you gather the grapes of your vineyard, do not pick it over again; that shall go to the stranger, the *fatherless*, and the *widow*" (Deuteronomy 24:19-21; italics added). Moreover: "You shall not ill-treat any *widow* or *orphan*" (Exodus 22:21; italics added).

Why are the fatherless child or orphan, and the widow, singled out along with the stranger? What special claims on justice do the orphan and the widow have? Surely there are others, too, who may be in need, and who certainly should not be ill-treated. But we tend to feel sorry for the orphan and the widow above others, and the authors of the Torah appeal directly to that sympathy by merely invoking these categories. As for the stranger, the evocation of sympathy may require elaboration: "You shall not oppress a stranger, for you know the feelings of the stranger, having yourselves been strangers in the land of Egypt" (Exodus 23:9). This appeal to both individual remembrances and group history of having been strangers in Egypt is made several times in the Torah. We should have sympathy for the stranger for the reason that we were once strangers in a strange land, and know the feeling.

But where has principle gone? Is need to be addressed on principle, or are we to be guided by our sentiments? If we take principle to be a rule of conduct, or guide to behavior (e.g., to address need, or not to ill-treat individuals), then sentiment, defined here as feeling or emotion, often moves us to apply that principle selectively, targeting certain groupings of individuals for that behavior while excluding other individuals. I suggest that justice must involve principles that promote equal application to all, whether those principles pertain to need, due process, compensation, civil rights, taxation, fair distribution of the common wealth, or even desert. Yet to complicate matters, even though our sentiments are selective, principle itself may derive from sentiment. After all, what moves us to aid those in need altogether, or view such aid in terms of justice? Inquiry into the nature of a just society must include the disentanglement of sentiment from principle, as well as an analysis of the relationship between the two.

Sentiment over Principle in Contemporary Policymaking

In the Torah, statements of principle and appeals to sentiment are interwoven and dispersed throughout, and thus we do not witness in it some ancient phase in a gradual evolution of reliance on principle from reliance on sentiment. The frequent conflict between principle and sentiment in social policy continues throughout history, with sentiment often trumping principle. England's Elizabethan Poor Laws divided the needy into those considered to be worthy of relief, including the lame, "impotent," old, and blind, and those who were to be set to work (see Axinn and Levin, 1982, pp. 9-13). The American Social Security Act of 1935 divided the needy into separate programs for the elderly, the blind, and children. This Act even provided higher cash benefits for the elderly and the blind than for children. That this differential treatment was likely due to negative sentiment toward, or suspicions of, the parents is supported by the fact that needy children, to this day, are more generously supported in foster homes and institutions than when residing with their parents. The elderly also might have fared better than children due to their stronger lobbying power as a group. But the blind, without equivalent power, fared equally well, and this can only be attributed to the uniquely deep sympathy we have toward them, perhaps grounded in our own special fears of the loss of sight. After all, the deaf and other subcategories of physically handicapped people were not designated for benefits, even though their basic subsistence needs (of food, clothing, and shelter)—which is what these policies were meant to address—may have been the same.

The triumphs of sentiment over principle are legion in modern social policies, arguably indicated by many such categorical distinctions, in the United States as well as many other countries. Our dislike of "welfare mothers" have prompted policies that place time limits on the provision of cash benefits to address their need, and other restrictions that penalize their children for the supposed sins of their parents (see Pelton, 1999b). Meanwhile, our positive sentiment toward needy elderly and disabled people, driven by images of frailty and helplessness, allow for policies that differentially address their need indefinitely and with relative impunity. Shelter is denied or provided only temporarily to homeless people, based on policies inspired by affective stereotypes of homeless people as freeloading bums who "enjoy their lifestyles."

Sentiment, not principle, is appealed to by affirmative action policies that create preferred-group status, much as racist policies of the past and welfare policies favoring the orphan and the widow have done. Special "sin" taxes, their very appellation revealing their origins in antipathy, are selectively applied to the purchase of cigarettes and alcoholic beverages, and thus to consumers with preferences for such products. Selective drug prohibition laws have their origins in racist beliefs that cocaine induced superhuman strength in black people, that opium incited sexual relations between Chinese men and white women, and that marijuana caused violence by Mexican immigrants (Musto, 1987). In California, the public's positive sentiment toward certain groups of people allows special laws to be passed granting property and renters' tax assistance to senior citizens, and property tax exemptions to disabled veterans.

Special laws are passed containing greater penalties for the murder of children and police officers than for the murder of other individuals, and for so-called hate crimes. Such laws appeal directly to our heightened sympathies and antipathies toward the victims and perpetrators, but ask us to value the lives of children, police officers, and victims of group hatred differently than other human lives. And while capital punishment continues to be permissible in the United States, the Supreme Court has recently declared, in a ruling arguably based more on sympathy than principle, that execution of mentally retarded people constitutes "cruel and unusual punishment." The principle that certain crimes are to be addressed by capital punishment will be applied selectively. At the same time, the principle that capital punishment constitutes "cruel and unusual punishment" will be applied selectively.

Sentiment can violate principle not only in policies, but also in the course of their application. In fact, in recent years, "abuse excuses," such as the "battered women's syndrome" and "black rage," have been imaginatively invoked in the courtroom (see Dershowitz, 1994; Pelton, 1999a, pp. 130-135). The defense presumably attempts to establish, as required by criminal law, that the past victimization of the defendant affected his or her state of mind at the time of the alleged criminal behavior in such a manner that he or she had little or no choice. Yet, in practice, the altered state of mind is seldom established, and the outcome of the trial depends upon whether the jury is convinced that the alleged past victimization took place, and whether such belief has evinced a substantial degree of sympathy for the defendant from the jury. To be sure, that is what such defenses are designed to do. "Black rage" and "urban survival syndrome" defenses have been less successful on behalf of African-American men on trial for murder, perhaps because there is less sympathy for poor people or the realities of black ghetto life than there is for battered women. And the inconsistencies of sentiment cut two ways—if evidence can be produced to show that you were under the influence of drugs or alcohol at the time of the alleged crime, this might contribute to conviction and a harsher sentence, but if the judge and jury can be convinced that you were under the influence of mental illness or previous abuse, this might bode well for you.

Our likes and dislikes, preferences and prejudices, strong as they already are, can be strengthened by powerful images, and cultivated through stories pertaining to particular individuals and groups. Movie stars, sometimes motivated by their personal experiences with particular diseases, are enlisted to lobby for governmental funding of research for those diseases, as well as to appeal for charitable funding of such research. Displays of horrible images, such as of battered children, often presented along with misleadingly bloated statistics, often draw our sympathy and unequal attention to particular situations and issues and away from other issues of equivalent moral gravity that leave individuals no less injured or dead. Indeed, those who seek justice (or even charity) for people dying of hunger and starvation on another continent are obliged to resort to such imagery. And, often necessarily if the purpose is change, historical accounts of group oppression are used to draw attention not to oppression per se but to the oppression of particular groups selected from all those who have suffered group oppression. The upshot is frequently policymaking guided by sentiment, with concomitant avoidance of the task of constructing principle. Surely, policies are often made on the basis of such sentiment selectively aroused, and rationalized in the name of justice. We even say that we are addressing particular injustices to particular individuals and groups. Yet when we stop at sentimental reaction, acting on it alone, rather than upon a principle that may be derived from it, we favor those to whom our attention was drawn while ignoring others who are similarly situated, thereby in effect treating them dissimilarly or in a discriminatory manner.

Sympathy for the victims of the September 11, 2001 attacks and their families compelled millions of Americans to contribute to various funds set up on their behalf. Although charity obviously follows sentiment, we might expect public policy and law to follow principle. That sympathy alone is not a guide to justice is seen in the fact that imbalances quickly arose in the proportionality of the amounts contributed to funds for the families of the firefighters and police officers who died at New York's World Trade Center on the one hand, and for those of others who were murdered there (Sun, Cohen, and Salmon, 2002). But it is also seen in the government policies formulated to compensate all of these families and the questions raised of equivalent policy concern for the families of victims of the Oklahoma City terrorist attack a few years earlier

(Lagnado, 2002). Indeed, questions of compensation for families of victims of myriad other disasters, caused by terrorists or not, and involving large numbers of people or only a few, could be raised. No clear path through the morass of compensation issues is readily discernible or perhaps even possible to formulate, but it is clear that whatever constructive and positive results sympathy may produce for the families involved, sympathy and justice are two entirely different guides to compensation and policy. Only government can do justice when it comes to social welfare, yet, as seen in the legislation passed by Congress for compensation to victims' families in the September 11 attacks, its policies often embody sentiment rather than well-formulated principles.

Sentiment and Narrow Reasoning

Rationales or justifications are often provided for the shaping of policies by sentiment. They can be used to rationalize sentiment already present (such as motives of revenge in regard to the issue of capital punishment) and/or to cultivate sentiment in others. Why it is presumably just or reasonable to grant benefits or greater benefits to some individuals, or to some groups of individuals, rather than to others, must be explained. Rationales are needed not only to salve the consciences of the beneficiaries, but to win the sympathy or at least the passivity of those who will not directly benefit.

A few years ago, California Governor Gray Davis proposed to reward teachers by exempting them from state income taxes (Purdum, 2000). Much reason can no doubt be garnered to support such laws. Sentiment focuses discussion on the important work that school teachers do, the relatively low pay they receive, and their worthiness of reward. For those who admire teachers, arguments that we should make policies that reward them for their important work can be very convincing at first blush. If this can be simply done by exempting them from state income taxes, why not do it? The solution seems reasonable, even logical. But principles of justice stand outside the narrower reason of sentiment to question the act of selection itself. Principle asks why, if teachers are to be exempted from state income taxes, everyone who does important or societally beneficial work should not be exempted also, if anyone at all. To do otherwise is to raise a contradiction that principle does not abide. Selective sentiment encourages narrow reasoning, while narrow reasoning elicits selective sentiment. (Although the exemption was not enacted, California now provides teachers with special income tax credits.)

Narrow reasoning supports sentiment and charity, but it is too limited to support justice. When narrow reasoning is used to generate public policy we have, in effect, government engaged in charity while violating justice. Narrow reasoning can in fact initiate and promote concerns of justice by calling attention to the plight of particular individuals or groups. But when we fashion government policies that respond in limited and categorized kind to those individuals and groups—rather than extract the principles that may in fact be pointed to by that narrow reasoning and that can be applied to all and codified in new laws and policies—what results are policies that conform to sentiment and selective self-interest but not to justice.

Sentiment, not principle, is appealed to when policy proposals are put forth to help senior citizens pay for the costs of escalating prescription drug prices, but not others equally in need of such assistance. In this case, the argument that such need is more prevalent among the elderly uses aggregated statistics as well as stereotypical images of "old age" to appeal to sentiment rather than logic. Unless we were to accept some type of crude utilitarianism that would violate or favor individuals for the sake of the "common good," the only purpose that such group statistics can serve is to bolster an appeal to sentiment.

In modern times, social science is often willingly enlisted to fuel and support narrow reasoning. If empirical evidence seems to show that cigarette smoking and alcohol consumption are detrimental to health and public safety, and incur monetary costs to society, it appears reasonable to propose special cigarette and liquor taxes. Sentiment does not even seem to be involved here, nor the judgment necessary in the reasoning for the teachers' policy: the arguments seem to be based on empirical evidence. Yet it can be asked if empirical evidence shows the consumption of other products to be equally hazardous, and if so, how and why have cigarettes and liquor been targeted for special taxation? Did previous sentiment guide the selection, and hence the selection of which products to research? Moreover, it can be asked if the use in policymaking of the frequently aggregate form of the empirical evidence collected is not prejudicial to those particular individuals who consume cigarettes and alcohol without detriment to health or safety. To enlist group statistics is to engage in the same narrow reasoning referred to previously, but now with the appearance of scientific reasoning and backing. Much compelling reasoning can be involved, and often is, but such reasoning is narrow, often driven by and in the service of sentiment, and contrary to the requirements of justice. Reflection is needed to take consideration of the policy proposals out of the realm of sentiment and into the realm of justice, but a guide is needed against which to evaluate them. It must be asked: By what principle or standard is this policy just? Principle asks why certain products, and those who have preferences toward using them, should be singled out and targeted for special taxes, empirical evidence or no. More silently, it asks who will judge.

Historically, perhaps it has been assumed that orphans and widows are more likely to be in need than others, or in greater need than others. But so too, perhaps, are the abandoned child or wife, the physically or mentally ill, the blind or deaf or otherwise physically disabled, or the victim of natural disaster. To be sure, one or another or all of these categories have at one time or another been introduced into social welfare policies. But why single them out? Surely, there are persons in need who fall outside any of these groupings. Why then specify orphanhood or widowhood in policies meant to address need? Whatever reasoning is involved here is of the narrow sort, in that it is not in accord with the full array of facts. But it *is* in accord with our sentimental attachment to orphans and widows.

Putting aside the fallacious reasoning from aggregated statistics to the individual, we may ask what factors might render the individual orphan or widow in need more *deserving* of support than others equally in need. We may consider that the needy orphan or widow has become destitute due to no fault of his or her own. We may consider it legitimate to address only need that is not due to individual fault, while not addressing need due to an individual's own character or actions. In this case, we would not be acting in accordance with the principle that need must be addressed, but rather in accordance with the principle that need not personally caused must be addressed. In fact, this latter principle, sometimes explicitly stated and sometimes implicit, underlies the abundant and familiar policies of social welfare that profess to separate the worthy poor from the unworthy. But it can be argued that even if the precept that only the need of "worthy" (defined as the absence of individual fault) individuals must be addressed could be considered legitimate as a principle of justice, once we allow factors other than individual need itself to enter policies ostensibly aimed at addressing need, we open the door to the influence of sentiment, in this case through judgment of desert and greater worthiness.

The widow may be able-bodied, and thus, although she has lost her husband, quite capable of earning her own living. If she does not do so, we could consider her need to be personally caused. Therefore, although the "able-bodied" is a category often excluded from policies that ostensibly address the need of the worthy or deserving, it overlaps with the widow category, which has been historically included. Yet the woman whose husband abandoned her, being in the same situation as the widow, may be excluded from policies for want of being a widow, and for being able-bodied. And the child whose parents are able-bodied but in need (thus presumably due to their own fault) will not have his or her own need addressed by such policies, even though he or she is similarly situated as the orphan in regard to need and desert (although policies might remove this child from the home in order to address his or her need without addressing that of the parents). On the other hand, jobs might not be available for all able-bodied people who want to work, or some may be victims of employment discrimination in the job market, obviously due to no fault of their own. Moreover, many disabled people may be capable of work.

Yet the orphan, the child, the widow, the elderly, the blind, the disabled, and the able-bodied have been entrenched categories in welfare policies. Since neither rational thinking nor justice is satisfied by these categories, they likely derive from sentiment. We pity the orphan over other children, the widow over the abandoned wife, the blind foremost among the disabled and the disabled over the able-bodied adult, the elderly over the middle-aged adult, the child over the adult. And because of our sentiments, individuals similarly situated in regard to need will be treated differently, raising the specter of discrimination, while the judgment of worthiness is executed in a crudely stereotyped manner.

In reality, such policies can be more accurately viewed as merely instituting a form of compensation for certain sentimentally selected needy people based not on any judgment of worthiness, but upon our sympathy for their loss (e.g., of eyesight or a husband) and our stereotyped imaginings of what sorrow they have been through and the condition they are in (e.g., the elderly must be frail and ill). After all, whereas the alleged conformance of the individuals in the selected categories to the definition of worthiness is problematic, it can be said that every blind person is without sight, and every widow has lost a husband, by definition. Only the consequences of these statuses need be imagined, or "confirmed" by group statistics.

Now while compensation has its place in law and justice (although it is not clear why the government should be involved in it for the categories of people in question here), it is not the same as the addressing of need. Moreover, it is due the wealthy as well as the poor. Be that as it may, one might suggest that if the categories don't do justice, then why not form policies based more closely on the principle that "worthy" need must be addressed, simply by mandating that each person in need must be judged on an individual basis? Aside from the question of justice raised about a society that would not adopt the principle of addressing need without judgment, the nature of the act of judgment itself raises questions of justice. How is it to be determined if an individual's current need is due to his or her own fault or not? And who is to do the determining? A person who refuses any employment offered to him or her may have mental problems even if we have not learned to detect them or, on the other hand, may be lazy. We will declare as "worthy" the persons whose mental problems psychologists have learned to diagnose (although even many mentally ill persons may be capable of working, and so we enter a regress of ill-fitting categories), but not the others. We do this because we have sympathy for the mentally ill, but not for the others.

As discussed earlier, the proliferation of "abuse excuses" used within the criminal justice system have been designed to win the sympathy of juries. The logic of the acceptance of these excuses is faulty, since it presumes that we can distinguish between legitimate and illegitimate excuses (and that the excuses matter). In the welfare policy arena, where no violent act has been committed that might dampen our sympathy, we would have a far greater proliferation of factors proffered to qualify people as "worthy" of receiving welfare support, while decisions would be determined by the petitioner's skill of argumentation in eliciting the judging person's sympathy more than anything else. One of the early administrators of the Social Security Board in the United States, mindful of such problems, "called disability a matter of 'conjecture,' because the state of disability rested not on a set of facts but on the conclusions that were drawn from the facts" (Berkowitz, 1988, p. 283). Indeed, we resort to fixed, relatively determinate categories in our welfare policies in order to avoid these problems. Yet, as we have seen, the fixed categories themselves may be driven by sentiment.

In actuality, the "disabled" category has proved to be quite elastic, requiring highly indeterminate individual judgments. In recent years in the United States, more and more blue-collar workers have decided to drop out of the labor force rather than to accept the lower-paying jobs now available to them. Many of them have turned to the Social Security disability insurance program for support, and the number of recipients in this program has nearly doubled within the past decade or so. Apparently, many of the people who, in the past, would have proved themselves capable of working with bad backs and other injuries now apply for and are accepted for disability benefits (Leonhardt, 2002). Perhaps a backlash will build against them, but the sympathy drawn by our sacrosanct stereotypes of the "disabled" may mitigate against that. Yet the fact that the meager level of benefits afforded to these people by the disability program holds attraction for them, relative to their alternatives, speaks to their state of need, whether they are "able-bodied" or not. However, the benefits are not given to everyone similarly situated, but only to those who decide to petition the program on the basis of "disability," and successfully do so.

Whether an individual is able-bodied, or refuses to work, or is a widow or an orphan, or whether there are jobs available, simply determines whether we will have *sympathy* for that individual's present state of need, not whether that state of need exists or not. It exists: what it is due to is another matter, and this matter determines our sentiment toward him or her, or toward his or her need. We derive satisfaction, no doubt, from a sensed fittingness between deed and desert, from people getting what they "deserve" (whether that desert be positive or negative). But the sentiment that drives or derives from the application of desert, when set into policy, may violate, rather than do, justice.

Although desert is a legitimate concern and enters into countless everyday transactions, arguments for desert, as we have seen, can be used to violate principle or its application. We can never be confident that arguments for desert are not merely serving selective sentiment, narrow reasoning, and interest, all of which act counter to principle, and are the very things that principle should overcome and negate. If we were to speak of a principle of desert, we would have to say that policies that would reduce taxes for teachers but not others, or benefit needy orphans and widows and "the elderly" but not others, or benefit victims of a particular disaster while ignoring those of others, or victims of natural disasters but not those of economic disasters or even individual economic circumstances, all violate that principle. Yet such policies have been propagated allegedly in the service of a principle of desert. Of course, it is possible to incorporate need into the principle of desert, by asserting that need is a form of desert, whether or not one is at personal fault for his or her own need.

But the principle of desert would then dictate that if people in need are deserving of having their need addressed, then all people in need are deserving of that, without exception.

It can be objected that it is self-interest, not sentiment, that guides the development of many of the kinds of social policies criticized here. We readily find justification for acts and policies that benefit ourselves. But even powerful interest groups seeking special benefits, such as exist on behalf of the elderly today, must appeal to the larger public for political support, and the success of this appeal must ultimately depend on positive sentiment. Self-interest may indeed motivate many campaigns for special treatment, but the rationalizations and arguments for "deservingness" of such treatment are necessary to successfully appeal to the wider public's sentiment.

Moreover, even self-interest is based on sentiment—toward oneself. Self-interest stands in direct opposition to principle. Policies that favor ourselves over others, or benefit ourselves but not others in similar circumstances, are in contradiction to principle. Principle is not needed to favor ourselves. It is needed to embody disinterest in policy and law, and to ensure that the narrow self-interest of the powerful does not determine what those policies and laws will be, for policies and laws not based on principle ensure that self-interest, not justice, will be served.

The Derivation of Justice

Yet, ironically, one's sense of justice may be derived from sentiment toward oneself. The famous biblical phrase, "Love your fellow as yourself" (e.g., Leviticus 19:18), has often been taken as the core moral teaching of the Bible, the basis for all morality and justice. It assumes first the valuing of oneself, and then the application of that sentiment to other (human) lives. It reflects a sense of justice based upon sentiment toward (love of) oneself, that implies, as a principle, similar valuing and treatment of other selves as oneself. It is thus a principle derived from sentiment, and expresses reverence for human life.

However, it can be conjectured that the author of this maxim might not have been driven by any sense of justice, but merely by the wisdom to foresee that such a principle must be aspired to if an orderly and viable community is to be built and sustained. Justice has practical purposes, and is implemented to achieve them. But this conjecture begs the question, Why does the author of this maxim desire an orderly and viable community and the ensuing good of the community? The answer must be, if we are to continue in this practical vein, to benefit himself. Yet here we are back to sentiment toward oneself as the generator of principle, in the form of self-interest. And if we say that the author wants to benefit others as well as himself, then we are again back to sentiment as a basis of moral principle.

For David Hume (1740/2000; 1751/1975) and Adam Smith (1759/1966), the morals derive from the sentiments. Smith began his treatise on *The Theory of Moral Sentiments* (1759/1966, p. 3) by saying that even in the nature of a selfish man, there are factors "which interest him in the fortune of others, and render their happiness necessary to him, though he derives nothing from it, except the pleasure of seeing it. Of this kind is pity or compassion..." Immanuel Kant, however, argued that his formula of humanity, "So act that you use humanity, whether in your own person or in the person of any other, always at the same time as an end, never merely as a means" (1785/1998, 4:429), is derived from reason alone, without resort to sentiment. What has been most contested, by Arthur Schopenhauer (1839/1995) and others, is not the ethic itself, but Kant's contention that it "is not borrowed from experience" and "must arise from pure reason" (4:430-431).

To accept Kant's arguments claiming the objective valuation of humanity through reason is to deny any role whatsoever to sentiment in the formulation of morality and justice. If the principles of morality and the foundations of justice are the product of pure reason alone, then I could simply conclude, as I have shown here, that sentiment violates justice, and be done with it. Yet, contrary to Kant, it is still possible to maintain that value stands prior to reason as well as to fact, that a value on life must be derived from sentiment. From sentiment toward oneself is derived the valuing of (human) life, and thus the possibility of a sense of justice.

If we grant that reason cannot posit its own end (humanity) without deriving such valuing of human beings from experience, and further, without presupposing the subjective valuing of oneself, then there are still two ways in which concern for oneself can extend to concern for others: through reason and through sentiment. Principle involves extension through reason, because if life is to be valued in accordance with *principle*, then all life is to be valued, and to prescribe the valuing of my life and not others' is to raise a contradiction. (Yet it can be said that it is precisely because reason cannot posit its own end or object, that reason can be enlisted in the service of self-interest and sentiment, as well as principle.)

We also value others' lives in accordance with *sentiment*, but although we can conjecture that sentiment (originating toward oneself) is necessary for a sense of justice, it cannot be a sufficient basis for justice itself, since it frequently directs us to overlook some lives in violation of justice. Hence we can say that although sentiment may give rise to a sense of justice, to formulate that sense into principle and justice takes reason. Schopenhauer (1839/1995), in the course of proposing compassion (which is a form that sentiment toward others can take) as the source of morality and justice, does not consider the ways in which compassion can lead us astray in regard to justice, and so confuses compassion and philanthropy with justice. Thus he seems to consider the selective favoring of "widows and orphans," as well as the poor over the rich, as the promotion of justice (p. 173). Moreover, he poses a case in which one man desists, on the basis of principle, from carrying out his original intent to kill his rival, while another desists due to a sudden burst of "compassion and pity" for his intended victim (pp. 167-169). Schopenhauer wishes the reader to conclude that he or she would more readily entrust his or her own destiny to the second man than to the first. But he ignores the fact that, in this case, the reader must hope that the second man will not be distanced from the intended victim, either physically or psychologically, to such an extent that the compassion and pity that Schopenhauer is banking on will not be aroused. Yet, curiously, Schopenhauer himself says, elsewhere in his treatise: "Without *principles* firmly held, we should inevitably be at the mercy of antimoral tendencies when, through external impressions, these tendencies were stirred to emotions" (pp. 150-151, italics in original). Principle also allows for the possibility that we will positively address those toward whom we have no particular sentiment one way or the other, while sentiment does not.

Although it can be said that the choice of the object of principle is subjective, principle itself then works to suspend judgment in regard to that object. Overcoming the biases of sentiment is precisely what principles of justice demand of us—to treat equally those we like and those we despise, those we pity and those we envy, and the wealthy and the poor, without favoring either one or the other. The Torah exhorts us to neither side with the mighty or show deference to the rich, nor show deference to or favor the poor (Exodus 23:2-3; Leviticus 19:15), and to help even one's enemy (Exodus 23:4-5). Our sense of justice, therefore, may be said to be derived from sentiment, yet the principles derived from our sense of justice have a life of their own, so to speak, devoid of sentiment by definition.

If our sense of justice references life itself, and not only human life, and if life is to be valued in accordance with principle, then the logic of principle must necessarily extend the valuing of life beyond human life, to all life. In this case, Kant's thesis of morality, which regards human beings, by virtue of their rational nature, as ends in themselves, but animals as means or mere things, could, in effect, be seen as a rationalization for limiting the realm of moral principles to all rational beings, and not extending it to others, and Kant could be accused of narrow reasoning that stems from sentiment. That our sense of justice does indeed extend to animals is indicated, however weakly, in the Torah's admonitions not to eat "the blood of any flesh, for the life of all flesh is its blood" (Leviticus 17:14), and to reduce the suffering of animals and refrain from being cruel to them. Yet Schopenhauer, after criticizing Kant by raging against a morality that "knows and respects only its own worthy species, whose characteristic *reason* is the condition on which a being can be an object of moral consideration and respect" (1839/1995, p. 96, italics in original), blithely proceeds to employ rationalization in the service of sentiment (and self-interest) by saying that "sympathy for animals should not carry us to the length of having to abstain from animal food, like the Brahmans" and that "man would suffer more by going without animal food, especially in the North, than the animal does through a quick and always unforeseen death" (p.182).

Yet, despite the viability of vegetarianism, reasoning in accordance with principle to all life does have its practical limitations. It would be impossible to continue to live in this world if principle were to be followed to its ultimate limits in regard to all forms of life. Yet our experience tells us that our sentiment does extend beyond human lives to other forms of life. To where it does, our sense of justice derived from sentiment may or may not follow. It is indeed clear that our sentiment can extend to animals, without our sense of justice following.

What we can learn from all this is that sentiment stands in complex relationship to principle. While our very sense of justice may be derived from sentiment, sentiment also serves to violate justice. Paradoxically, it can also serve to extend it. Yet, in the absence of principle, justice cannot be said to exist. Principle, which by definition admits of no exception—and hence justice—is violated by sentiment even within the always-limited domain that is claimed for justice. In addition, whenever principle does not follow sentiment into a wider domain, then wherever sentiment goes, we have sentiment without justice.

Yet the fact that we value justice for its own sake, and not only for our own, is obvious. We take an interest in justice. We feel offended—because our sense of justice is offended—when we learn that people in a distant country, strangers to us, have been treated unfairly, deprived of their belongings, or falsely accused, much less brutally handled or murdered. Apparently, the sense of justice is a strong motivating force for some people and in some instances. We say that their sense of justice has been offended, but wherefrom does the intense interest arise, that provokes outrage? Even "the pleasure of seeing" the happiness of others (Smith) does not apply to those who have striven to extend justice through principle to individuals they despise (such as murderers), or to individuals whose fortunes they envy. Nor does it apply to those who have sacrificed their own lives for the sake of justice or principle. Schopenhauer (1839/1995, p. 204) would claim that such people make less distinction between themselves and others, than do other people, but this explanation, in absence of separate empirical evidence, appears circular and explains nothing. Having a *sense* of justice, we may develop a *passion* for justice, but the two are to be distinguished from each other. In any event, from whatever sources we may draw our passion for justice, justice itself must reside in principles, and not in passion or sentiment.

The Power of Principle over Sentiment

Appeals to sentiment are so pervasive and commonplace in the public policymaking arena that many of us have come to accept this situation as inevitable, an unalterable result of human nature, and a reflection of the immutable entanglement of sentiment with principle. To be sure, in everyday life—not only in government, but in our workplaces, civic associations, and other social institutions—many principles are constructed only to be routinely violated through sentiment in practice. The most cynical commentators, such as Stanley Fish (1994), claim that there exists, in the social realm, only a clash of competing interests, and nothing more. The mere notion of principle is derided. But even the more sanguine are convinced that those who seek to promote principle over sentiment are naively idealistic and, well, sentimental. The serious discussions about caring versus justice in the feminist literature (e.g., see the various views reported and discussed in Sunstein, 1990, and White, 2000) question the virtues of principle, and some feminists, rather than seeking ways in which care can be incorporated into social policies generated from principles of justice, ignore the dangers to justice posed by the sentimental aspects of care entailed in promoting care *over* principles of justice.

Principle as a tool (much less as a requirement) of justice has been subjected to suspicion: Is it really just not to acknowledge personal or group history, when addressing need, for example? Some would argue that adherence to principle favors those who have been advantaged in the past and disadvantages the (previously) oppressed. But others would argue that the presence of principle allows the oppressed to win their rights by appealing to it. In leading the civil rights movement, Martin Luther King, Jr. insisted on holding America to the fundamental principles of liberal democracy and justice embedded in its own Constitution. He had no need to speak against these principles or to propose divergences from them. The defense of principle, other than this, is that its absence invites endless claims to special treatment and clashes of selective interests and sentiments, leading to a concept of "justice" as mere endless power struggle.

Of course, a particular principle itself can be questioned in regard to its justness. For example, is it just for a community to address need? The question can be raised, Why address need at all? These questions concern our values, and what we choose as objects of our principles, but not the concept of principle itself. We address need because we value human life. If my life is to be valued, then all lives are to be valued. And if all life is to be valued, then dire need that threatens the survival of life (such as the lack of minimal food, clothing, and shelter) must be addressed without exception. Principles generated to address need must address that object without condition or exception. And, similarly, if all life is to be valued, then killing is morally wrong, without exception, condition, or regard for social context. Principles are abstract and absolute, not relative to context. Hence they are nondiscriminatory, and the principle of nondiscrimination itself must be the first principle of justice.

Principles are ideals that we may aspire to, but never attain or perfectly achieve, in that they are in continual conflict with sentiment, narrow reasoning, rationalization, and self-interest. Reason in the service of self-interest may lead us to kill individuals who are about to kill us, but principle proclaims that killing is wrong, and that if killing is wrong, then it is always wrong. We have more sympathy for the person who killed in self-defense than for the one who did so in "cold blood," but principles are not refuted by feelings. To preserve principle, we should say that while killing was necessary to protect ourselves (given our present ignorance of alternative means to do so), it is no less morally wrong for that. But why preserve principle? Because it is a guide to achievement of justice in the future; it is an ideal to strive for.

Yet principle is always limited in its application. We apply many principles within our national community, but not beyond. Even after we have defined the limited sphere of application, we may allow sentiment to determine how the sphere will be sub-divided. We may do this when we address, in our social policies, not only the object of principle, such as need, but the designation of beneficiaries on the basis of possessing or being ascribed particular personal or group characteristics (such as being an orphan, racially white or black, a member of the community); a certain individual history presumed to cause that need (such as death of parents or husband, job loss, natural disaster, disability [depending on how they are phrased, these histories may or may not already be described by such ascriptions as "orphan" or "widow"]); and/or a certain group history (such as being ascribed as a member of a racial or religious group that had been targeted [by government or others] for discrimination) presumed to cause that need.

The factors limiting the sphere of application itself (let us take for an example here humanity, rather than the national community) may include sentiment (I can identify my own needs with those of other human beings, but less so with animals, and thus I have greater sympathy for human beings), or rationales (perhaps derived from sentiment, such as the proposition that animals do not experience pain in the same way as we do, or do not have consciousness or reasoning powers [Kant's rationale], which set them apart from us), or practicality (we need to eat animal meat in order to survive) and desirability (we enjoy eating meat), bringing us back to sentiment.

We can formulate principles concerning the nonviolation of life, and limit their application to human life, or only to human life within the boundaries of our own society. We can formulate principles to address human need, and limit their application to those incapable of working. Acquired sympathy for animals, for the lives of people of other nations, for those who cannot find jobs, for those who work but are not paid enough to support themselves, may move us to extend the scope of application of such principles. Or antipathy toward other nations, or the jobless, may move us to maintain the narrowness of their application.

However, principle itself allows for the *possibility* that those we despise will be regarded or treated similarly to those we like, while sentiment does not, unless we speak of a sentiment for justice itself. Principle can transcend sentiment, but sentiment cannot transcend itself. Sentiment can be supported by narrow reason, and can even be generated by such reason, but it is transcended only through principle. Only the construction and application of principle, even if based on our narrow experience, which is then generalized to others, can do justice. Only principle can safeguard us against the known and dangerous human tendencies to rationalize one's emotional inclinations in the name of justice.

The human mind is capable of generating (moral) principles to govern one's own behavior, or that of a society. It is the ability to generate principles that gives human beings the potential to liberate their behavior from determinism by sentiment, and to transcend sentiment. Once generated, principles become forces that can determine human behavior much as sentiment can. They represent the mind's determination of behavior and in this sense, the self-determination of behavior as opposed to determination by sentiment, biological motives, and external forces. They may conflict with sentiment, but there is no necessity that they become subordinate to sentiment. People throughout history, relatively few though they may be, have died rather than violate their principles. Hedonistic explanations, such as behavioral reinforcement theory, have to be stretched to the point of incredulity or circularity in order to account for this fact. There is no question but that from time to time individuals manage to subordinate their sentiment to moral principles, and thereby demonstrate the human capacity to do so. We must consider the potential of an individual to resist the pull of sentiment through the formulation of principle. But principles are ideals to strive for, not always winning out over sentiment in determining behavior or, for that matter, in determining social policy.

4

Social Science and Public Policy

Throughout the second half of the twentieth century, the use of social science research to influence—or at least rationalize—social policy has grown exponentially. Government funding for policy-relevant social science research projects has increased enormously, while private foundations now routinely funnel hundreds of millions of dollars annually to social scientists at universities and "think tanks" for such enterprises. These researchers, who presently constitute a well-established growth industry, insist that rational social policy must be informed by social science data, and that they are the ones most qualified to draw conclusions and policy recommendations from their own findings. Their funders apparently agree, and listen when they want to.

Virtually all American social scientists consider themselves to be politically liberal in the classical sense of liberalism, and many are furthermore liberal in the modern sense of that term, that is, in the meaning that liberalism takes on when contrasted with conservatism. Yet the focus of liberal political philosophy is the individual, while the emphasis of much social science is on aggregate data. This fundamental discrepancy and its implications are the subject of this analysis.

In classical liberalism, the focus on the individual is manifested in concern for protection of individual freedom, especially against the potential encroachment of a coercive government. In modern liberalism, it is additionally expressed in the use of government to actively promote equal opportunity for all. In some societies, government may exist to protect and enhance the well-being of some individuals only, or some groups of individuals. It follows that a *just* society must be one in which the government protects and benefits *all* of its individual members. Liberalism, as well as justice, mandates that laws and policies must be fair to each and every individual, as individuals.

Yet the policy implications that social scientists often draw from their prevalent aggregate-data and group-difference findings are more often compatible with strict versions of "the greatest good to the greatest number" and the "common good" that overlook fairness to each and every individual, than they are with the basic tenets of liberalism and a just society. Violation of just process for the sake of intended collective good ends is compounded when applied selectively to certain groups. I will argue here that social science data analyses, to the extent that they are used to form and maintain group constructs, are a poor basis for policymaking.

My concern, then, is not merely that social science often generates aggregate data from which generalizations are derived. Much important knowledge is produced in this manner. Rather, I am concerned that in the policy arena, such data often lend themselves to, and are used for, the promotion of a narrow form of utilitarianism that is incompatible with liberalism.

My aim here is to suggest a new lens (which I maintain is a liberal lens) through which to view policy, and through which to examine social science applications to policy. Policies that address people on aggregate or group bases, often encouraged by social science data, ignore individual qualifications (such as need) or supplement such qualifications with group criteria. A public health insurance program that addresses the health needs of those aged sixty-five or older, but excludes younger people similarly situated in regard to health needs, is discriminatory. Yet oddly enough, if such a policy merely were not to contain financial eligibility requirements for the receipt of benefits, scholars in the field of policy analysis would identify it as a "universal" policy. I maintain that liberal policies would address individual qualifications only, rather than group generalizations. I believe that while some policies should be means-tested, and some not (e.g., public libraries), none should be group-tested. Truly "universal" policies would address criteria relevant to their provisions on an individual basis. Unless *all* are to be included, any inclusion or exclusion must be based on individually relevant criteria, such as individual need.

Yet group-based policies pervade our policy arena. They do so with the aid of social science data that are collected in the very service of group interests. Here I primarily examine the nature of the problem, and make only a beginning attempt to answer the questions raised, such as whether policies, as products and outcomes, can be formulated in any other way; whether the policymaking process can be something other than the narrow placation of group interests; and what roles social science can constructively play in informing public policy. At the same time, I point to the desirability of a more limited role for social science in the policymaking process than it currently enjoys.

Aggregate Reasoning

Currently, social scientists throughout the country are in the process of tracking and evaluating the various "welfare reforms" that have been implemented under the so-called Personal Responsibility and Work Opportunity Reconciliation Act of 1996 (P.L. 104-193). Such research questions as the following are being asked: Do family caps (the disallowance of benefits for an additional child born to a mother while she and her other children are receiving Temporary

Assistance for Needy Families [TANF]) reduce the number of children born to mothers while on TANF? Do school attendance requirements, which may reduce TANF benefits to mothers based on their children's school attendance records, reduce truancy? Do time limits on the receipt of TANF leave families better off than they were on the old AFDC (Aid to Families with Dependent Children) program? Do new welfare-to-work programs succeed in moving welfare mothers into jobs? Is child poverty reduced? All of these questions will be answered in an aggregate manner, in a statistical-probabilistic sense.

Speaking of the discretion given to states, under the federal law, to impose family caps, Gary Burtless, R. Kent Weaver, and Joshua Wiener (1997, pp. 96-97) state: "Giving states flexibility on this issue is sensible because evidence on the impact of family caps on additional births to welfare recipients...is still being gathered and analyzed." The "evidence," of course, will pertain to "welfare recipients" as a group. But what if the evidence were to show that family caps were successful in reducing such births? Such births would still occur, and those children born would be denied benefits.

While Burtless, Weaver, and Wiener indicate their dislike for the new welfare law, they nonetheless say about "safety net" policies in general: "Where the benefits of policy change are almost certainly large, the federal government should move boldly to change current policy. Where there is a major risk of harm to the nation's poor...the federal government should move more cautiously—through sponsored state experimentation and state waivers, for example. And where the risks of potential innovations clearly outweigh their likely advantages, the federal government should prohibit states from taking those actions" (1997, pp. 90-91). It is obvious here that the arena of policy analysis has shifted away from individual need as addressed by AFDC as an entitlement, to questions of aggregate benefits to society as a whole, to harm to poor children and their mothers as a group, and to aggregate risks and advantages. In other words, it has shifted to "the greatest good to the greatest number" and the elusive "common good"—and to the province of social science.

To be sure, before the federal law was passed, many social scientists challenged states' federal waiver requests for programs, incorporating many of the restrictions mentioned above, that became the predecessors of the new law. But they did so on the basis of aggregate data tentatively indicating that the proposed policies would cause harm to children as a group, rather than on ethical grounds pertaining to the processes that would be set up.

Certainly, too, many social scientists expect to find that the behavioral and time restrictions have hurt impoverished children and their mothers in the aggregate, and if and when they do, they anticipate using that data to argue against continuing those restrictions. But what if they do not find aggregate harm? Will harm to individuals go ignored? Will the same social scientists maintain credibility if they shift the grounds for their opposition in midstream?

Irwin Garfinkel and Sara McLanahan (1994) note that government can reduce the economic insecurity of single-mother families, but doing so will increase their dependence on government, as well as their prevalence (by lowering the costs of family dissolution). They state: "Reducing insecurity would be called for if the relationship between insecurity and children's future well-being turned out to be strong, while the relationship between government support and prevalence and dependence turned out to be weak" (p. 205). Thus they neatly turn a question of value choices and political philosophy into a project for social scientists, who will presumably resolve the policy issues involved through the collection and analysis of aggregate outcome data. To be sure, they then go on to argue from the available data that reducing economic insecurity is called for, but social science is further established as the court of resolution for policy-premise alternatives.

Thus the collection of aggregate data is consistent with, and indeed supports, a policy-debate focus on empirical outcomes as opposed to principles of justice pertaining to individuals. The special interests of social scientists in this emphasis on "the greatest good to the greatest number" are obvious, in that policy issues are framed in terms of empirical questions that are most suitable to their methodological tools and skills.

Group Justification

Additionally troubling is the differential application of aggregate reasoning, with the compliance of social scientists in terms of their data collection, to some groups of individuals and not others. There has been no challenge, from social scientists or elsewhere, to the proposition that such policies as discussed above should be selectively applied to the group constructed as needy children and their mothers, but not to programs for other constructed groups, such as veterans, or the needy elderly, or the disabled.

Most of the myriad group constructions of public policies pre-date social science empirical findings. Throughout history, there are numerous examples of public policies that have prescribed differential treatment of individuals grouped by age, gender, race, ethnicity, and so on. These groupings in policy have been justified by stereotypes concerning, for example, the frailness and poverty of the elderly, or racial inferiority. Oftentimes the validity of the generalizations seemed self-evident to the policymakers, even if the result of self-fulfilling prophecies (for example, barring members of a group from education and then stereotyping them as "ignorant"). In modern times, however, aggregate data and group-difference findings are often employed to maintain, support, and justify the group constructions inherent in group-oriented policies. Sometimes they are used to generate new group constructions.

Research supporting group stereotypes that, in turn, are used to misinform, initiate, maintain, and extend social policies run the gamut from the mere collection of descriptive statistics to studies employing sophisticated methodology and analysis. Some states now have laws that require vision and other tests for driver's license renewal, only for people over a certain age, based on statistics indicating that elderly people, as a group, are involved proportionately in more fatal accidents than most other age groups. Our eyes are diverted from the injustice of age discrimination to the seeming reasonableness of policies that may, indeed, reduce fatal accidents.

As another example, statistical analyses inform us that the Social Security program has lifted many elderly people out of poverty. Social scientists as well as others utilize such aggregate facts to support current Social Security policy. Thus aggregate data are used to rationalize policies that selectively address the needs of individuals grouped by age.

Dinesh D'Souza (1995, p. 259) uses aggregate reasoning to support "rational" or "statistical" discrimination. He cites the case of a shopkeeper in Washington, D.C., who decides whom to let in on the basis of physical appearance, employing "race as one factor, but not the only factor, in her decisionmaking." D'Souza sees her as a "prudent statistician" who, in an effort to reduce risk to herself, is practicing "rational" discrimination. Since some stereotypes—or generalizations about groups of people—are valid, such as that young black males commit a greatly disproportionate number of all crimes (as compared to other young males, presumably), people such as the shopkeeper are acting on reasonable generalizations and, in such contexts, "a bigot is simply a sociologist without credentials" (p. 268). Speaking of "legitimate economic reasons" for "rational" discrimination based on accurate group generalizations, he suggests that private companies be allowed to discriminate in transactions such as "renting an apartment or hiring for a job," and states that "if there are differences in accident rates and life expectancy between whites and blacks, as there are, that would constitute a valid business criterion for insurance companies to take into account" (pp. 281, 544).

Richard Posner, in advocating greater use of social science in helping to resolve legal issues, faults the United States Supreme Court for failing to consider gender differences in its decision against the Virginia Military Institute regarding its refusal to admit women (1999, pp. 165-173). But he refers only to *group* differences, between "the average man and the average woman." He suggests that if individual consideration of women's applications were to "benefit few" women, then the exclusion of women "would make compelling sense."

Even more bewildering than D'Souza's and Posner's endorsement of group statistics as justification for discrimination is others' use of potential aggregate outcomes to combat such arguments. David Strauss (1991, p. 1648) argues that "it is not the fate of the individual victim of discrimination that makes statistical discrimination troubling," but rather, "the aggregate effects of statistical discrimination on the minority population." For example, it "discourages investment in human capital" among members of the group that is discriminated against. Commenting favorably on Strauss' stance, but not wishing to leave out individuals, Jeffrey Lehman (1994, p. 241) asserts: "When one considers both the frequency with which individuals do not fit racial stereotypes and the extent of harm inflicted on such individuals by statistical discrimination in employment, the practice seems morally intolerable."

Thus moral issues are seemingly converted into empirical questions. Presumably, if "aggregate effects of statistical discrimination" could not be found, then Strauss would have no grounds for objecting to it. Moreover, whether or not group discrimination is justified awaits empirical data concerning the frequency with which members of the group fit group stereotypes and the extent of harm that results. Once again, social science data collection, and not ethics and political philosophy, is legitimated as the arena for debate about policy premises.

Individual Rights vs. Group Outcomes

Despite their own tendency toward aggregate reasoning, Burtless, Weaver, and Wiener (1997, p. 85) acknowledge that under an entitlement program such as AFDC, as opposed to a block grant program such as TANF (which replaced AFDC), "governments are required to treat persons in the same circumstances in the same way." Treating individuals in the same circumstances in the same way is, of course, the principle of nondiscrimination, associated with the "equal protection" clause of the Fourteenth Amendment to the Constitution.

But according to this principle, to deny benefits to a child born on welfare, through no fault of his or her own, while providing such benefits to other children on welfare, would be wrong. Time limits also deny equal protection, in that some children similarly situated in regard to need will be denied benefits, while others will receive them. Yet the principle of nondiscrimination goes further: it does not abide the differential addressing of need on the basis of factors irrelevant to that need (or for that matter, the differential addressing of circumstances, merit, competence, or responsibility, on the basis of factors irrelevant to those factors). Thus the child who is truant from school, or whose mother fails to find an adequately paying job or comply with job-training requirements, is unfairly discriminated against if other children in similar need are provided benefits. It would be wrong to evaluate these policies on the basis of any empirical evidence of aggregate success, because they violate the principle of nondiscrimination. These policies would deny benefits to some children and women in dire need for the sake of presumably benefiting society as a "whole."

Moreover, if individuals in the same circumstances should be treated in the same way, then need must not be conflated with group constructions that assign individuals in the same circumstances to differential treatment. For example, under current policies, a needy child of a widowed mother will receive higher benefits (without time limits) under the Supplemental Security Income (SSI) program than those whose fathers are living and who therefore qualify for the TANF program, even though such factors are irrelevant from the perspective of the child's need. Under current policies, too, a needy elderly person will have his or her need more adequately addressed through SSI than a needy child would through TANF.

An individual has the right to be responded to on the basis of his or her need, or even individual culpability, rather than on the basis of group stereotypes formed out of ignorance or even through scientific group-difference findings. In short, people have the human right, the most basic right of all, to be responded to as individuals, not as members of groups. All else is discrimination.

Yet, as we have seen, aggregate-data and group-difference findings are often used to justify special benefits or penalties for certain groups of individuals. But the question of why these groups, and not others, should be selected, is not and cannot be answered by the data. In a fair scheme of things, the question of which individuals shall be differentially treated in which ways can only be decided on the basis of a priori principles to which data collection is irrelevant, that is, that no amount of data can either support or nonsupport.

For example, in discussing the advisability of increasing the retirement age as a means of restoring long-term financial solvency to the Social Security system, Henry Aaron and Barry Bosworth (1997, p. 279) state: "There is little evidence on whether the health condition of the elderly and their ability to continue working at a given age has increased along with the increase in life expectancies." By comparing "the elderly" with younger groups, evidence could establish statistically valid stereotypes about "the elderly" and their health condition, but stereotypes nonetheless, since they would be generalizations about arbitrarily constructed groups (using age sixty-five, sixty-seven, seventy, or whatever you will, as the group boundary). What is in question is the ethical rationale for any individual to begin receiving retirement benefits at some point in life, an issue to which the statistical relatedness or "group relevance" of the health condition of "the elderly" is irrelevant.

Is the rationale that an individual who was employed for a particular number of years (say twenty, thirty, or forty?) is "deserving" of Social Security benefits while others are not? In other words, do we consider the individual who has worked for a designated number of years differently situated in regard to merit than those who have not? Or do we consider the individual who is elderly differently situated in regard to need than those who are not? Is the rationale that the individual has "paid into the system" for a designated number of years? Or that the individual (presumably by dint of having reached a certain age) is not physically or mentally capable of working any longer? Or that an individual should be "rewarded" a set amount, which he or she would exceed if he or she lived "too long" or started collecting benefits "too early"?

But these are questions of values and principles, not statistics. Moreover, they pertain to the individual, and not the group. And if the Social Security system is in financial trouble, this might be the impetus to confront the underlying value-assumptions upon which this system is presumably based, and indeed, the inconsistent, conflicting, and contradictory underpinnings of the haphazard admixture of social policies that comprise the entire welfare state (and which support the social science enterprise).

Debate is needed concerning ethical societal conduct and the nature of social justice, with some consensus reached on principles, which must precede any call for data. Justice demands that any principles decided upon must be relevant to the individual, and applied equally to each and every individual. The health status of "the elderly" does not address the health status of the individual elderly person, nor does it address the health status of individuals who are not elderly. Criteria for inclusion or exclusion of individuals within policy prescriptions, depending upon the principle employed, must address need, merit, or responsibility in an individually relevant manner.

In his well-known 1968 *Harvard Educational Review* article, James Coleman (p. 15) suggested that the 1954 Supreme Court decision in *Brown v. Board of Education* should have been based solely on the premise that "the use of race as a basis for school assignment violates fundamental freedoms," rather than confounding this argument with one based on differential *effects* of racially-segregated schooling.

In the 1970s, in an article in *Law and Contemporary Problems*, Henry Levin (1975, p. 217) noted that education reform measures, such as school desegregation and reduced reliance of educational financing on local property taxes, could be defended on grounds of fairness alone, yet arguments that such reforms are essential to a just society have been overshadowed by claims based on social science research outcomes. "At this stage, the issue has...been cast in terms of the achievement scores of blacks rather than in terms of the larger moral and human dilemmas raised by segregated public institutions. There is little doubt that the research agenda has framed the issue" (p. 239). He concludes that "if social science findings increasingly are used to create what appear to be technical issues out of essentially moral dilemmas, this presents a potential social danger" (p. 240).

Reflecting on these comments, Henry Aaron suggests in his 1978 book, *Politics and the Professors* (pp. 97-98), that the "single-minded focus of analysts" on educational outcomes succeeded "in diverting attention from education as a right." The reason for this concern undoubtedly is that if empirical group outcomes ultimately do not bear out the social scientists' claims, then there would be no grounds to continue the policies. Yet, in the realm of rights and fairness, even the fact that discrimination has caused individual harm need not be shown. Perhaps the social scientists' claims that they support the policies on empirical grounds are disingenuous, but they were not forthcoming as to what their grounds were.

Recently, in *The Shape of the River*, William Bowen and Derek Bok (1998) have defended the use of race as a factor in college admissions policies by presenting aggregate data indicating that African American students who matriculated at twenty-eight of the most selective colleges and universities in the country did well in terms of graduation rates, subsequent obtainment of professional and other graduate degrees, and careers and salaries. Bowen and Bok argue from additional data that race-based admission policies at these schools have benefited society as a whole.

Claiming that the goal of race-based admission policies has been to increase "diversity," they defend the fairness of such policies in this manner: "It may be perfectly 'fair' to reject an applicant because the college has already enrolled many other students very much like him or her... When making a stew, adding an extra carrot rather than one more potato may make excellent sense—and be eminently 'fair'—if there are already lots of potatoes in the pot" (p. 278). Such a comparison not only promotes the crudest racial stereotyping, but obliterates the concept of individual human rights. Through this clumsy argument for "fairness," Bowen and Bok implicitly acknowledge that policies cannot be defended on the basis of group outcome data alone. Yet, at the same time, they turn group diversity, which itself is an outcome of policy, into a principle of fairness—fairness to groups. The question that liberalism must ask, however, is whether or not race is a criterion that similarly situates all individuals in regard to need, merit, competence, or responsibility.

Certainly, social science's seat at the policy table has become well entrenched. I am suggesting, however, that our faith in social science to resolve social policy issues has been somewhat misguided and misplaced. Issues concerning such values and principles as human rights and nondiscrimination cannot be enlightened by resort to group statistics. We have allowed social science to overwhelm and confuse our deliberations in areas of policy in which it has no appropriate place. Only when we sort out the morality of means from the empiricism of ends, and the rights of the individual from the measurement of the "common good," can we begin to identify the appropriate application, nature, and areas of social scientific examination in regard to policy-related issues. While many factors and kinds of input can usefully inform policy debate, I am suggesting that matters of individual justice should first and foremost inform it, and that the liberal version of justice does not abide violations of the individual for the sake of some aggregate good.

Obscuring Causation

There are an infinite number of ways to divide up any pie into smaller units. When that "pie" consists of a universe of human beings, it can be divided up by grouping individuals by height, weight, eye color, age, race, place of residence, food preference, alcoholic consumption, drug use, family status, gender, religious affiliation, and on and on. In regard to one or another dependent variable, group differences can always be found. But it will by no means be obvious what the reasons for or "causes" of these group differences are.

Suppose that upon division of the "pie" into black people and white people, we find a greater statistical probability of car accidents for black people. (In that case, if we had divided the pie in accordance with eye color rather than race, we would be likely to find a statistical difference in accidents by eye color, since eye color is correlated with race.) Few liberals would condone racial categorization for car insurance purposes, simply because of empirical group-difference findings in accident rates. They would call it discrimination. Despite such statistics, it could not be said that any individual, by virtue of being black, was differently situated in regard to responsibility for car accidents than other individuals.

Yet the same logical objections can be applied to differential car-insurance premium payments for teenagers and adults, or suburban and urban dwellers, despite differential group statistics in regard to accidents. One's chronological age does not cause one to have a car accident, nor does being an urban dweller, even though the probabilities of having an accident when living in an urban area might be greater. Policies that address individually irrelevant factors on the basis of their statistical relatedness or "group relevance" are nonetheless discriminatory. Yet many of us become concerned about the actuarial construction of such groups and statistics for differential-premium purposes only when we are reminded, for example, that black people are more likely to live in urban areas than are white people, and so urban-suburban categorization will discriminate against black people. It is, however, all discrimination.

Suppose that studies show that those who use certain types of drugs, on the whole, are more violent than those who do not. This would not mean that every user of these drugs, even within the samples studied, had been found to be more violent than every non-user. What we have here is a scientifically generated (or supported) stereotype that is valid in a statistical sense. It is not valid in an individual sense. Individuals are convicted and imprisoned for possession of certain arbitrarily designated drugs, not because they have harmed or robbed anyone, but because use of the drugs is thought to be statistically correlated with violence and other felonies. Our prohibition laws are based on group assumptions about the drugs, not on individuals' violation of other individuals. Individuals are prosecuted for their group identity as a drug user or seller. Drug laws, like many others, are discriminatory in that they address individually irrelevant factors on the basis of their "group relevance."

In fact, many possible causal factors are routinely obscured through group-based policy construction. For example, laws against driving while intoxicated are supported by a statistical relationship between drunken driving and accidents. Drivers can be arrested for driving while intoxicated, even if they were not driving recklessly. By the same token, a person who was apprehended for driving recklessly may get a lesser penalty if he or she were to pass a blood-alcohol test. Yet sleepiness at the wheel is a factor in at least as many vehicular accidents as intoxication, and cocaine and marijuana are factors in many others. Thus, by putting so much emphasis on one possible cause of reckless driving, rather than the reckless driving itself, we deflect attention from the other causes at the same time that we penalize individuals for "possessing" a group factor. In addition, we overlook individuals who committed wrongful acts while not possessing that factor. Moreover, even if intoxication is a partial cause of reckless driving in a statistical sense, it would not be clear that a particular intoxicated driver's reckless driving was caused by his intoxication.

Some opponents of affirmative action policies in college admissions have criticized them in like manner. That is, by targeting group representativeness and diversity rather than wrongful acts of discrimination, the policies have not only been unfair to innocent individuals who have not engaged in such acts, but have deflected collective attention from possible root causes of low representation (or unequal opportunity), such as inadequate K-12 education, and gross disparities in the quality and funding of public education across school districts.

Group Appeal

Yet group-based policies are well entrenched because they have served political purposes in the past. Public opinion research produces another kind of aggregate data that is often collected and used with the express purpose to inform the development of group-based policies and policy proposals. For example, Lawrence Bobo and James Kluegel (1993) conducted a survey in which some white respondents were asked if they favor specific need-targeted policies, such as providing special college scholarships for children from economically disadvantaged backgrounds who maintain good grades. Others were asked the same question in a race-targeted way, such as if they favor providing special college scholarships for black children who maintain good grades. Based on the findings, which indicate that far higher percentages of whites are in favor of need-targeted policies than of race-based policies, although substantially high percentages are in favor of race-based policies, Lawrence Bobo and Ryan Smith (1994, p. 393) remark: "Race-based policies that are clearly tilted toward enhancing opportunities or the ability to take advantage of opportunities appear to have a sufficiently broad base of support in white public opinion that they could be pursued without immediately provoking controversy and conflict." Nowhere do they ask, however, whether such policies would be fair to poor white children who maintain good grades.

Paul Starr (1997) concerns himself with identifying which *groups* (the elderly, the young, Hispanics, etc.) the Democrats must appeal to in order to corral a new majority of voters. Their voting patterns must be ascertained, as well as their "salient issues." The pollster Stanley Greenberg (1997, p. 295), in his chapter in the same book, suggests that by "focusing single-mindedly on the bold project of helping working and middle-class families to improve their lives...a popularly oriented progressive Democratic Party can come to dominate America's politics again." In a national survey, he tested a "progressive story" which asserts that "working middle-class families" "need somebody on their side" and found that three-quarters of the electorate finds it "convincing" (p. 282). There is no place in his "progressive story" for raising ethical issues concerning the recent "welfare reform"—that's history, and poor unemployed single mothers (not to mention their children) don't vote in very large numbers anyway. What Greenberg has apparently learned from the decline of the Democratic Party on the slope of race-based policies is that new group-based policies must be devised to mollify the group that the old policies offended, so long as it has a large vote.

In effect, through survey research, we can poll the American public, conceptually slice it into any number of pieces (the elderly, those about to become elderly, young adults, unmarried women, working middle-class families, Hispanics, African Americans, ad infinitum), and ascertain recent voting trends, special interests, salient issues, and favored programs of each of these groups. Then, by packaging a hodgepodge of proposed discrete mini-policies, each having appeal to one or another of the groups, we can put together a "coalition" of enough groups to constitute a voting majority.

Yet Greenberg (1997) himself cites survey findings indicating that three-quarters of the public say that they would have more confidence in the government if it had programs that benefit all Americans rather than particular groups. Perhaps, then, an appeal to the public's sense of justice, rather than to its various group interests, and policy proposals consistent with principles of justice held by all, would be a better political strategy.

Indeed, in recent American politics, as group-based policies have come to be perceived by many Americans as promoting the differential treatment of individuals based on group membership, catering to group-based claims has become less politically viable, save for the desperate ploys just noted. Policies formulated to appeal to people's sense of justice by promoting fairness to individuals rather than "fairness" to groups might be more politically viable at the same time that they would promote justice in actuality. There is nothing inevitable about the political viability of group-based policy development, whose persistence at this point is due more to inertia than to continued political success. Unfortunately, however, social science continues to play an important role in buttressing group-based claims with aggregate group data that, in turn, divert our attention from the discriminatory nature of the policies then proposed.

Appropriate Policy Uses of Social Science

Certainly, I have not been suggesting scientific censorship here. Social scientists should be free to gather data on anything they want and to present them in any form they please. Moreover, there is nothing wrong with looking at whether or not a policy has achieved its own intended aggregate outcomes. We do wish to have policies that, for example, will reduce harm to as many individuals as possible, if not all, and aggregate data can suggest the policy measures and programs needed to achieve this result. These are certainly legitimate areas of social-scientific investigation. However, I am suggesting that policies must first be evaluated in terms of agreed-upon principles of justice and fairness; that no amount of social-scientific data can inform such evaluation; and that social scientists should not pretend or represent otherwise. Furthermore, I am suggesting that of all the possible kinds and forms of data there are to collect, they have often collected those kinds and forms that they themselves have expressly used in a manner that would promote policies that serve group interests while obscuring issues of justice and fairness to individuals.

If fatal automobile accidents are reduced for the elderly by testing their driving periodically, then why not test all drivers periodically and reduce accidents even further? Likewise, if all of the needy are addressed in supportive policies, and not just the elderly, then poverty can be reduced still further. Social scientists should not advocate from their group-circumscribed data in a manner that would obscure these policy issues.

Because today social scientists are so prevalently looked to as policy experts, I would even urge them to overstep their bounds somewhat, by actively pointing out that findings of group differences have nothing at all to contribute to issues of justice to individuals. To wit, the question of aggregate race (or any other group) differences is an empirical one, but one that has no bearing whatsoever upon the moral question of rightful actions toward individuals. Even the question of whether any aggregate differences that may be found have genetic or environmental origins—also an empirical question—has no relevance whatsoever. The common presumption that it does—and hence that science matters in this context—is responsible for a particularly misleading and illiberal approach to education against discrimination, one that would, through its own inadequate logic, actually provide a rationale for condoning discrimination if group differences were to be found.

Of course, in the United States, we continue to generate a growing body of research literature to evaluate whether or not certain policies and programs are effective. Such studies produce aggregate results in the form of scientific group-difference findings. They are potentially useful, and not necessarily inappropriate from the point of view of justice. The findings, of course, are provided in the form of statistical group differences, on various outcome measures, between those who were assigned to groups that received the "treatment" in question, and those assigned to groups that did not. There is a place for such evaluative research.

Perhaps the difference between using group outcome data to evaluate many social intervention programs, on the one hand, and the "welfare reform" system, on the other, is the following. In the former, the "treatments" tested are not intrinsically violative of individuals, and we use group comparisons as the only procedure we have to evaluate whether or not a method or program is potent enough to benefit *any* individual.

There are surely other constructive uses of social science data in informing public policy, but we should more carefully consider their ethical implications than we do at present. For example, interest-group politics currently influences the distribution of federal research and other monies targeting various diseases and other social problems. Social scientists have served the interests of child abuse crusaders by using broad and vague operational definitions of "child abuse and neglect" that produce "alarming" statistics that stereotype impoverished families and support increased funding of coercive "child rescue" policies (as I have argued in previous books; see Pelton, 1989, 1999a). To counter the influence of interest-group politics, we could rank-order diseases and other social problems in terms of fatality statistics. Yet to determine, say, the distribution of research monies solely on this basis would not be entirely satisfactory, since it would make sense to disproportionately fund disease research in areas where scientists are close to finding a cure. My only point here is that we should begin serious discussion concerning the appropriate and inappropriate applications of social science to public policy analysis.

Social science has its place, but we must understand the importance of the fact that it produces aggregate group data. Such data can be used, and often are, to form group constructs. Group constructs are generalizations, and that is to say that they are over-generalizations. Policies based on group constructs, statistical or otherwise, are discriminatory in that they make a fiction of individual realities. Group-difference findings have some constructive uses, but informing social policies in regard to differential treatment of individuals who are arbitrarily grouped is not one of them. There is no ethical basis for limiting this liberal edict to some groupings, such as by race or gender, and not applying it to others. Yet in countless areas of public policy, social science findings have been used to legitimate discrimination.

5

Need, Desert, and Nondiscrimination

Individuals come together to form a community, and maintain its existence, in order to benefit themselves and others. There is no rationale for the existence of a community other than to benefit the individuals within it. This concern for the individual, as we have seen, is manifested in liberal philosophy. The founders of the United States surely formed a union for the purpose of benefiting the people within it. Liberal philosophy expresses concern and respect for the individual, posits that the goal of the community is to benefit (i.e., to protect and enhance) human life, and requires that laws and policies be fair to each and every individual, as individuals.

Liberalism (in philosophy at least, if not always in practice) particularly specifies that no individual may be used as an instrument for the benefit of others, or ignored by government in the process of benefiting others. The individual must not be violated within the means, or sacrificed for the group. Hence the emphasis of liberalism is on individually beneficial procedure, and equality of treatment, not on equality of beneficial results. A society that would ensure equal results would benefit some through the violation of others, as surely as would a society that did not actively pursue nondiscrimination. A society that would ensure equal results would deny individuals the freedom to reap the rewards of their own unequal labor, efforts, and abilities, and thus would involve the undue encroachment of coercive government feared by classical liberalism. Yet a society that would deny or fail to promote equal opportunity of individuals to develop or use their own unequal potential abilities would fail to benefit everyone within it.

Therefore, although not always cast as a moral philosophy, it is possible to view liberalism as stemming from a single moral value, the sanctity of individual human life, and a single first principle of social justice, or fairness, that of nondiscrimination. All else can be derived. My task here is to rethink the social policy implications of liberalism as a system of justice.

A liberal community, in choosing among schemes for the distribution of benefits, is obliged to rationalize its policy choices in terms of justice. Why it is presumably just or fair to grant certain benefits to some individuals, or some groups of individuals, rather than others, or to grant greater benefits to some rather than others, must be explained. The grounds most commonly put forth for the differential granting of benefits include the "deservingness" of the intended beneficiaries, their need, and the indirect benefit that will presumably result to all—or at least to most, in the form of the "common good."

Thus, while all distribution of benefits are intended to enhance human life, we must face the issues of fairness of distribution, and what social policy arrangements constitute fairness. These issues are complicated by the fact that because our individual circumstances in life inevitably will differ from each other, what benefits might be valuable to you might not be valuable to me. We must of course also face the issues of contribution: Who shall pay, and how much? Is it fair that some contribute more than others, and if so, in accordance with what criteria? We establish a community treasury to benefit ourselves, but we must set up fair principles to govern both contribution and distribution.

Need and Desert

A community whose central value is the sanctity of human life must protect life, and therefore such a community could not allow anyone within it to go hungry, shelterless, or unclothed, nor anyone in need of medical attention to go without it. An individual whose basic survival needs are not met cannot be viewed in any way as benefiting from the community. If a just community exists to benefit everyone within it, then it must benefit the needy. If a community did not benefit *anyone* within it, it would cease to exist, but if the community exists and does not benefit the needy, then it must be benefiting some and not others, and the wealthy if not the poor. It would not be operating in harmony with the sanctity of human life as a moral value, but in accordance with the selective valuing of some lives and not others.

This selectivity would be based on need, but in a perverse way: those in need would be discriminated against. Thus we see that the moral value of the sanctity of human life, in a community context, is inextricably related to the principle of nondiscrimination, both of which are violated if need is not addressed. This violation would occur if the community did not address need at all. But if a community decides to provide benefits to some of the needy and not others, such as to those among the elderly who are needy, but not to the needy among the young, it again violates the moral value and again practices discrimination.

Hence a just society would affirm the sanctity of human life by addressing need, at least at some minimal level, without reference to differential conditions, circumstances, or characteristics. Differential treatment of need (here in the sense of treating some people's need and not others) on the basis of any differentiating factors whatsoever would constitute discrimination, because the moral value of the sanctity of human life dictates the only relevant dimension to be need itself. The question of desert is not raised, because everyone is deserving of regard at this minimal level of sustaining human life.

In truth, however, most societies have distinguished between the "deserving" needy and the "undeserving" needy in their social welfare policies. Only such implicit distinctions, often made on the basis of arbitrary group constructions, can account for the fact that policies often assign individuals with identical need to differential treatment. I have already described several examples of this in the United States, in regard to TANF, SSI, children, and the elderly.

If we were to adopt an unconditional criterion of need—which I posit stems directly from the basic tenets of liberalism—then needy children, for example, would fare much better in the aggregate than they do now. Presently, at least partly because of the differential treatment of children and the elderly as categories of people in social policy, the poverty rate is far higher among children than among the elderly. However, it is not this differential group statistic that warrants revised policies, but the differential treatment itself. In sum, I maintain that on grounds of both the moral value of the sanctity of human life and the principle of nondiscrimination, a just society must address individual poverty in a nonjudgmental manner.

Desert and Nondiscrimination

I have suggested that, at least in terms of liberal philosophy as I have portrayed it here, the concept of desert poses no problem for determination of the appropriate response to need, since all of the needy are deserving of minimal benefit sufficient to address need. Moreover, policies that provide minimal benefit to all those in need are nondiscriminatory, in that they distinguish only between those who are similarly situated in regard to the relevant dimension of need, and those who are not. However, when we move to consideration of benefit beyond need, or when a benefit is to be given to some but not to others, we confront the concept of desert. But invocation of the concept of desert presents major challenges to justice.

While nondiscrimination dictates that individuals similarly situated be treated similarly, the concept of desert is often used to argue that certain individuals are actually situated dissimilarly from others, but similarly to each other, in regard to some relevant dimension that policy should address, and therefore constitute a group "deserving" of dissimilar treatment. Arguments for differential treatment of individuals and groups based on assertions of differential circumstances (and histories) permeate the political arena, and are the crux of modern politics in the United States. Such arguments are used to establish the "justice" of differential treatment, to appeal to the sympathies of the electorate, and to tempt that segment of the electorate that would qualify for differential positive treatment (that is, qualify as "deserving") under the proposed policies.

In applying nondiscrimination, we seek to ensure that arbitrary criteria (those not intrinsically relevant to the object at hand) are not being used to exclude otherwise eligible individuals. Desert arguments, on the other hand, are attempts to distinguish one's circumstances from those of others, to establish that one is deserving of something that others are not. Moreover, claims of desert are frequently made not on the basis of current individual need or other qualifications, but on the basis of past circumstances and events. When such claims are made individually, they are often addressed individually through awards of compensation, either through the courts, or privately in such forums as the workplace. When such claims are advanced through government policies, they are usually made on behalf of groups of individuals, not all of whom have experienced the same past circumstances and events.

In arguments for *government policies* that will provide differential treatment, a class of individuals is construed based upon some common characteristic (e.g., veterans, children, people aged sixty-five and over, people previously employed) and a rationale is developed to support the claim that the designated individuals are "deserving" of special benefits for which only they shall be eligible. The challenge—and, surely, the test of legitimacy in the eyes of justice—is to establish the relevance of the class construction to the benefits to be claimed, and to distinguish the circumstances of this class of individuals from everyone else. Many arguments are compelling and convincing until examined more closely to determine the relevance of the benefits to the alleged differentiating circumstance, and the fairness to those excluded. Often the rationale is based on group generalizations, statistically accurate or not.

The question that nondiscrimination must ask is whether the difference is relevant to the individual, and to the issue at hand, or to the provision or treatment in question. The challenge to justice presented by the desert argument is that it often includes some individuals situated in circumstances to which the proposed provisions are relevant, but excludes other such individuals, at the same time that it also includes individuals to whose circumstances the provisions are not relevant. Hence, as compelling as the argument might be on an emotional level, it nonetheless violates the principle of nondiscrimination. If the argument is accepted into policy, individuals similarly situated will not be treated similarly. To illustrate, here I will examine these propositions in relation to the American Social Security program, and particularly that part of it that deals with old age and retirement.

The Case of Social Security

The funding of retirement benefits for the elderly in the United States, under the Social Security Act of 1935, has been largely on a pay-as-you-go basis. That is, payroll taxes taken from employed individuals (and their employers) are transferred to retired people in the form of cash benefits. In actuality, there is no sizable common trust fund that has been built up over the years through the accumulation and investment of (and interest upon) the payroll taxes that had been paid in the past by those who are currently receiving retirement benefits (see, e.g., Longman, 1996; Graetz and Mashaw, 1999). Moreover, the taxes are regressive in that they are not paid on wages above a certain limit ($72,600 per year in 1999, and more recently raised to $90,000), and are not paid on other forms of income, such as from investments.

Complex formulas govern the amounts that retired persons will receive in Social Security benefits, but in general, one qualifies through having worked (in covered employment) a minimum of ten years, and the size of the monthly benefit is somewhat sensitive to need, but the maximum amount will vary—up to a low ceiling—depending on how many years (up to thirty-five years) one has worked, and how high one's income had been while working (Schieber and Shoven, 1999, pp. 290-298). Thus the benefit amounts are also somewhat sensitive to past earnings. Higher past-income earners will get greater benefits, and this is so regardless of current need for any benefits at all. In addition, spouses and children of retired persons can be included in benefit calculations, and survivors of earners—mostly widows, and children up to a certain age—will receive benefits. Many widows, based on their deceased husbands' history of earnings, qualify for benefits almost as high as those they qualify for on the basis of their own work history. Since they must choose one or the other, the widow's work history counts for very little in terms of benefits. Disabled people who are not elderly can also receive Social Security benefits.

We can ask, then, what is the justification for paying retirement benefits by transferring money from people of one generation to those of an older one? Interestingly, nowhere in the Social Security Act of 1935 is there a statement of its original goals (except to provide for the "general welfare"). However, we can turn to the statements of the architects, administrators, and defenders of the American Social Security system, who have claimed its rationale to be to insure or protect people against (or against loss of income due to) unemployment, illness, disability, and old age. As Wilbur Cohen (former secretary of the federal Department of Health, Education, and Welfare) said in a debate with Milton Friedman: "Social security is a form of income guarantee for the aged, the disabled, the widow and orphan. As a nation we are committed to that principle for these groups" (Cohen and Friedman, 1972, p. 15). Furthermore, it is clear that the intent of the Social Security part of the Social Security Act, as distinct from the public assistance parts, is to protect (members of) such groups only among people who had incomes from past employment, and their dependents. Public assistance would provide benefits to others, but only if they are in poverty, and again only if they belong to certain groups (such as the elderly, the disabled, and single mothers with children). In the popular view, however, Social Security is above all a system of guaranteed income to people upon retirement above a certain age, which they deserve because they have worked most of their lives, and are entitled to because they have paid taxes during those working years specifically earmarked for Social Security. This is precisely the view that the architects of Social Security intended the public to have.

But what is the justice of such justifications and arrangements? It must first be said that protection, in the form of monetary benefits, against old age, disability, widowhood, and other such personal circumstances makes little sense if taken literally, because monetary remuneration has no intrinsic relevance to such circumstances. There are wealthy widows and wealthy elderly people, and some of the greatest achievements in the arts, sciences, and business have been made by elderly (Picasso comes to mind) and even severely disabled people (Stephen Hawking readily comes to mind), with at least a few of these people having been handsomely financially rewarded for their accomplishments.

Unless one considers old age or widowhood as a need in itself—or as an "accomplishment" in itself—addressing it financially makes no sense. The only possible logic involved is based on prejudicial thinking: If we assume that older people, for example, are poorer, in the aggregate, than younger people, we might conclude that older people, as a group, should be targeted for financial benefits. Such policy would be wrong from the standpoint of liberal philosophy because it is based on stereotyping. Even if the stereotype were statistically valid, we would be speaking of a "group relevance," whereas the focus of nondiscrimination is the individual. Group generalizations do not respect the individual and his or her deviation from the group on one or another relevant dimension. Action toward the individual based on prejudgment from group generalization—whether or not the generalization is accurate qua generalization—constitutes discrimination. Such policy discrimination is never harmless. If need is addressed arbitrarily, for example, through arbitrary rules and arbitrary group construction, then some people in need will not have their need addressed, and some people not in need will be unjustly benefited from the community treasury.

In other words, arguments for desert of the "protection from old age" variety implicitly are based on need, but in an aggregate manner that is discriminatory, because they support the exclusion of some who are in need, and the inclusion of some who are not in need. "Old age" as a factor in policymaking merely plays on stereotype and sentiment.

Rather than protection against such conditions as old age, it would seem more reasonable to posit the goal of Social Security as protection against loss of income due to such conditions. Yet loss of income is not independently assessed, but merely assumed. And even if an individual were to report no loss of income, he or she would be eligible for the Social Security benefits on the mere basis of age. Some elderly people who are currently retired have experienced no loss of income. Hence, although this rationale seems more reasonable, it is not the operative one. Secondly, this rationale is subject to some of the fallacies already mentioned, in that it provides no reason for protecting from loss of income only those within the groups specified.

Moreover, it is at least reasonable to raise the question of why government should protect people against loss of income altogether. Many elderly retired people have experienced loss of income that in no way has degraded the quality of their lives. Is government obliged to compensate a top executive for the loss of income he experiences when retiring with a private pension of half a million dollars, from a position that paid an annual salary of one million dollars? In truth, the Social Security benefit that this retired executive receives will constitute a tiny fraction of his loss, but why should this be paid? In addition, many elderly people have paid off the mortgage on their home during their working years, and for that reason alone require less annual income to maintain the same standard of living as previously, not to mention the cessation of their previous support of their children and the costs of their children's college educations. The policy on its own does not make sense. Yet if we were to try to sort out by reason those circumstances of loss of income that we will address in policy and those we will not, there is no end to the distinctions that can be reasonably proffered and contested at the same time. Thus we could decide that it is not government's place to address loss of income. If loss of income happens to bring one below some minimal level of need, then that person's need would be addressed similar to others in need, without differentiation. But it would be need, not the loss of income, that would be addressed.

Indeed, many people have voluntarily retired, although entirely capable of continuing to work. In recent years, less than 35 percent of all Americans aged fifty-five and older have been working full time (Brewer, 2000). Arguably, senior citizens, as a group, currently include the largest number of able-bodied (and voluntarily) unemployed in the nation. While some senior citizens might have "retired" nonvoluntarily due to age discrimination in the employment arena, others retired willingly. As already mentioned, people are considered deserving of retirement benefits both on the basis of having worked a number of years and having paid into the system. Yet some implicit belief regarding age itself must be part of the mix of deservingness, since one is not eligible for full benefits until age sixty-five (and this age of eligibility is set to rise slightly over the next several years to sixty-seven by 2025).

There is much arbitrariness and confusion here. For example, there is no ethical rationale for establishing a retirement age at sixty-five, as opposed to sixty-seven, seventy, or fifty-five; for saying that an individual who was employed for a particular number of years (say twenty or thirty as opposed to fifteen or ten) is deserving of benefits while others are not; or for saying that an individual is deserving of one amount of benefits as opposed to another.

To be sure, the very concept of retirement itself, at least as a concern of government, is rarely if ever debated or questioned. Of course, a person has the right to stop working whenever he or she wants. Surely, there can be no objection if a person builds up savings while working for the purpose of supporting himself or herself after ceasing to work at some point in time. Nor can we object if a group of employees and their employer decide to develop a private pension fund for similar purpose. The need for analysis of the concept of retirement arises only when government is asked to participate in it, either through a public Social Security system or through the granting of tax breaks on private contributions to private pension funds. The concept of retirement seems to carry the connotation that one has "earned" paid retirement through one's previous work. But why should government be involved in this, and why should government reward a person for ceasing to work?

And if the rationale of Social Security is not retirement, but that one is deserving for having worked for x number of years, or has reached the age of sixty-five, then why should his or her benefits be reduced or eliminated if he continues to work? In fact, in what amounts to the ultimate obfuscation of the goals of the old-age Social Security program, the so-called Senior Citizens' Freedom to Work Act of 2000 (P.L. 106-182) has amended the program by eliminating the earnings test for individuals who have attained "retirement age." Now, there is no earnings limit for a person aged sixty-five or over to receive his or her full Social Security benefits. In truth, the earnings test had been eliminated for Social Security recipients aged seventy-five and over as early as 1950, and the age was further reduced to seventy-two, and then seventy, by laws passed in 1954 and 1977, respectively (DeWitt, 1999).

What, then, remains as a possible rationale for the old-age Social Security program? If the intent is to protect people against loss of income, it is surely a very poorly targeted program. We are left only with Social Security benefits serving as supplements to income for those over a certain age. In fact, one need not retire at all to receive the benefits, but merely "attain" the arbitrarily designated "retirement age." But if the government is going to hand out supplements, why not give them to everyone? Either that, or to those most in need. We are left with the notion of Social Security benefits as a reward for a certain minimal number of years of past employment, to be granted only after one reaches a certain age.

I raise the question if the provision of "rewards" in the form of monetary benefits, and decisions as to who shall receive such "rewards," are proper functions of the policies of liberal government. It is, after all, through "reward" as a dimension of social policy that current inequities in the addressing of need are currently justified and through which, for example, many elderly who are well off receive Social Security payments while many children remain in dire need due to the presumed "undeservingness" of their mothers.

One can counter that since Social Security policy and other policies that reward individuals with monetary benefits enhance individual well-being, they are consistent with the basic precepts of liberalism and the proper role of liberal community toward the individuals within it. For after all, the rationale for the formation and maintenance of community is to benefit the individuals within it. But these precepts also hold that in a *just* community, all individuals, and not only some, or some groups, will benefit. The "reward" dimension serves to justify discrimination by obliging us to judge who are the "deserving" and "undeserving" among those who are already similarly situated. We claim that some have "earned" and others have not "earned" the "reward." When we allow a government to be in the business of financial reward, we foster a patronage system whereby politicians pander to politically powerful groups for their votes by promising them rewards for their loyalty, as has been the case with Social Security. If, after addressing need, we wish to go beyond need by fashioning policies to enhance well-being, why not seek to enhance the well-being of everyone?

If there are no *a priori* grounds for proposing that government should be involved in "retirement" in any way, then the only remaining rationale for continuing the current system is that people have already paid into it, on the promise that they would receive retirement benefits. While this is true, and government should keep its promises, it is no grounds for continuing the system beyond what is needed to deal fairly with those who have already paid in. As already mentioned, although a special category of taxes is dedicated to Social Security, and current retirees have paid those taxes, in actuality their benefits are paid through the taxes that current workers are paying into that category. This remaining rationale begs the question of why such a generational transfer of tax money should be considered just. Surely, in many cases these transfers of tax money are going from people who need it more to people who need it less or not at all. The fair *transition* from our current jumble of social policies to something quite different is a topic I will not discuss here, although reasonable suggestions have been made in the past (see, e.g., Milton Friedman's suggestions in Cohen and Friedman, 1972, pp. 44 ff.).

A Community of Unearned Abundance

Suppose the existence of a national community that is able to fill its treasury through common ownership of a natural resource, such as oil within its lands, rather than through taxation. In fact, there are some nations that have operated on this basis. Even the state of Alaska has had no state taxes, actually giving every individual an annual check, all the consequence of state oil royalties (Egan, 1994; Schmidt, 1997; Van Parijs, 2000; Alperovitz, 2000). Such individual incomes are, in a sense, unearned. The individual members of the community would not have put forth any effort, nor even taken any risks. Foreigners could be contracted to run the entire operation, from extraction of the oil from the ground, to refinement, sale, and delivery. The incomes would accrue to individuals solely through common ownership of the oil itself.

Yet, regardless of such arrangements, if in fact individuals have benefited from the formation of a community, then those benefits—above and beyond the wealth that would have accrued to individuals in the absence of a community—are a form of common wealth, akin to the common ownership of a natural resource, in this case, community itself.

John Locke, in his second treatise of government, emphasized the role of government in protecting and preserving one's property, including one's life and liberty (Locke, 1689/1963, see esp. pp. 411-415, 416, 418-421). But we know now, by looking from our vantage point of living in the modern world, that liberal national communities produce great wealth beyond the mere preservation of what one would have been fearful of losing in Locke's "state of nature." The wealth-producing potential of community itself was not foreseen, or at least not addressed.

The profits to an individual who owns a restaurant would be reduced to a sliver in the absence of roads, bridges, and water and sewer systems built by the community. In this case, the community will withhold or take back some portion of this "excess" or "unearned" income, and redistribute it, perhaps to the building of more roads. As a university professor in a near-anarchic society such as Somalia, I would obtain an exceedingly small fraction of the wealth and well-being that accrues to me by occupying the same position and putting forth the same effort in the United States.

Indeed, as members of a community, especially of a prosperous one, we have all gained benefits (both monetary and nonmonetary) beyond our individual efforts, and often without even the need for our individual efforts. Such benefits accrue to us, in part, from having a liberal-democratic form of government and the rights and freedoms we do. In the United States, some people have devised innovations, new products, and marketing networks, and have made discoveries and inventions that have created countless jobs and opportunities for others. But they were enabled to do so through our ideals of individual freedom, free speech, nondiscrimination, and democracy, and the governmental structures that support these ideals, not to mention the physical infrastructure the community has built, its public school system, and its universities. We who were born in the United States have derived many benefits since birth simply from that fact alone, and not only from our individual efforts. Our lives would be shorter and more brutal if we had been born, say, in Afghanistan, rather than in America.

Yet there is no reason to say that people should not gain through benefits not earned through work and effort. Even if the community had accumulated enough wealth—for example, through royalties for a natural resource commonly owned—to make everyone individually wealthy, is there any reason that such wealth should be denied to certain individuals on the grounds that they are not "deserving" of it or did not "earn" it? The answer, as far as I can see, is no.

The monetary (as well as nonmonetary) wealth that accrues to one is a function not only of one's labor, ingenuity, and risk-taking, but also of the particular national community that one happens to be situated in. It can only be concluded that the community can produce a common wealth that accrues to many, if not all, of the individuals within that community. The taxing of such excess monetary wealth by the community is not theft (although the act of tax collection can still be characterized as coercion), in that such wealth is produced by the community structures beyond individual efforts, and thus can be said to belong to the community as a whole. Yet we must not presume to take it all, because the precise quantity of this unearned wealth is not measurable, and the receipt of individual benefits from it is the rationale for forming a community in the first place.

In an endless circle, the community benefits individuals, these "excess" benefits are taxed, and the taxes are then used to benefit the community, both through cash and in-kind benefits. In a just community, these resources would be distributed in a manner that would benefit everyone, without discrimination, as well as in a manner that would combat discriminatory exclusion. What is left to determine is the nature of a system that would accomplish distribution of benefits in this manner, as well as the nature, on the contribution side, of a taxation system that would embody fairness and nondiscrimination in taxation.

Fairness in Taxation

In lieu of the existence of a community-owned natural resource, the royalties from which are used to fill the community treasury, a community resorts to taxation. The purpose of taxation, then, is to pool resources to benefit the community, meaning all of the individuals within it, if we are speaking of a just community. If this is indeed the purpose of taxation, then the sole challenge on the taxation side is to build and implement a system of taxation that is fair to everyone within the community.

Yet in the past and present, other functions besides the pooling of resources through fair-share taxation have been advocated and implemented. In the time of the French Revolution, progressive taxation was advocated as "a mild form of income redistribution" (Gross, 1997, p. 123), and as a means of "removing extreme inequalities of fortune" (p. 124). The Report of the Ontario Fair Tax Commission endorsed progressive taxation as a means of making the tax system in that Canadian province "a more effective instrument for income and wealth redistribution" (Ontario Fair Tax Commission, 1993, p. 12). Recently, as noted in chapter 3, the governor of California proposed to exempt public school teachers from state income taxes, no doubt in special recognition of, or as a "reward" for, the important work they do (Purdum, 2000). So-called "sin" taxes have been instituted in the United States, such as higher taxes on cigarettes or alcoholic beverages than on other commodities. The rationale here is that the consumption of "bad" things should be penalized, or that taxes should be employed as disincentives to the use of "bad" things, or that because the consumption of cigarettes or alcohol can lead to illness whose treatment the community must pay for (e.g., through Medicare), the users of these products should be taxed more than nonusers, or a nebulous combination of all of these rationales.

Moreover, tax breaks for selected "social goods," such as childcare expenses, have been built into income tax systems. Ontario, for example, has provided an "age credit" for every taxpayer sixty-five years of age or older. "This special treatment of seniors in the tax system has been justified in several ways. First, it is a way of recognizing the lifelong contribution of seniors to Canadian society. It is argued that this contribution merits a social benefit to all seniors regardless of income... Second, it is based on the recognition that seniors *generally* experience a drop in income upon retirement and *on average* have significantly lower incomes than other Canadians... Third, it is argued that because a *high proportion* of seniors have low pension incomes, they merit special assistance, in this case in the form of tax relief" (Ontario Fair Tax Commission, 1993, pp. 322-323, italics added).

In the United States, we are all familiar with many other tax breaks for selected groups, such as the homeowner's deduction for mortgage interest payments. The rationales are easy to contrive, both for the groups chosen to be favored, and those not yet chosen. For example, we can say that it is a benefit to the community to encourage home ownership. Just as easily, we can propose that tax breaks should be provided to slim people, because they incur less health expenses, on average, to the community. Or in a similar vein, we can propose a special tax on fat people. To be sure, to maintain the community treasury at a particular level to pay for its distributive and other policies, tax breaks for one group must mean tax increases (or tax penalties) for other groups.

If homeowners are to receive tax breaks on their housing loans, then to fill the community treasury, non-homeowners will have to pay more in taxes, if they cannot receive tax breaks on other types of loans. But there is the question of why there should be tax breaks on any loans at all. If those who purchase alcoholic beverages pay more in taxes than those who purchase other products instead, then others pay less. Rationales may be proffered, but they cannot negate the fact that individuals similarly situated as equal members of the community will receive differential treatment in regard to their tax obligations.

To summarize, tax systems have been intended not only as a way of raising money to fill the community treasury, but as a means of compressing the range of inequality of incomes, of implementing moralistic judgments by rewarding "good" behaviors and penalizing "bad" behaviors, of behavior modification, of providing for social services through tax breaks rather than through direct provision, and of simply benefiting individuals falling within certain groupings deemed to be "deserving" of special favor in regard to tax treatment by dint of certain group generalizations. Of course, in addition to the "goodness" of these uses meant to be accepted at face value, each use has been rationalized, ironically, as promoting tax fairness.

Thus, much as, on the distribution side, policies have been burdened with multiple goals that have obfuscated the issue of fairness, and have made fairness of distribution more difficult to conceptualize and to achieve, the collection side, too, has been saddled with multiple goals that have obscured the straightforward (though not simple) issue of fairness in collection. And just as these practices have raised the specter of discrimination on the distribution side, they have violated the principle of nondiscrimination on the collection side.

Progressive income tax structures—in which the proportion of income that one must pay as tax rises with the level of income—have been defended as means to compress income inequality. Although the intent, and the result, has never been the equalization of incomes—for one thing, it is feared that if marketplace incentives for people to build new wealth that would benefit the economy would be severely attenuated, wealthy people would slack off—the implication is that to redress income inequality to whatever extent is to act in the direction of fairness. Liberalism, however, promotes equality of treatment rather than results, and it is against its tenets to compel equality of results. For this reason, attempts have been made to buttress the fairness claim for progressive taxation with separate arguments. It has been claimed that as one moves up the income scale, one experiences diminishing increments of satisfaction or utility from additional income increments. Therefore the "sacrifice" that one makes by giving up the same amount or even the same percentage of one's income at higher levels of income is not as great as at lower levels. To achieve fairness in terms of equivalent "sacrifice," so this reasoning goes, tax rates should be progressive.

In practice, progressive income taxation is more show than substance. The progressive tax rate that applies to one's income bracket is not applied to one's entire taxable income. So, for example, if one has a taxable income of $400,000 for the year, putting her in the top tax rate bracket of, say, 40 percent, her tax liability will not be $160,000. Rather, only the amount above, say, $250,000 will be taxed at 40 percent, while the amount between, say, $120,000 and $250,000 will be taxed at the next lowest rate on the progressive tax scale, say, 35 percent, and so on. Her tax liability can end up being less than $135,000, for an effective tax rate of less than 34 percent. Yet the person with an average income may end up with a tax liability that amounts to 25 percent. The point is that the range of effective tax rates is far more compressed than the appearances given by the range of marginal tax rates.

The appearances, however, contribute toward placating the public's desire to "soak the rich." Indeed, most of us have at least a vague sense that there is something obscene about a corporate chief executive or basketball player receiving an annual income equivalent to that of 100 people with average incomes. The appropriateness of a government role in this matter, however, is debatable. Perhaps the matter should be taken up with the people who, directly or indirectly, consent to the provision of such high incomes (including stockholders and basketball fans). Our desire to enlist government in penalizing the rich might stem more from sentiment than principle.

But let us return to the original purpose of taxation. It is to fill the community treasury, and to do so in a manner that is fair to all contributors, with each paying his or her fair share. To target some to pay excessively relative to others in order to fill a treasury whose purpose is to benefit everyone would constitute discriminatory unfairness. In the United States, even moderate-income citizens are enjoying extremely high standards of living, which in fact have been aided by the common treasury to which their taxes have gone. The issue is not "sacrifice," but simply fair tax shares.

It is true that our taxes "purchase" specific services, such as police and fire departments, and the repair of roads we travel on. If this were the whole story, the high-income person should pay no more in taxes than a person of moderate income, for each in effect would be "purchasing" specific services, and achieving equivalent benefit, much as we regard it as entirely appropriate for the high-income person to pay the same price for a hamburger at McDonald's as a person of more moderate means. If McDonald's charged the high-income person more, it would be engaging in discrimination, just as surely as if it were to charge different prices for the same product based on the race of the purchaser. But in forming and maintaining a community, we have achieved levels of wealth in this country that would have been impossible to achieve without community. This is not a matter of this or that service, but a result of the form of government we have established and maintained, the regulations we have imposed on ourselves, the liberties we protect, the manner in which government encourages and supports invention and discovery, the services themselves, and so on, in synergistic combination. McDonald's itself, or any business, could in no way have achieved its level of economic success without it.

It is for these reasons that we should find it ludicrous (as we do, whether for these reasons or not), if a person with an income of $50,000 and another with an income of $500,000 should pay the same amount in total taxes of, say, $10,000. This would represent a tax rate of 20 percent of income for the former person, and 2 percent for the latter. Such a regressive taxation structure does not recognize the fact that whereas both persons have benefited from the community, the higher-income person has benefited far more, at least in monetary terms, which indeed is the coin of taxation. The case can reasonably be made that the higher-income person's fair share should be proportionate to his or her income, that is, also 20 percent, or in this case, $100,000, amounting to ten times the tax payment of the lesser-income person.

Income is a measure of how much one has benefited from a combination of his effort and abilities, luck, and the community structures. It is because of the contribution made to his benefit by community structures that it is fair to tax his income in the first place. What he does with his income, except for the part taken in taxes, is his business. But the larger the benefit, the more he has benefited from community structures—at least in a monetary and materialistic sense—and so it is fair that he pay more taxes than those who have benefited less. Yet he still has plenty of leeway to profit from his own efforts and abilities virtually without limit. Arguably, however, there are people who "deserve" more for their efforts and abilities than they are getting, but this is not a matter for welfare or taxes.

At the very least, the grounds for proposing the fairness of progressive taxation, as opposed to proportional taxation, are arbitrary and nebulous. If tax is progressive, what real grounds are there for deciding what the rate steps should be, what the tax brackets should be, how many tax brackets there should be, and at what levels of income they should begin and end? And just why should higher-income people pay at a higher rate than others? We are left adrift in a sea of arbitrariness. In fact, in the United States, the top rate once stood at more than 90 percent, then declined to 70 percent, and then to 50 percent. It dropped further to 28 percent in 1986, but then rose to 39.6 percent in 1994 (Slemrod and Bakija, 1996, p. 25). A rationale for one or another of these rates, or for one over the others (except to say that it is better to soak the rich more rather than less), would be unfathomable.

There is certainly also a degree of arbitrariness in setting a proportional (or flat) rate at, say, 20 percent. Arbitrariness is not intolerable in itself, so long as it treats all people equally (as would a proportional tax rate arbitrarily set at 20 percent, or 22 percent, or so on). The problem arises when different rates are applied to different people, as it does in progressive taxation schemes. Indeed, leaving sentiment aside, it is possible to construe progressive taxation as class discrimination, and no less discriminatory for the probability that the majority would vote for it.

Most so-called proportional income tax structures, however, are actually progressive in that they contain two steps. That is, they include some exempt level of income (as do progressive tax structures) below which the tax rate would be zero, a level at which we decide to impose no taxes. Anything beyond that, no matter how much, is taxed at the same flat rate. Yet, although the progression here is based upon a minimal amount of tax-exempt income that we have decided should be afforded to all, the "all" refers only to those who have an income at all. No unearned benefits from community, to be distributed in some manner to all members of the community, are recognized.

Alternatively, we can say that income under a certain amount not only should not be taxed, but should be supplemented by government support up to that amount. This can be counted as one variant of what has been called a negative income tax structure (Friedman, 1962, pp. 191-195; Atkinson, 1975, pp. 227-233). Further, we can decide that this amount be set at a level sufficient to address minimal human need. The only problem here is that if we set the minimal amount at, say, $10,000, then a person who chooses not to work will have the same income as one who holds a job paying $10,000 per year, and we do not consider this to be fair. In fact, in that the government transfers $10,000 to the former and nothing to the latter, this arrangement can be considered discriminatory against working people.

Thus we would need two minimal levels, one which no one is allowed to fall below for whatever reason, say, $10,000, and one, say $20,000, at which and below no taxes are taken. In between no income and an income of $20,000, the minimal income support would be reduced by $500 for every $1,000 of income, and so would be reduced to zero at $20,000. This would constitute another variant of a negative income tax structure. Since the income support is usually designed to diminish to zero at fairly low levels of income, the rate at which the income support is reduced (here, 50 percent) is often set considerably higher than the positive income tax rate for the next income bracket starting at $20,000. The problems here are that we are back to a tax structure with multiple tax brackets—one, in fact, in which the tax structure is regressive in that the "tax" on income below $20,000 is, in effect, higher than the tax on income above $20,000—and that tax policy is, in effect, deliberately being used to provide "incentives" for work rather than solely for filling the treasury in a fair manner.

A Universal Social Dividend and Taxation System

To summarize, beyond the proposition that the community exists to benefit the individuals within it, I began with the moral value of the sanctity of human life and the fundamental principle of nondiscrimination, and construed these to comprise the moral foundation of liberalism. From this foundation, I drew the implication that a liberal and just community, through its instrument of government, is obliged not to allow basic human needs to go unaddressed, and must address such need without judgment or discrimination. Further, I concluded that the common practice of utilizing the concept of desert as a dimension of social policy is highly problematic in that, at the very least, it constantly challenges the principle of nondiscrimination, and therefore justice, with debatable claims and distinctions. I also suggested that the community, being more than and different than the sum of the individuals within it and their individual efforts, has qualities of its own that do not reside in individuals, such as a democratic form of government, or environmental regulations, that in synergistic combination may produce wealth above and beyond individuals' efforts, and which, in a sense is not "earned" by most, if any, individuals within that community. It can be considered a communal wealth, in that it is in excess of that which would have accrued to individuals, despite their efforts, in absence of community. The existence of this excess wealth is certain, even though we have no means of measuring its precise quantity.

In addition, on both the contribution and distribution sides, I discussed policy dimensions that compel arbitrary cutoffs and distinctions to be drawn, many of which, in treating individuals differently, may be considered discriminatory. I also noted the obfuscation of goals in policies, and the unfairness inherent in the use of a tax system to do anything other than to fill the treasury by collecting taxes in accordance with formulas that are fair to all individuals. My task, then, is to propose a set of policy arrangements that would be informed by the observations made here, that would avoid the pitfalls and dilemmas noted, and that would be consistent with or fit the foundation and derived tenets of liberalism as depicted here.

Variations of the concept of a "social dividend" combined with a flat income tax structure have been proposed at least since the 1940s, and in several countries (see, e.g., Rhys Williams, 1943; Atkinson, 1975, 1995; Parker, 1989; Funiciello, 1993; Murray, 1997; BAG SHI, 2000; and Krebs and Rein, 2000, for proposals, reviews, and critiques). The variant I will suggest here is substantially similar to some of the previous proposals, and seems to fit the foregoing discussion in a logically consistent manner. Indeed, a value of this discussion, I believe, is to contribute to the development of a sound rationale for such approaches.

I propose that an annual common monetary benefit, at least of sufficient size to address the basic human needs of an individual in a minimally adequate manner, be allocated (without transfer) to every member of the community, adjusted only for size of household. This benefit would, at the least, set a floor under which no one would be allowed to fall. Let us say that this amount has been determined to be $10,000 per year for an individual in a single-individual household, with combined amounts for more than one individual per household increased by $3,000 for each additional individual.[1] Then, if we decide to raise the common monetary benefit to above a minimally adequate level, we will always do so by some multiple of this same combined amount. Hence, even if the common benefit decided upon is to be more generous than a minimally adequate amount, it will be tied to individual needs, and as such done in a fair manner. Even for a very wealthy man, the amount allocated would be his fair share that he would have used to meet his basic needs, or somewhat beyond (depending on the level of common benefit that the society has decided upon) had he lost his wealth.

If a society is to respect human life without discrimination, its policies must enhance the lives of all regardless of economic station. True, the degree of one's wealth is itself an indicator of the extent to which one has benefited from the community, but this will be addressed on the tax contribution side. At issue here are deliberate social welfare policies that allocate money from the treasury in the form of individual cash benefits. The question is whether those benefits should be larger for some than for others, or whether each should not be allocated an equal share.

As part of this arrangement that allocates common benefits, the tax on all other income would be flat, or strictly proportional. That is, unlike other "proportional" tax schemes, there will not be a zero percent rate on any amount of income (other than the common benefit, which will simply not be taxed). Everyone will be taxed at the same rate. Now let us consider a woman living alone who, under the prevailing level of provision, is allocated $10,000 as her annual benefit. Further, let us suppose that the prevailing income tax rate is 40 percent. If her nonbenefit income for the year is $25,000, she would owe $10,000 in income tax. But the government owes her a $10,000 benefit, and so she would pay the government nothing, $25,000 being the break-even point.

A single mother with two children who has a nonbenefit income of $25,000 would owe $10,000 in income tax. But the government owes her $16,000, and so her net income would be $31,000. Her break-even point would be $40,000. For a four-person household, most often consisting of a two-parent family with two children, or a single mother with three children, the social dividend would be $19,000, and the break-even point would be $47,500.

Although the proposed system does not, strictly speaking, contain a negative income tax scheme—since set benefits are allocated to everyone (including the wealthy) and there is no special percentage rate applied only to incomes below the break-even point—those with low income benefit considerably. In fact, if the woman living alone had a nonbenefit income of $20,000, she would have owed the government $8,000, but since the government owed her $10,000, her net income would have been $22,000. If she had a nonbenefit income of $15,000, her net income would have been $19,000. And if her nonbenefit income had been $10,000, her net income would have been $16,000. That is, the lower one's income, the more that gets added to it, in a negatively progressive manner. Yet the same tax rate applies to all. If she did not have any nonbenefit income, the government would have paid her the full $10,000.

Going the other way on the income scale, let us suppose that this woman had $30,000 in nonbenefit income. At a 40 percent tax rate, she would owe $12,000 in taxes, but because the government would owe her a universal income benefit of $10,000, she would pay only $2,000, or less than 7 percent of her nonbenefit income. If she had $100,000 in nonbenefit income, she would owe $40,000 in taxes, but because the government would owe her a social dividend of $10,000, she would pay $30,000, or 30 percent of her nonbenefit income. Similarly, if she had $1 million in nonbenefit income, she would owe $400,000 in taxes, but since the government owes her $10,000, she would pay $390,000, or 39 percent of her nonbenefit income. The point is that although the proposed tax system does not contain a progressive tax scheme, the tax payments are progressive with higher incomes. A person with 20 times the income of one with

$50,000 will pay 39 times more in tax. Although not the object, the range of income inequality would be compressed.

In truth, the effective tax rate would reach an asymptotic level of 40 percent at higher income levels. That is, for incomes over $1 million, the effective tax rate will rise negligibly, always remaining between 39 percent and 40 percent. Hence the progressivity is greatest at lower and middle income levels. In fact, progressive tax schemes also have a maximum tax rate, with all income levels beyond an arbitrarily chosen level being taxed at the same exact rate. The tax scale in the currently proposed scheme is continuous, having no differential tax brackets or arbitrary cutoff points.

In the proposed system, in accordance with earlier discussion, no tax breaks whatsoever would be allowed. As argued earlier, the making of policy through tax breaks blurs and obfuscates the goals of tax collection, and the fairness of taxation schemes. Tax breaks end up favoring the most powerful and wealthy, consequently loading an unfair share of the tax burden onto the shoulders of the less well off. A fair tax system must be simple and clearly discernible in design.

There should be no special categories of taxes (such as for Medicare or Social Security), because such divisions confuse the issues, and are necessary only if special categories of people are to continue to be addressed through discriminatory policies. Otherwise, all taxation should go into general funds. Indeed, taxation into general funds is already a form of insurance. If every single member of society is to be recognized as covered, then no special employee contributions are necessary. We need only figure out a fair system of contribution (taxation) and distribution (social welfare policies).

Additionally, under this proposal in the United States, the social dividend would replace the Old Age, Survivors, and Disabilities Insurance (OASDI, or Social Security), Unemployment Insurance, SSI, TANF, and other such group-specific public assistance and "insurance" programs, as well as tax credit programs such as the Earned Income Tax Credit (EITC) (see also Funiciello, 1993, p. 302; Murray, 1997, pp. 192-193). Private retirement pensions would be taxed the same as any other types of income. This would mean, for example (utilizing the same parametric values as above), that a single man living in retirement and collecting various pensions and income from his investments would break even if his total income were $25,000, collect some payment from the government if it were below that amount, and make some payment to the government if it were above that amount. He would be actually paid the full social dividend of $10,000 only if he had no income whatsoever.

It should be noted that one's assets are not taken into account in the proposed scheme (although the income that one's assets may produce would be). Thus it is possible for a person to own outright an expensive house and car and yet, if having no income, be paid the full social dividend of $10,000. It is assumed, of course, that taxes have already been paid on the income used to purchase the house and car in the first place. Assets could be taken into account in this scheme only if we were to allow that the same assets should be taxed over and over again on an annual basis. Barring that, the person with assets is as entitled as anyone else is to the social dividend, to be collected in whole or in part in cash or to be used to offset income taxes. However, if the house were to be passed on as an inheritance, we may want to tax it as income to the inheritor at that point. If the inheritor were to sell the house at some later time, we would tax only the income attributable to the increased value of the house at that point. Retired and unemployed single persons, if receiving less than $25,000 in income, will be paid some amount by the government, no matter what assets they may hold, yet this would be true of everyone, regardless of retirement or unemployment status.

Finally, under the proposed system, it turns out that there are powerful built-in incentives to work, although this was not the deliberate intent. A single man who works for a $10,000 income will net $16,000, as opposed to $10,000 if he did not work (again using the same parameters as above). There is no disincentive to work unless one is fully content with minimal survival, since no matter what a man makes, he is allocated the common benefit, offset only somewhat by taxes at the lower income levels. Yet everyone not only is allocated a fair-share benefit or stake in the community, but also (if having any income at all) pays taxes into the community.

Is such a proposal so radically different from what we have now? Old-age Social Security is already a "universal" benefit system, quite similar to the one proposed here, but only for those above a certain age. Currently, if a man attains a certain age, he will begin to collect some minimal monthly benefit for the rest of his life (although the amount of the benefit will vary somewhat from person to person). He will receive this benefit whether he is "able-bodied" or not, whether he works or not, or whether he is wealthy or not. Also, similar to the proposal presented here, he can use his benefit to offset his income tax. (The difference is that in the proposed system, income is taxed from the first dollar.) The major difference is that the old-age Social Security program is limited to those above a certain age. In the proposal presented here, we are simply applying a program roughly similar to the Social Security program to *everyone*, in the name of nondiscrimination.

Surely, under this proposal, some people might opt to live within the minimal level of comfort that the social dividend may afford. Some of these people might use the time freed up by minimal benefit to support themselves through college, finance the early stages of an artistic career, take full-time care of their children, or study Torah. Others, to be sure, will make no effort to do anything, or perhaps play checkers all day. But these are among the options we already provide today, albeit for only certain classes of people, such as the "aged." On the other hand, some people are forced to not have jobs, either because the jobs are not available, they do not have the skills for the jobs that are available, or they have suffered types of incapacitation that preclude their continuation in the jobs at which they were working. Why not grant the benefit to all of us, without distinction? Differential benefit allocation based on arbitrary distinctions and differential sympathy is unfair and irrational.

It is clear that the social dividend and tax system proposed here is truly universal in the sense that everyone, even the wealthy person, is allocated the same income benefit (adjusted only for household size), and that everyone pays tax on his or her income, no matter how small that income is (and at the same tax rate, at that). Thus there are no group distinctions or encouragement of group stigmatization. I would make one caveat in regard to potential stigmatization, however. Theoretically, it is possible to assume that some people with no income, and therefore in actual receipt of the full social dividend, might spend so much of it for nonessential items (such as liquor, illicit drugs, or gambling), that they would still be left without adequate food, clothing, and shelter. Since an essential obligation of the community is to ensure that the essential survival needs of everyone within it are addressed, I would propose that in such cases protective voucher payments of rent and the like be made by government officials, thus changing the social benefit into an in-kind benefit for the protection of the individual.

Such a system, however, does not isolate the poor from the wealthy, but actually allies the interests of the wealthy with those of the poor. Reduction of the size of the social benefit, or the increase of the tax rate, both of which would be to the detriment of low-income and poor people, would likewise not serve the interests of the wealthy. If high-income people wish to advocate for higher common benefits to offset more of their taxes, then if they are successful, low-income people, and the poor without earned income, will benefit too, for they also will be allocated higher benefits. And if retired elderly people, through their organizations, successfully lobby for higher common benefits, then children will gain also. All of this would be true at the same time that wealthier people would pay far more taxes, and progressively more, than others, that no one would go hungry or homeless (depending on the size of the common benefit agreed upon), and yet everyone would pay a fair share and get a fair benefit. There would be no discrimination, such as against working people or children, or in favor of the elderly, or even against the wealthy.

Yet the system is by no means inefficient or wasteful, in that far more will be contributed into the treasury per person by high-income people than by low-income people; poor and many low-income people will draw money from the treasury; and the considerable bureaucracies and administrative costs necessary to operate public assistance programs that purport to divine the "deserving" from the "undeserving" will be eliminated. The Internal Revenue Service could handle the entire system without much modification or expansion, or even with a reduction in its bureaucracy due to a greatly simplified tax system.

The point of this discussion is merely that such a universal social dividend program as proposed here is consistent with the moral precepts of liberalism as posited here, not that it is mandated by them. We can hypothetically consider a community that is not wealthy overall, and has scant communal unearned abundance. Shall benefits be credited to all, necessitating a tax rate that would truly burden those with moderate incomes? Shall alternatively, the benefits be made so low that they leave the poor still deeply mired in poverty? Rather than these alternatives, a just community which, for reasons I discussed earlier, is obliged to address need primarily, might choose to set up a welfare system along the traditional lines of a means-tested program such as AFDC, but noncategorical. Such a system would have its drawbacks, in that up till and even somewhat beyond the earned-income equivalent of the minimal welfare benefit decided upon, people might have little incentive to hold a job. Hence there would be some "leakage" or "waste" in this system set up by an unwealthy society that aspires to be just. Yet there can be no doubt that a community, rich or poor, having members who have acquired considerable unearned abundance from the fact of the existence of the community, or not, has a moral obligation, to be implemented through government as instrument, to benefit its needy members.

Since government is a form of collective behavior, and a product of individuals, it has moral obligations similar to those of individuals. We can thus talk about the rightful conduct of a community (or nation) not only toward the individuals within it, but also toward the nations and individuals outside it. Consistent with the moral foundation of liberalism—the sanctity of individual human life—it has a moral responsibility for the survival of others. While the universal social dividend and taxation system proposed here is based on the sanctity of human life, it also depends on a common treasury and excess community wealth. But the moral foundation of liberalism by itself takes us to another level of concern—the entire world, which does not have a common treasury. If a common treasury does not exist, then we are thrown back entirely on our moral responsibility as the rationale and guide for redistribution, although it is possible to additionally maintain that our own community's excess wealth is partially a product of the existence and labors of the world outside of our community (an argument that I will not pursue here).

Promoting Nondiscrimination

When we go beyond cash-benefit programs to in-kind programs, we often ask whether a proposed program would promote the "common good." But such a justification is frequently offered for programs that would not individually and directly benefit everyone. The claim that a program, although used only by some, is likely to result in indirect benefit to all, or to the community as a whole or group, stands in danger of violating the more basic matter of fairness to each and every individual, as individuals. Judgments of the "greater good" or "benefit to the community" often foster and disguise discrimination against some for the sake of the good of others.

We might even agree that certain benefits to some individuals, such as public education, increase the overall wealth of the society, thus allowing greater benefits to be distributed to all individuals. But that should not be the litmus test for instituting such a program, because while an individual should not be violated for the sake of the common good (such as to increase the wealth of the community as a whole), neither should an individual be favored for that purpose, or any other purpose. Rather, the main rationale for instituting such a program should be the promotion of the good of people in a nondiscriminatory manner, or the promotion of nondiscrimination itself.

Hence, individually relevant criteria should take precedence over "common good" criteria in determining the most essential programs. Public education should be a function of government because it is essential for promoting nondiscrimination. Theoretically, at least, public education ensures that individuals will not be denied the opportunity to develop their own abilities—and thus not be denied comparable and reasonable opportunity to reap the other benefits of community—due to a factor irrelevant to those abilities, namely, whether they or their families can financially afford the education. A society that would not promote such opportunity would fail to benefit everyone within it.

Likewise, a truly universal health care system (and not just for the elderly nor even the poor) is essential, because in deciding whether or not to institute a governmental program at all—why have public education and public health care systems in the first place?—priority must be given to those programs that promote the good of people in a nondiscriminatory manner at the most basic levels of protecting and enhancing individual human life.

The national community, via government, has the responsibility to ensure that whatever programs are instituted to promote nondiscrimination will *operate* in a nondiscriminatory manner. In the United States, one of the most pressing issues in this regard concerns the nature of funding mechanisms for public education. Due to the fact that public primary and secondary school education has been, and largely continues to be, funded through local property taxes, many of the poorest children in the most impoverished areas of the nation receive the most poorly funded education. Although many states currently attempt to offset the disparities produced by a property-tax-based funding system by providing supplemental state funding in disproportionately greater amounts to poor districts, and there is some federal funding, gross disparities still exist in some parts of the country. For example, as Jonathan Kozol (1992) has documented, the impoverished children of the devastated town of East St. Louis attend dilapidated school buildings containing outdated, shoddy equipment and few books, while children from financially better-off families in nearby towns attend schools that are extravagant by comparison, in beautiful buildings stocked with many books, the latest computers, and modern teaching devices.

Children similarly situated, theoretically at least, in regard to membership status within the community, have the right to be treated similarly. The fundamental concept of local funding of primary and secondary schools through property taxes is discriminatory in that it predetermines gross inequalities in educational opportunity. If we have a national community, as surely evidenced by the fact that we have a federal government, then public schools should be funded through the federal treasury, in order to ensure nondiscrimination in educational opportunity. Variation from state to state, and town to town, promotes discrimination. In regard to school funding, taxes are currently being used in a manner that promotes class discrimination.[2]

More than the availability of comparable educational opportunity, however, is needed to promote nondiscrimination. If liberalism values the individual, then a liberal community must be one that values, benefits, and supports each and every individual. Through the instrument of government, it must actively promote nondiscrimination through, at the very least, the reduction of barriers and obstructions to comparable treatment and consideration of all individuals. If a person who is qualified for a civil engineering job is barred from consideration for that job solely because her wheelchair cannot get through the doorway of the firm's offices, then she is the subject of discrimination, since her disability and her need to use a wheelchair are not relevant to her qualifications to do the work of civil engineering. To promote nondiscrimination, public policy must provide for the widening of the office doorway. The need in such cases is not financial need warranting monetary benefit (unless the benefit is in the form of a cash grant expressly for the purpose of buying, e.g., a specially adapted computer for a blind or hearing-impaired person), but specific in-kind benefits. In the past, it is likely that discrimination, not handicaps per se, was responsible for the impoverishment of many people with disabilities.

Yet we face the seeming paradox that programs that are used by only some and that benefit only some are necessary to promote nondiscrimination. On the one hand, since many needs and problems are not universal, the only way in which a community can address the needs of all of its members in a manner that is beneficial as well as fair to all is to mount such programs. On the other hand, what is to prevent this whole enterprise from deteriorating into the very prospect (or current reality) that we wish to avoid—policies being made on the basis of pervasive invocation of selective claims of desert that set up privileged categories of people for the receipt of special benefits?

First, we must distinguish programs that would cater to mere preference (e.g., free-cigar programs) and thus discriminate in favor of some and against others, from programs that are necessary to support human life in fundamental and nondiscrimination-promoting ways, even if benefiting few individuals. Government-funded research and technology to combat sickle-cell anemia and breast cancer will benefit only some—in fact, such programs would even disproportionately benefit black people and women, respectively. But if the community is to even minimally benefit all of its members, it surely is appropriate that it utilize some of its pooled community resources to combat debilitating and life-threatening diseases, regardless of their demographic distribution, which is irrelevant to the task at hand.

Second, the programs would have to operate in a nondiscriminatory manner—they must be available to all. Programs to combat sickle-cell anemia and breast cancer are not discriminatory so long as white people and men are not arbitrarily excluded from benefit. A college that offers increased time on examinations to certain students (who have been classified as having learning disabilities) should offer the same amount of time to all students. If a benefit or support is to be offered to some, then it should be offered to all, even though only those who believe they can benefit from it will partake of it. Unlike cash benefits, many in-kind benefits—such as the provision of computer-screen magnifiers, educational materials in Braille, or sign-language interpreters in the classroom—would be of no use to most of us, and so we would not partake of them. Other benefits, such as the installation of new elevators and outside ramps in public accommodations to ensure accessibility to all those who use wheelchairs, would be used by others, too.

We should strive to design programs that provide in-kind supports as specific to the need as possible, and which do not necessitate the development of eligibility criteria to distinguish groups for inclusion and exclusion. For example, the common practice of providing special parking spaces for the handicapped necessitates group-eligibility requirements and promotes special treatment. It would behoove us to search for alternative approaches for the specific need in question—in this case, the need to promote painless access, for everyone, from parking lots to buildings—that will not require the categorization of people. Yet many supports addressed to specific needs (such as the elevators just mentioned) will benefit us all. Indeed, in seeking new ways to benefit some individuals in life-sustaining and barrier-reducing ways, we will find new ways of helping and supporting the lives of all of us.

In the quest to promote nondiscrimination, there will still be gray areas in regard to what benefits should be provided altogether. For example, should public childcare be funded? We must ask whether such a program would serve to reduce inequality of opportunity, or remove barriers to comparable treatment and consideration, and thereby promote nondiscrimination, even if benefiting only some. For some parents who must go to jobs outside the home, daycare may indeed be a necessity of justice that should be provided regardless of whether or not the parents can financially afford it. However, for some parents, it might only be a preference, and still others might wish to stay home to care for their children. Therefore we have a benefit that promotes nondiscrimination for some, caters to others' mere preferences, and constitutes a service that still others are providing for themselves. I would argue that if the benefit is necessary for the promotion of nondiscrimination for some, then it should be instituted; and if instituted, it should be available to all. However, the principle of nondiscrimination leads us to consider that if public daycare is to be provided to those with children, perhaps it should also be provide to those who need such care for adult relatives. The implications of adherence to the principle of nondiscrimination will require ongoing debate, clarification, and reflection, but I contend that consideration of the issues raised by this principle will serve justice better than devotion to the concept of desert in policymaking.

Finally, it is true that when people are wealthy, they can purchase their own education, daycare, or other benefits that may be necessary to ensure that they receive nondiscriminatory treatment. Yet, I propose that all in-kind benefit programs provided by government should be available to rich and poor alike, with no payment or sliding fee scales. The rationale here is that, with the taxation system being reduced to one clear goal, we can assume that all people have already paid their fair share to the community through their taxes. It would not be fair to exclude some members of the community from the receipt of services that are offered to others, nor would it be fair to double-charge the wealthy. This would amount to class discrimination.

Likewise, if the community is committed to promoting nondiscrimination, the burden of its costs must be fairly shared by the entire community, and thus should be paid for out of the common treasury, which we have already satisfied ourselves has been funded in an equitable manner. Provisions of current laws that require the civil engineering employer, for example, to pay the costs of the supports necessary to provide opportunity for the wheelchair-bound civil engineer can be viewed as discriminatory against the employer. If nondiscrimination is a responsibility of the community, then the community as a whole should pay to support it, not just a few individuals.

In conclusion, I have argued that judgment of desert cannot be a just basis for governmental allocation of resources, beyond the desert that applies to all individuals based upon the intrinsic value of human life. Through government policies, we should enable people in the present without discrimination, and not attempt to reward and compensate them for past deeds and events. The government of a liberal community that aspires to be just must shift its focus from the questionable judgment of desert to the active promotion of nondiscrimination.

Notes

1. Although I have set the single-individual benefit considerably above the 1999 poverty threshold, I have based the additions to the combined amounts (at $3,000 for each additional individual) upon the roughly average percentage of 30 percent of the single-individual amount indicated in the Census Bureau's table of poverty thresholds (U.S. Bureau of the Census, 2000).
2. The shift in the funding of public education proposed here, from property taxes to federal income taxes, might offset the possibly depressing effect that the elimination of the mortgage-interest tax break might have on the value of a house.

sury. Only a moral obligation based upon the sanctity of human life, which converges with justice in the life-affirmation frame, would compel us to address need outside of our community, and this principle of life affirmation would require us to strive to address need without discrimination.

In Las Vegas, as in other parts of the country, there are age-"qualified" housing development "communities" in which only people over age fifty-five may live. By contractual agreement, a person buying a house in such a development is assured that other houses within the development will not be occupied by younger people. But such policies that exclude people on the basis of arbitrary factors amount to discrimination, and should be seen as having no more moral (much less legal) standing than color-"qualified" "communities." A challenge to the exclusion in either case could be met by the argument that to change the rules now would violate contractual promises made to current residents of the development. My point is that—although most of us see it in the case of race discrimination but currently fail to acknowledge it in the case of age discrimination—moral obligations, such as nondiscrimination, precede and override contractual obligations. This is why preconditions must be placed on contract formulations of justice, such as those that accompany the hypothetical original position.

Group-Oriented Policies

Given the emphasis on the individual, individual rights, respect for the individual, nondiscrimination, equal opportunity, and means and process in liberal philosophy, it is surprising how pervasively the group-justice frame is manifested in the public policies of the United States as well as other modern liberal democracies.

The group-justice frame, it will be recalled, distinguishes between groups in social policy, and applies the notion of desert not only to groups rather than to individuals, but even across generations yet unborn within a group. Actually, there are many manifestations of the group frame in contemporary policies in which the notion of desert does not even appear to be involved. That is, no attempt is made to justify the policy in terms of desert. Rather, the grounds are either utilitarian, or completely oblivious to the plight of group members other than the intended victims or beneficiaries.

When God instructed King Saul to put to death all of the Amalekites for the assault that Amalek made upon the Israelites on their way up from Egypt two centuries earlier, the only possible connection of these unfortunates to the earlier crime was group membership. We can speak of a "group desert," but this concept defies logic since there was no conceivable way in which the Amalekites to be slaughtered could have been responsible for that earlier crime. We can speak of the emotion of revenge, or justification in terms of utility (e.g., if the opportunity were left for Israelites to mingle with members of other groups, the latter would have a wayward influence on them, and undermine the traditions, culture, code of justice, and other strengths of their own group), but not of justice.

What does the plight of the Amalekites in the Bible have to do with the policies of modern liberal democracies? Again, I must emphasize that my concern is with the most abstract cognitive core of justice formulation in the human mind that may yield apparent differences on the surface level of policies that mask an underlying identity in regard to the more fundamental frames from which they stem. Although it is rarely claimed, in defiance of logic, that individuals not responsible for a crime "deserve" to be violated for it, attempts are made to claim that those who are to receive benefits or penalties are deserving of, or responsible for, that which they will receive. Arguments are made on the basis of presumed utility as well as deservingness.

Group-frame policies pervade every area of the American public policy landscape. The federal income tax code is riddled with tax breaks for various categories of people, such as those who own the homes they live in and have mortgages on them, people who have one type of income as opposed to another, and those who are elderly or blind. Oil and gas companies, and the timber and agricultural industries, receive special tax breaks that other industries do not. In effect: "Tax breaks allow some people to pay much less tax than others with the same income" (Century Foundation, 2002, p. 12). This is group discrimination, much as is discrimination based on race.

As we have already seen, we have separate welfare categories for separate groups of people of equivalent dire need, such as poor children and their mothers, poor elderly, and veterans. Governmental health care programs cover only certain groups of people, such as the elderly and the poor. Federal administrative regulations and court decisions sanction affirmative action policies that favor members of particular racial and ethnic groups in hiring and college admissions. Social Security benefits go to certain classes of people and not to others. Federal relief is selectively extended to certain industries, such as farming. Industries and even specific companies lobby Congress for special tax breaks and other types of policy provisions favorable to them, and often achieve them, with even the names of specific companies written into federal law. State laws favor certain groups, such as teachers, with tax breaks. Private and public universities are allowed to discriminate in admissions on the basis of so-called legacies (giving preference to descendants of alumni), as well as race and ethnicity.

In chapter 1, I noted that war itself is the practice of the group frame in its most deadly form. Modern liberal democracies still practice it, and justify it in terms of necessity. Mindful of the fact that individuals do not "deserve" to suffer merely by dint of being a member of an enemy nation, they do seek to limit infliction of enemy casualties to combatants and, much in evidence lately, to inanimate military targets. To be sure, in the latter there is recognition that even individual combatants do not "deserve" to die. If all else fails, long-standing "just war" propositions are invoked, such as proportionality and discrimination. But the latter are *group* concepts. Proportionality speaks of *how many* people it is justifiable to kill, and discrimination speaks of *which* people it is justifiable to kill (soldiers, for example, are presumed less innocent than noncombatants). Moreover, according to just-war doctrine, war can be justified on the basis of being fought for a "just cause" and as a "last resort" (see Pelton, 1999a, pp. 166-168).

In regard to domestic policies, I pointed out (in chapter 1) that the group frame exerts its influence in the very attempts of policymakers to distinguish between the "deserving" and "undeserving." This influence is reflected in their construction of groups for the purpose of targeting the individuals within them for separate and unequal programs for the distribution of financial benefits. Yet the individuals within those groups do not uniformly differ from one group to another on any conceivable notions of desert. Moreover, if there is any "principle" of addressing need involved, the policies violate it by insuring that individuals similarly situated in regard to need will be treated differently. Through the TANF program, for example, children situated similarly in regard to need as needy elderly, first are treated differently in accordance with different programs for children and elderly, and second are treated differently, one child from another, through arbitrary restrictions (i.e., those not relevant to need, or even to desert) unique to that program. Thus they are targeted for double discrimination. We have seen that attempts at social engineering in policymaking often—perhaps inevitably—end up as group-frame policies in that many individuals do not in any sense get what they deserve, such as children who are denied welfare benefits in clumsy attempts to sanction their mothers. Although the policies' intentions are expressed in terms of incentive and desert stemming from the desert frame, the children are used merely as props, much as in the story of Job, in concert with the group frame. Moreover, the policies are built on group stereotypes and statistical generalizations (which are themselves stereotypes). Particularly in regard to those disfavored or excluded by the policies, the concept of desert contradictorily serves to justify (e.g., in TANF and affirmative action policies) that which cannot conceivably be deserved.

Other group-frame policies discriminatory toward children seem to exist by default or inaction, such as the fact that TANF benefits vary greatly from one state to another, or that children residing in impoverished localities will be provided less-adequately funded public education than other children. Yet there are always defenders ready with justifications: states' rights (a group concept, in this case in conflict with individual children's rights) or local control can be invoked.

In chapter 3, additional examples of current-day group-frame policies were provided, and it was argued that many such policies are driven by sentiment, yet sentiment is not a sufficient basis for individual justice, which cannot exist in the absence of principle. We are drawn to support "sin" taxes, selective drug prohibition laws, tax breaks for members of selected groups, and even affirmative action policies, through sentiment. Such policies are then justified through narrow reasoning, the collection of aggregate statistics, and assumptions of desert, although our sentiments can be derived from as well as cultivated through these processes. Such group-frame policies not only condemn equally-deserving individuals in "groups" outside of the designated ones to unequal treatment, but also rest on the false assumption that all individuals *within* the designated groups are equally deserving (either of reward or penalty). In chapter 4, such currently operative group-frame policies as driver's license renewal tests for "the elderly" were added to the list. Finally, in chapter 5, the American old-age Social Security program, a prime example of a group-frame social policy, was scrutinized in terms of generational transfers of funds, and its implicit generalizations about the poverty or need, low income, loss of income, desert, and frailty of "the elderly." Other current group-frame policies were noted along the way, such as Medicare, but one can already see that the list is quite lengthy.

In recent years, in the face of adverse court decisions, the defense of affirmative action policies in college admission practices has shifted from that of overcoming past discrimination (with desert argued on the grounds of group history) to the presumed need of a racially diverse student body for educational purposes as a "compelling state interest." Affirmative action, we are told, will be beneficial not only to the favored groups, but also to the community as a whole. Judges have said that there must be shown to be some overriding substantial common good involved—a compelling state interest—and so supporters have scrambled, over the past few decades, to claim diversity as that good, but this claim is then backed by attempts to show group results, such as in the data presented in *The Shape of the River* (Bowen and Bok, 1998). Social scientists hope to gain evidence of favorable aggregate outcomes showing that even white students benefit from affirmative action at a particular college (although not those who were denied admission through such discrimination), and that "society as a whole" is benefited. One of the most "compelling interests" that a just society could have, however, is that individuals not be violated through discrimination, even in the process of society pursuing a common good. Racial diversity may indeed be a desirable goal, but the end does not justify the means, according to both liberal philosophy and the principle of life affirmation. Affirmative action is a form of social engineering in which, eschewing principle, self-designated sages presume to divine which individuals, and groups, are deserving and which undeserving, and what higher goals the populace should be manipulated toward, regardless of the fact that some individuals will be violated in the process.

6

Justice and Social Policy

In this book, I have contended that three ancient frames of justice—group, desert, and life affirmation—continue to serve as the major policy frames from which the policies of human society emanate. In this chapter, I intend to further examine the cognitive foundations of modern social policies, to extend and deepen my analysis of the separate policy implications of the three frames, and to review how these frames and their policy implications are manifested in current social policies, particularly in the United States. I especially wish to more thoroughly examine the underdeveloped implications of the third frame, which I have referred to as the principle of life affirmation.

Of Frames and Contracts

Although all three frames of justice can find expression in contract formulations of justice, they can be seen to precede them. Kant and Rawls spoke of the inviolability of the individual. Rawls said that the principles chosen in the original position are to be acceptable from a moral point of view (1971, p. 120). The choices open to those in the original position are limited by the "constraints of the concept of right" that are imposed upon them (p. 130). They are to be universal in application, in the sense of Kant's formula of universal law. There is a question of whether the universality of nonexception must be imposed upon the parties in the original position, or whether through conditions set upon the initial situation, such as having no specific information about themselves, they are "effectively forced to stick to general principles" (p. 131) anyway. At any rate, the moral necessity of the universality-without-exception formulation of principles can be derived from the fundamental value of reverence for human life, itself, without recourse to a constructed original position or to contracts to be drawn up and agreed to within that position. A value on life makes no distinction between my life and others' lives. If my life is not to be violated, then equivalently, others' lives are not to be violated. Hence reason leads us to formulate the principle of nondiscrimination. Once the moral value of the sanctity of human life is accepted, the obligation to respect life and to strive not to violate it is a *moral* obligation, not a contractual one. Morality would oblige us to hold ourselves to it in our conduct (hence the notion of morality as referring to right conduct), regardless of contracts, or others' broken contractual obligations, or so is the case from the perspective of the life-affirmation frame of justice. The concept of a "right" is really too weak to describe the notion of the inviolability of human life.

According to John Locke, in his second treatise of government (1689/1963, p. 341): "The state of nature has a law of nature to govern it, which obliges every one: and reason, which is that law, teaches all mankind, who will but consult it, that being all equal and independent, no one ought to harm another in his life, health, liberty, or possessions... Every one, as he is bound to preserve himself...so by the like reason, when his own preservation comes not in competition, ought he, as much as he can, to preserve the rest of mankind, and may not, unless it be to do justice to an offender, take away or impair the life, or what tends to the preservation of life, the liberty, health, limb, or goods of another." Thus Locke implies a sense of justice that precedes contract, in the state of nature, but at the same time, he acknowledges both the frames of life affirmation and individual desert. Although he emphasizes the desert frame throughout this treatise, he also speaks of "a right of war" (p. 349), and a war of conquest or aggression as "an unjust war" (pp. 443-444). Yet by illustrating his arguments pertaining to war mostly with metaphorical examples concerning individual aggressors and thieves (pp. 347-349, 443-445), he is able to ignore the group-frame realities of war (which he addresses only in regard to the aftermath of war [pp. 445-455]).

According to Jean-Jacques Rousseau (1762/2002, p. 178): "Without doubt there is a universal justice emanating from reason alone; but this justice, in order to be accepted among us, should be reciprocal. Regarding things from a human standpoint, the laws of justice are inoperative among men for want of a natural sanction; they only bring good to the wicked and evil to the just when the latter observe them with everyone, and no one observes them in return. Conventions and laws, then, are necessary to couple rights with duties and apply justice to its object. In the state of nature, where everything exists in common, I owe nothing to those to whom I have promised nothing; I recognize as belonging to others only what is useless to me. This is not the case in the civil state, in which all rights are determined by law."

Thus, according to Rousseau, justice, as does a contract, refers to reciprocity. I promise to do this, and you in turn promise to do that. No doubt, the "this" and the "that" are in our respective interests. There must be sanctions for breaking the contract, lest both the wicked and the just get what they do not deserve. But in the absence of a contract, I have no obligations. If there is a sense of justice, it is not consulted in a supposed earlier state of nature, and thus man's actions become imbued with a moral quality only when he transits from this state to the civil state (p. 166).

Yet what if we were to stand by silently while citizens of another society were being slaughtered? We have made no contract with them: wherefrom does our duty, if any, arise? At best, we could intellectually contrive the notion that there is an implicit social contract between all human beings that they should come to each other's aid if the other is being violated. But then this would only be another way of saying that we have a sense of justice prior to any notion of desert, and that this sense concerns the violation of human beings. Yet, ultimately, Rousseau justifies his scorn of the notion of doing good to the wicked (while making no acknowledgment of the group frame in war) in terms of utility: "Christianity preaches only servitude and dependence. Its spirit is too favorable to tyranny for the latter not to profit by it always" (pp. 251-252). So much for the Sermon on the Mount.

If there is a contract, even an implicit one, that we will not deliberately harm each other, there is an expectation of reciprocity: I will not harm you, and you will not harm me. If you harm me anyway, we can say that you have broken the contract, that you are not entitled to my abidance by it. But if you keep to the contract, you will be rewarded with my reciprocity. Therefore desert is the currency of contracts (although the *concept* of desert, surely, precedes contracts). But the moral obligation of the life-affirmation frame is not constrained by contract concepts, in that even if you violate me, I will strive not to violate you.

Contract formulations of justice concern interests and demand reciprocity. They confine, or extend, their provisions only to the contract community, and require desert. Yet justice is not merely a matter of interests, but of principles concerning moral conduct. The principles of life affirmation and desert are expressions of a universal sense of justice that precede contractual formulations or agreements. Contracts certainly do not require the group frame (although they seem to be able to accommodate that frame as well), which thus must precede the contract, too.

It will be recalled that Kant justified state coercion in the defense of freedom, and that Rawls claimed that principles of justice are those that "free and rational persons concerned to further their own interests" would choose in the original position. While it is true that they also spoke of the inviolability of the individual that, in Rawls' words, "even the welfare of society as a whole cannot override" (1971, p. 3), the ambiguities of liberalism arise from the mixture of life-affirmation frame reasoning with that of social contract formulations, or the desert frame itself. Moreover, the ambiguities arise from the fact that contracts concern individual and mutual interests, not justice, unless we were to define justice in terms of interests, which is what contract formulations do.

Persons might be willing to live by laws that they believe would serve the collective interest, and may be willing to accept those same laws in the original position. Because all three frames of justice can arguably find expression in the unique contract formulations of liberalism (in which life-frame preconditions are placed on them), the policy implications of liberalism are vague and ambiguous. This may be why Rawls' theory of justice has little to say specifically about the most controversial policy issues of our time, such as abortion, capital punishment, affirmative action, or indeed, the Social Security system. For example, would people in the original position support affirmative action policies, or not? Would they support policies that transfer tax contributions from younger working people to those over sixty-five years old in the form of monthly cash benefits, whether the latter are working or not, or wealthy or not? And on what grounds? Would they support governmental health care insurance limited to people over age sixty-five? On what basis? Would people in the original position subscribe to the establishment of separate programs, rather than one, to address the dire need of orphans, widows, children, the elderly, and the disabled? Liberalism can accommodate capital punishment as well as its abolition, or the desert frame as well as the life-affirmation frame. It is not clear whether liberal philosophy can also accommodate the group frame. Nondiscrimination, reasoned from the moral value of reverence for human life, or the inviolability of the individual, would seem to exclude it. On the other hand, in accordance with the formula of universal law, perhaps many of us would be willing to live by certain group-based policies, such as affirmative action. In fact, at least one commentator has argued that Rawls' theory can accommodate affirmative action policies as a derivative, partly on the basis of desert in the form of compensation (Jones, 1980). In addition, we are faced with the fact that people in other liberal democracies seem willing to live by at least some policies that are discrepant with our own, such as universal health care coverage, or the abolition of capital punishment.

Buchanan and Congleton (1998, p. xii) have said: "Politics by principle constrains agents and agencies of governance to act nondiscriminatorily, to treat all persons and groups of persons alike, and to refrain from behavior that is, in its nature, selective." On these grounds, they (Buchanan, 1997; Buchanan and Congleton, 1998) favor a variant of the flat income tax/social dividend proposal discussed in chapter 5 to perform the function of welfare state transfers. The flat income tax/social dividend concept superbly meets the criterion of nondiscrimination, and that is why we were led to it in chapter 5. Yet if social policies are to be just, they must address need. If we did not believe this, then we would not be motivated to think up demogrant (social dividend) proposals to begin with. From a contractual formulation, which Buchanan and Congleton explicitly subscribe to, it may be said that the task at hand in devising a demogrant proposal is to benefit all of the individuals in the community, and the needy as well as the wealthy. Yet perhaps their unacknowledged motivation stems from their implicit acceptance of the moral value of the sanctity of human life, which is conflated with the contractual formulation in the ambiguity of liberalism. However, such proposals, as I have said, do not extend to addressing the survival of others in need, outside of our own community with its common trea-

Even more recently, policies have emerged—in California, Texas, and Florida—that guarantee admission to the state university system of everyone within the top designated percentage (e.g., 10 percent in Texas) of his or her high school's graduating class. Because of such percentage plans, many students who were highly qualified on the basis of individual merit and competence, but were not in the top designated percentage of their high school's graduating class, have been rejected, while others with lower qualifications from other schools, but being among the designated percentage, have been accepted. Hence group constructs have been allowed to trump individual qualifications, and this again constitutes discrimination. There may, of course, be disagreement of how to best assess individual merit or competence for a particular object or task at hand (such as college admission), but once the criteria are developed, they must be equally applied to all, regardless of such irrelevant factors as race, ethnicity, geographical location, or even socioeconomic class. There are, in fact, other college admissions policies that require socioeconomic disadvantage to be assessed, even taking into consideration whether a candidate will be the first one in his or her family to attend college. But these factors, too, are irrelevant to the assessment of individual merit at the time of consideration for admission. Criteria of need are conflated with criteria of admission. Once a student qualifies on the basis of admission, consideration can be given to economic need itself, in a nondiscriminatory manner, by awarding him or her a financial-need-based scholarship if he or she qualifies on that basis alone.

The principle of nondiscrimination requires that each individual be responded to on the basis, and only on the basis, of factors intrinsically relevant to the determination of individual need, merit, competence, and/or responsibility, depending on the object of the policy. Nondiscrimination is so important for the life-affirmation frame of justice because the principle of life affirmation refers to respect for individual lives without exception. If human lives are to be valued, then all are to be equally valued, and life must be so affirmed in the means or process, so that no one will be violated for the sake of a presumed common or "higher" goal. Even slavery, in its time, was "justified" by its supporters as benefiting the country as a whole. But justice in accordance with the life-affirmation and also the desert frame demands that the individual must not be used as an instrument for the achievement of some intended group end. Each and every individual must be supported by a community that professes to value the individual.

The Policies of Individual Desert

As already noted in chapter 1, the individual-desert frame, when applied to distributional social policies, invariably becomes entangled with the group frame. Although the principle of desert is often invoked to justify group-frame policies, it is contradictorily violated within the policies themselves. In the previous section, it can be seen that a distinction can be made between policies that stem from the group frame as a core cognitive formulation of justice, even if "group desert" is not invoked, and group-based policies that stem from attempts to implement the individual-desert frame. But attempts are also made to justify group-frame policies in terms of utility, the common good or collective interest, as well as individual desert, and can be driven by the sentiment of revenge or even sympathy.

But group-based policies can stem from attempts to provide individuals with what they presumably deserve, and thus from the individual-desert frame. Yet the distinctions may be more apparent than real, and are not clear. For example, the TANF policy may be driven by an individual-desert frame, but it is also driven by the group stereotype of single mothers on welfare as "undeserving," and by the sentiment toward them as a group, based upon this stereotype. Affirmative action policies are currently justified in terms of the utility of diversity, but were originally driven by an individual-desert frame, designating black people for compensation, although not without the stereotyping of blacks as disadvantaged, poor, and exclusively victimized. As we have seen in chapter 3, narrow reasoning driven by and/or derived from sentiment readily accommodates group-frame policies, even if the formation of those policies is ostensibly driven by considerations of individual desert. Yet we are not unaware of the group-frame nature of these policies, and develop and endorse them nonetheless. Hence these policies can be said to stem from a core cognitive formulation of the group-frame of justice, with all their attendant justifications of necessity and utility, much as policies of war are.

The principle of desert requires that the factors that are claimed to qualify an individual for the benefits to be offered or the punishments to be imposed are individually relevant. This requirement excludes such provision or imposition on the basis of statistical relatedness or "group relevance." For example, if old age were found to be statistically related to loss of income, and it was claimed that loss of income establishes a claim to monetary compensation, then a policy that would compensate individuals on the basis of old age would violate the principle of desert, because while statistically related to loss of income, old age is not individually related to the factors claimed to qualify the individual for compensation. The principle would be violated, because not only would unqualified individuals receive the compensation, but also many of those who qualify on the basis of loss of income would not. This would constitute discrimination. There is still the question, of course (raised in chapter 5), of why government should compensate loss of income altogether.

We must distinguish here between merit and desert. Indeed, David Miller writes: "In contemporary discourse we use the term 'merit' to refer broadly to a person's admirable qualities, while tending to reserve 'desert' more specifically for cases in which someone is responsible for the results he or she brings about" (1999a, p. 125). We may add that "desert" is also reserved for cases in which a person was presumably wronged by the actions of others. For example, affirmative action policies depend (or once did) on arguments of desert, not merit.

But what is it that can be said to be deserved? A person who is most qualified for a job through his or her merit and competence in relation to the job may not have "earned" those qualities, but merely have been endowed with them. He or she does not "deserve" a reward, but gaining the job is not a matter of desert for past efforts or deeds, nor of being responsible for the results (whether in terms of the qualities themselves, or obtaining the job). It is a matter of not being excluded arbitrarily, on the basis of factors, such as race, irrelevant to the object at hand, for instance, the tasks of a civil engineer. Desert looks backward and forward (references the past and the future), while nondiscrimination focuses on the present. The question is whether or not a person is being violated in the present. People are unequal in their talents and abilities. To choose whom to hire on any basis other than the relevant abilities is to disrespect the individual and to deny him or her the opportunity to reap the benefits of them. The individual is sacrificed to group goals, such as diversity, or to group interests and biases of every sort. Of course, once we start down this road, and make claims on the basis of desert, one group after another steps forward to make that claim.

Hiring on the basis of merit, in relation to the qualifications for the job, is not a matter of predicting meritorious performance on the job, but of choosing the person who is most competent in terms of the job's qualifications. Hence this is not a matter of probabilities or statistical relevance, but of individual relevance. We are concluding that the person is most competent. Moreover, we are uncertain what—such as hard work, genes, or good schooling—contributed to this competence. If the inequality of our talents and capacities were not to be respected, then we would not be respected. The treatment of an individual on the basis of factors irrelevant to the task or object at hand (such as on the basis of skin color in consideration for a job) is the grossest disrespect, aside from the direct infliction of severe physical injury, that one could pay to an individual. If the relevant criteria are not being applied, then something else, such as color, is. It may be decided that some test that has been used in the past is not relevant. But whatever reasonable criteria are developed as being relevant must then be equally applied to all. It can then be said that people are being given equal consideration in regard to the object at hand. This constitutes nondiscrimination.

Policies of Compensation

We have yet to explore the separate policy implications of the individual-desert frame, other than its use, or consequence, as justification for what are seen, upon scrutiny, to be group-frame policies. It can be asked what policies exist, or what policies would look like, that are more centrally based upon the individual-desert frame, to the exclusion of the group frame. I have already claimed that when applied to distributional social policies, the individual-desert frame *invariably* becomes entangled with the group frame. In chapter 3, I argued that when we attempt to approximate the principle of individual desert more closely than such fixed, relatively determinate categories of orphan, widow, and age allow (here in regard to "worthy" need), we enter areas of highly indeterminate individual judgments and elastic categories such as "disabled" for distinguishing the "worthy" needy from the "unworthy" needy. Sentiment rather than principle continues to determine individual outcomes.

Surely, however, it can be argued that restitution, restoration, compensation, or reparation are justice functions of government policies. Government, through its courts, may order one party to compensate another, or may decide to set up policies of compensation for victims of disaster, such as the September 11, 2001 attacks on America, or may make reparations or pay compensation for crimes, injuries, or injustice committed by the government itself. All such matters involve notions of desert, but raise very thorny issues of individual justice.

Ideally, we might agree, restitution should go from those personally responsible to those personally victimized. Yet government may decide to pay compensation to those of its citizens who were victimized by others, or to the families of the victims, as in the September 11 attacks. We have already seen (in chapter 3) that such policies quickly raise questions of equivalent policy concerns for the families of victims of other terrorist attacks (such as the earlier Oklahoma City attack), or for victims of natural disasters, economic disasters, or individual economic misfortune, crime, or accident. The principle of individual desert is surely violated in policy if policy compensates some people but not others who are in equivalent positions of desert. This, again, is discrimination.

These difficulties could be overcome if we were simply willing to declare that dire need should be addressed, no matter what the presumed causes (or that all in dire need are "deserving" of having that need addressed by government). But policies of compensation go beyond need. In fact, the federal policy of compensation for the families of victims of the September 11 attacks specifies that each family is to be repaid for its economic losses, including those due to loss of earnings or other benefits related to employment, and to loss of business or employment opportunities (Belkin, 2002). Families of some stockbrokers killed in the attacks are thus potentially eligible for tens of millions of dollars, based on the victims' projected lifetime career earnings, while others, such as families of firefighters who died, will be eligible for far less. The question is again raised (as with old-age Social Security benefits) of why government should be compensating people for loss of income, since the practice can lead to grossly differential treatment of people similarly situated in regard to victimization and need. (Such compensation may be justifiable if the defendant was the one who caused the injuries, but government did not cause the injuries.) In Israel, for example, the families of victims of terrorist attacks receive monthly benefits equivalent to the average national monthly salary. As Belkin (2002) asks, how did our government get into the business of valuing one victim's life as several times more than another's?

But the desert principle itself is challenged, when consideration is given to the loss of human life no matter what the cause. Predictably and understandably, in the aftermath of the September 11 attacks and legislation, families of the victims of such tragedies as the Oklahoma City bombing in 1995, the bombing of the American Embassy in Nairobi in 1998, the 1993 World Trade Center bombing, and the attack on the U.S.S. *Cole*, have wondered why they are not included in that legislation, as well might the families of the victims of the accidental explosion in the Blue Creek No. 5 mine shaft in Brookwood, Alabama twelve days after the September 11 attacks. Referring to some of these incidents, Belkin (2002) opines: "Each of these groups has an argument for why they are deserving. As is the way of these things, the arguments that serve to include them simultaneously serve to exclude someone else." The embassy bombing victims were eventually included under the September 11 legislation. But the question remains—as Belkin puts it—"why is one group of victims more deserving than others?"

An additional set of questions is raised in regard to reparations for crimes, injuries, or injustice committed by the government itself. In Tulsa in 1921, a white mob intent on lynching a jailed black man who had been accused (falsely) of raping a white woman exchanged shots with a group of black men trying to protect him (Staples, 2003). City officials then deputized the members of the white mob, and handed out weapons to them. As many as 10,000 whites, including the police and the National Guard, entered the black community of Greenwood, "burning, looting, and shooting." Staples (2003) continues: "One white witness reported seeing officers in uniform robbing unarmed black citizens at gunpoint and shooting those who resisted. While the police were thus engaged, an execution squad composed of Klansmen roamed the riot zone, killing black men on site." As many as 300 were murdered in the so-called Tulsa Race Riot. All of the buildings in the community were demolished. Thousands of blacks were placed in prison camps, and others were forced to carry identification tags furnished by the city. The survivors and their families are currently suing the city and the state of Oklahoma for restitution.

Of course, what survivors remain are in their eighties and nineties. According to the individual-desert frame, they deserve to be individually compensated for any loss of possessions or property, or any injuries they suffered. Moreover, the individual children of deceased victims deserve to be compensated for their loss of possessions and property that we can assume they would have inherited. Injury to children who were not alive at the time would certainly not be physical, but perhaps psychological. Such injury would be more difficult to establish. It could also be argued that the children of those who were murdered should be compensated for the victims' projected loss of income, and thus we would be brought back to the question raised by the September 11 compensation policy, of attributing greater value to one victim's life than to another's.

But granted that the survivors and the children of other victims deserve compensation based on at least some factors, we are faced with the question of who should pay. There is little doubt that, along with the individuals who killed, looted, and destroyed, the government (city and state) itself was responsible for the atrocities of the Tulsa Race Riot of 1921, and thus incurred the obligation to make restitution. But government is the instrument of the community (in this case, the city and the state), and is established to benefit (protect and support) all of the members within that community. It has a common treasury to do so. Although government is a continuous, ongoing institution, intergenerational in nature, virtually no one alive today is personally responsible for the atrocities or the governmental decisions made, or was complicit in the atrocities, either through direct action, silence, negligence, payment into the treasury, or any other form of complicity. Moreover, it would be difficult to argue that the community, or those alive today, have benefited in any way from the atrocities. Yet because the monies that flowed into that treasury in 1921 are long since gone, any financial compensation paid out of it will be financed by the current treasury enriched through the taxes being paid by today's citizens, who are not responsible for the atrocities.

Nonetheless, as was argued in chapter 5, we have all gained benefits, beyond our individual efforts and contributions, as members of the ongoing community and because of that community. It is reasonable to argue that it is this communal wealth—which is in excess of that which would have accrued to individuals, despite their efforts, in absence of community—from which the claimants in the Tulsa Race Riot case will be paid, if they are successful in court. It is in this way that the community can take responsibility as a community for the undeniable wrongs done as a community to some of its members, through government as its instrument and representative, and for which the request for compensation seems reasonable and just, with nonetheless the important acknowledgment that there is no collective or intergenerational guilt, and that no living members of the community are personally responsible for the atrocities of 1921.

If we allow reparations to descendants for loss of possessions or property, but only to survivors for injury, then we are faced with the paradox that compensation might be paid to a maimed survivor, but not paid on behalf (perhaps to descendants) of a victim who was killed. This is perhaps a rationale for the German government paying reparations to the Israeli government (the latter presumably as the representative of the Jews who were slaughtered). On the other hand, this violates the individual-desert frame, for if the individual deserving compensation is not available to be compensated, then there is no one left to compensate. It would seem reasonable to propose that the individual-desert frame requires that compensation be paid to individual survivors, to deceased victims' children, and to even future descendants (if not already paid) for loss of possessions and property; and that it should also be paid to survivors for injury, as well as to deceased victims' children for direct injury to them due to the murder of their parents (which should be assumed without need for separate proof), but not to future descendants for injury. Moreover, it may be reasonable to suppose that the German government should be under no obligation to make reparations to the Israeli government (as opposed to individuals who qualify for compensation), although it may decide to do so, as the representative of the German people, on its own initiative, but then only with the proactive support of such a gesture by the German people as a whole. These restrictions are required by the desert frame if the group frame of "justice" is to be avoided.

The question of reparations to African Americans for slavery brings up additional thorny issues. In this case, future generations of Americans (even if recent immigrants) can even be said to have benefited from the slave labor that contributed to the building of the country. As Henry Louis Gates, Jr. (2001) suggests, "imported slave labor...did greatly enable the building of what we now consider modern economies" and "many Western nations reaped large and lasting benefits from African slavery." But who should be paid? In accordance with the principle of individual desert, only those individuals who are directly descended from American slaves, even if now several generations removed, should be compensated. But compensated for what? There is no loss of possessions or property, at least none that can be currently claimed. And there is no direct injury to living individuals that can currently be claimed (at least not individually, although higher rates of poverty and unemployment among African Americans as a *group* could be claimed as a result of a heritage of slavery). Whether or not Gates would agree with the latter two statements, he suggests that the fact that "slavery is embedded in American prosperity" provides a context for the United States to contribute at least $2 billion annually to a fund to combat AIDS, a disease that is currently devastating Africa, as well as lives in other parts of the world. He states: "Slavery will not disappear from our common history, but it may be mitigated by this type of *reparation*" (italics added).

Indeed, President George W. Bush, in his 2003 State of the Union address, asked Congress to commit $15 billion over the next five years to the fight against AIDS, particularly in Africa. But although Bush proposed this effort as "a work of mercy" rather than reparation, it should not be the former and it is certainly not the latter. Reparation is a matter of individual desert, while the proposal has little to do with desert, unless we were to say that those whose individual survival is threatened by deadly disease—or dire poverty, or any other factors—are deserving of assistance from the wealth of nations. If so, then Bush's proposal should not be put forth as a gesture of mercy, but as a matter of justice in accordance with the principle of life affirmation. But then, this principle would commit us to a systematic effort to combat hunger, poverty, and disease throughout the world, without discrimination in regard to continents, nations, or individuals. In the end, whatever compensation may be paid stands as nothing compared to past injury to life at issue, to policies that support life in the present, and to people's resolve not to be complicit with evil from here on out.

The greatest pitfalls of justice to avoid are those of pursuing group-based policies in the name of desert, of which I have already cited many examples. Some have defended affirmative action policies as a form of restitution. But such "restitution" is to groups (and to only the most competent members of those groups) based on generalizations that are not true for all individuals within the group (such as African Americans who are not descendants of slaves), and are "paid" at a cost not to the nation as a whole, but to individuals who may have played no role whatsoever in past discrimination, much less the institution of slavery, who are discriminated against on the basis of race or ethnicity in the course of applying for jobs or college admissions. We must eschew the danger of pursuing special claims for some groups rather than justice for all. When "reparations" treat other innocent people unfairly we begin to see that equally promoting the well-being of everyone in accordance with the life-affirmation frame is most just.

In Las Vegas, each of the thirty-eight members of the Las Vegas Paiute Tribe receives close to $100,000 annually, simply for being a member. The primary source of this revenue is the Las Vegas Paiute Smoke Shop, which substantially undersells its competitors due to exemptions from taxes on the cigarettes it sells. Native American tribes are regarded, under law, as sovereign nations. Predictably, disputes have arisen over who qualify as members based on blood-line percentages. Although the revenue is largely the product of special citizenship and group-based policies that are paid for, in a sense, by the state and national citizenship as a whole, the federal Bureau of Indian Affairs has no authority to approve or disapprove tribes' membership rolls (Puit, 2000a, 2000b). The tribes have certain inherent rights, such as to determine who is and who is not a member. Special laws exist that allow tribes to profit from gambling operations built on their lands in a group-discriminatory manner. Thus special citizenship status has been created for certain groups in a group-discriminatory manner that even yields special payments, presumably in the form of reparations for past unjust treatment of Native Americans by government. At least some Native Americans have come to expect such largess as their due, as individually deserved, and are proud of their special citizenship and privileges. Now a case can be made for the return of common lands owned by the forebears of current Native Americans under broken treaties with the United States government. But "sovereign nation" status paid for by the American nation as a whole, to people who benefit (or should) from the nation as a whole through equal protection, economic benefit, and equal rights, but additionally benefit through special tax exemptions and prerogatives based on ethnic identity, producing levels of citizenship, should be anathema to liberal philosophy. It is a contradiction of any notion of equal citizenship and the concept of nondiscrimination. This state of affairs is surely grounded in sentiment rather than any principle of desert, reparation, or life affirmation. American Indians being offered special treatment based on blood percentages is morally repugnant, and ruins the concept of equal citizenship.

Concepts such as compensation, reparation, and restitution apply to the positive side of desert, and there is no counterpart on the negative side. We are left only with the bare concept of desert itself, unless we were to say that the opposite of restoration or compensation is to take away or destroy. In the extreme, the individual-desert frame—in one sense, logically, and in another, contradictorily—merges with the group frame, in that the recompense for genocide, in accordance with a principle of proportionate punishment or the law of the talion ("an eye for an eye") would be the reciprocation of genocide. If your group murdered my children as a means of inflicting pain upon me, then how can I make you suffer equivalent pain except by murdering your children? As we are aware from events even in the world today as we speak, such a concept is not imaginary, but continues to be actualized in reality. To suggest that the group frame of "justice" in the form of genocide should be reciprocated upon the German people in response to the Holocaust is to suggest a moral absurdity and abomination, yet that would be the proportionate "desert" response. (To protest that most current Germans are innocent only reinforces the application of the concept of proportionality, since the victims of Nazi Germany were also innocent. Yet this type of response continues to occur in our world, with the events in the Balkans and Rwanda as recent examples.)

Desert in the Criminal Justice System

As already noted in chapter 1, the individual-desert frame dominates criminal justice systems throughout the world. Perhaps it can be said that it is within the criminal justice system that the individual-desert frame of justice is carried out in its purest form, without the conceptual confusion and complications discussed above. Retribution remains central to the system, even though the objective of retribution may be mixed with those of deterrence, rehabilitation, and incapacitation (physically restraining the criminal from the possibility of committing further criminal acts within the larger community). Yet even the policies for deciding guilt or innocence in individual cases, as is done within the criminal court, raise doubts as to the fairness with which the desert frame is or can be implemented. We have difficulty in deciding what factors should be taken into account in determining whether or not a person who has committed a criminal act should be held responsible for that act. As discussed in chapter 3, the proliferation of "abuse excuses" used within the criminal justice system have been designed, sometimes successfully, to win the sympathy of juries. These and other so-called "mental defenses" or "excusing states of mind," such as mental illness, ignorance, or not being able to distinguish right from wrong, have been offered, sometimes successfully, as defenses against the establishment of the defendant's culpability.

Modern man is sophisticated enough to know that all behavior is multiply determined. Partial determinants may include past and present external or environmental factors operating upon the individual, as well as genetic factors. Yet these factors converge within the entity we call the individual, and at the moment of the criminal act, the individual who perpetrated it was himself the necessary and sufficient causal agent. Whether mentally ill, in an altered state of mind, ignorant, or abused in the past, the suspect was a causal agent if at the moment of the criminal act he was a source of autonomous action or omission. Only if the action was not autonomous, as when one's body is thrown as a projectile by powerful external forces, and is hurtled against another person who sustains severe injury, could we say that the individual was not a causal agent at the moment of the act. Yet since all behavior is multiply determined, "abuse excuses" and mental defenses invite differential retribution on the basis of the irrelevant distinction (irrelevant to desert, at least) of whether or not some of the partial determinants can be identified and win our sympathy. Group-based claims for special consideration emerge, as when advocates for battered women who have killed their mates enlist social scientists to concoct theories about syndromes that presumably excuse a class of killers from ascription of desert (see Pelton, 1999a, pp. 130-135).

Questions of the desert of retribution also arise in decisions regarding which acts shall be designated as criminal by law. For what acts is an individual deserving of punishment? Many laws, such as drug prohibition laws, designate as criminal certain acts that do not directly or intrinsically harm others (so-called victimless crimes). People in possession of certain drugs, such as marijuana, heroin, and cocaine, can be imprisoned as retribution, and many have been. On what grounds do such people "deserve" to be punished? When we recognize that such laws are based on stereotypes, even if these in turn are based on valid statistical generalizations about the effects of drug use, then we understand that such laws violate the concept of individual desert, since they designate a class of people, that is, those who use certain drugs, as criminal, and mete out retribution to them on the basis of that class identity, and not on evidence of individually-perpetrated harm to others. Thus such laws bring us again to the group frame of justice. In fact, large proportions of those imprisoned in the United States have been imprisoned for violations of drug prohibition laws. It can be argued that imprisonment on the basis of such laws has become a proxy for the preventive detention of poor black men on the grounds that some among them would commit criminal harm to others if not confined in prison.

When we turn to crimes that have victims, there is also the question of what punishment constitutes just desert. Imprisonment, for varying periods of time, is widely used as punishment for crimes of severe harm to others, yet imprisonment bears little resemblance to most crimes that are committed. Proportionate "justice" in terms of "an eye for an eye" is not carried out in the United States, except in some cases of murder in the form of capital punishment, and in some cases of theft in the form of restitution or fines. Even in biblical times, we are told, the Hebrew community did not put into practice the law of the talion except for murder. But although imprisonment is generally a more humane form of punishment (in theory at least, because the statement is also dependent upon the actual conditions existing within the prison) than the law of the talion, it can be questioned whether imprisonment is appropriate desert for the least severe forms of crime, such as theft (in which no threat of violence is involved). To be sure, in regard to punishment other than that based on the law of the talion, there is no basis for calculating proportionate desert. How many years in prison does a person who has maimed someone in an assault deserve? We avoid the question by merely focusing on whether the sentences for the most severe crimes are longer than for the less severe. Even this guide for fairness of individual desert is frequently violated in practice, in terms of actual time spent in prison, if not in the original sentence (a matter that has been exacerbated by recent "three strikes and you're out" laws passed in some states, and overcrowded prisons necessitating early release of some prisoners).

These are some of the problems with the application of the individual-desert frame within the criminal justice system. They arise, ironically, because our sense of justice urges us to eschew (for the most part) the law of the talion—which is the most logical and exact, if inhumane, formulation of the principle of individual desert—and produces ongoing controversy over the practice of capital punishment. Although both emanate from people's sense of justice, the principle of desert sometimes defers to the principle of life affirmation. This deference might be due to sentiment, yes, but as discussed in chapter 3, the sense of justice from which principles of justice are formulated may itself stem from sentiment.

Ultimately, the life-affirmation frame dictates that if life is to be valued, then all life is to be valued, and we are all responsible for each other. But that does not mean that we deserve reward for fulfilling our responsibility, or retribution for failing or violating it. Holding people responsible does not mean giving them what they deserve.

The Policies of Justice as Life Affirmation

Our sense of justice is revealed in many ways. We can discuss as a community, as we do, who is "deserving" of receiving governmentally funded health care coverage, and who is not. But when it comes down to uninsured people dying because they would not be admitted to a hospital or emergency room, we are appalled and draw the line. We do, as a community, decide to pay for their medical treatment. One could say that whereas the intent of the desert frame is often contradicted in policy as well as in practice, here it is contradicted only in practice.

Health Care

Ultimately, the predominance of the life-affirmation frame over the desert frame in regard to policymaking on this issue would be the best solution on utilitarian grounds; the predominance of the desert frame over the life-affirmation frame in regard to policy, yet with neither forsaken, is the worst solution. Although government does insure many elder Americans (under Medicare) and many impoverished Americans (under Medicaid), 75 million Americans lacked health insurance at some point during 2001 or 2002 (according to the Robert Wood Johnson Foundation). The severe financial strain placed on community emergency care centers due to the treatment of uninsured individuals who could not pay has led to the recent closing of some of them, in turn affecting the availability of medical care even for the insured (Schmid, 2003). Hospitals raise their fees to insured patients to offset the cost of treating the uninsured. Moreover, the uninsured generally do not receive preventive health care, and so must be seen at later, more costly, and more life-threatening stages of treatment.

The point is that due to our sense of justice, we have *de facto* policies based on the principle of life affirmation, in that we have resolved, in effect, not to allow our citizens or even "the stranger" among us to die or suffer without treatment and care (I say "we" because much of the treatment and care of the uninsured falls to public hospitals). Yet our official policies, in effect, declare that only those who are elderly, very poor, insured through employment benefits, or have the means to pay for it on their own, are "deserving" of health care. The result is a health care system that is neither effective nor cost-efficient in saving lives (of those who are not insured and are treated only at the point of emergency), and that undoubtedly distributes the cost of health care among its citizenship in an unfair (i.e., discriminatory) manner. Policies (both de facto and official) based exclusively either on the desert frame or on the life-affirmation frame would be more cost-efficient, but only policies based exclusively upon the principle of life affirmation (unless we were to assume that all people in need of health care are deserving of it, bringing us to the life-affirmation frame anyway) would be more humane. Medicare could be extended to everyone, not just the elderly, producing a national single-payer system in which the enormous administrative costs of a system based on multiple private insurers would be eliminated (Angell, 2002).

Homelessness

It seems to me that in its treatment of homeless people within it, a society is directly confronted with the question of whether as a community, through government as its instrument and representative, it will value human life without exception, condition, or rationalization, or whether it will select, exclude, and deny responsibility through judgment of desert. I have come to see this issue as one of the ultimate tests of our commitment to the affirmation of human life. Since we do currently give a dying uninsured person medical treatment, whether he or she can pay for it or not, and without judgment of desert, we act inconsistently when we withhold from any individual the basic material necessities for survival. Yet in many cities in the United States, many homeless people are currently neglected, and denied shelter and social care. They are left to sleep in the streets, and then are chased, stereotyped, vilified, and despised. The mayor of Las Vegas, wanting nothing better than that homeless people would disappear from the city and valley, has shamefully and publicly characterized "the homeless" living in the streets as robbers, rapists, and murderers. Through a long night and Palm Sunday morning in 2002, I witnessed in astonishment the eviction by police of about 200 homeless people from their pup tents and blankets (donated by sympathetic Las Vegans) on the sidewalks in and near the so-called "homeless corridor" where the insufficient shelter facilities of various charity organizations (such as Catholic Charities and the Salvation Army) are grouped together, about three miles up from the fabulous casino-hotels of the famed Las Vegas Strip. Many of them had slept there through the winter, with nighttime temperatures often dipping to near and below freezing.

Government officials had claimed that they only wanted to clean the sidewalks, a task they could easily have accomplished in the broad light of day. But they came for the homeless in the middle of the night. Many of the homeless, with the help of others, relocated themselves to a nearby vacant lot on a small mesa overlooking Las Vegas Boulevard. In the early morning, a flotilla of police cars and paddy wagons gathered in a distant parking lot, poised for yet another assault. Soon the homeless campers were told that they had to leave immediately or be arrested. Bewildered and weary, forsaken and forlorn, these hapless have-nots gathered up their few belongings, some loading them on shopping carts, and slowly pushed onward once again in all directions from that lot, destinations unknown. With the lot cleared of people, the police made some pretense of separating valuables left behind from that which was to be destroyed. A dump truck appeared on the lot, and then a small bulldozer. By late morning, abandoned tents, blankets, bags, and whatever else was left, were methodically shoveled up along the mesa's perimeter, one "home" at a time, and deposited with a plump into the dump truck. So much for human dignity.

Attributions of desert serve as excuses not to house the homeless, even though the allegedly respected status of military veteran would, one might think, qualify some of the homeless as deserving of a roof over their heads in accordance with the judgmental and often arbitrary reasoning of the desert frame. It is clear that many people read into the situation of the homeless their desert, much as Job's onlookers did to the personal catastrophes that had befallen him. But just as only Job's circumstances were real and present, while onlookers' inferences of desert were in the realm of idle speculation irrelevant to the actuality of Job's suffering, so too is only the homelessness real. It is the principle of life affirmation that obliges us to address the homeless, not any notions or principle of desert. On the contrary, the concept of desert paves the way for condemnation, speculation, neglect, and inaction. It opens a door to the rationalization and justification of callous public and official disregard for (some) human life.

The collective community behavior of human neglect predictably turns to abuse, as a dynamic containing its own internal logic unfolds, and as was seen in the moral abomination and travesty of justice that occurred on Palm Sunday, 2002, in Las Vegas. The sidewalks and vacant lots are dirtied. The homeless become an eyesore, and worse still, a threat to the community's pretensions toward religiosity, morality, and justice. Homeless people must then be further vilified, and homelessness criminalized. Suspicions about homeless people's intentions are nurtured and given voice. It must be established that it is not the community that has wronged them, but they who have wronged us. They need to be evicted from even their makeshift "homes," their meager belongings confiscated. They must be chased, harassed by police, ticketed for jaywalking, threatened with arrest, roused from sleep. Perhaps then they will leave, but one way or another, we must rid ourselves of them.

At another time in another place, before they came for the Jews, they came for the homeless. Before they came for gays and lesbians, they came for "idlers," "loafers," and "those who had gone to seed." Before they came for handicapped children, they came for the "socially adverse," including drug addicts, prostitutes, vagrants, and the "irredeemably work-shy and uneconomic." Moreover, Professor Timm Kunstreich (2003) of Hamburg notes that even before the Nazi rise to power, welfare laws and guidelines had established a hierarchical differentiation between potential recipients of benefits. He writes that the changes precipitated by Nazi welfare amendments in the 1930s were partly of an incremental nature and thus went largely unnoticed, although more often they were greeted with general acceptance (and silence, one might add). He points out that "everybody" ceased to mean "all people," and now referred only to those deemed suitable to be part of the "healthy *Volks*body." Las Vegas had not become Nazi Germany, but "everybody" had surely ceased to mean "all people."

Even some of the advocates and service providers for homeless people have engaged in the language of rationalization and the rhetoric of exclusion. It is claimed that some of the homeless "enjoy their lifestyles" and do not "want" to sleep in beds in a heated environment. Presumably, they "want" to sleep on cold sidewalks in below-freezing weather. There is talk, too, of "service-resistant" homeless people, the "root causes" of homelessness, and roads to self-sufficiency and spiritual recovery. And in desperate attempts to get help for at least some of the people sleeping in the streets, some advocates have acceded to talk of the "good" as opposed to the "bad" homeless.

A government-appointed regional homeless task force formed in the Las Vegas valley participated in the stereotyping of "the homeless" through the development of a "philosophy of service" that "recognizes" the existence of three types of clients: the Have Nots ("situationally homeless," due to job loss, for example), the Can Nots, and the Will Nots. The Will Nots are characterized as "able-bodied, mentally capable clients who refuse structured services." Government, it is suggested, should focus on the first two categories. As for the Will Nots? "Government must prioritize and limit its role due to the limited availability of resources." In addition, the "emphasis is to be on work as a therapeutic measure," and those capable of employment should provide community service and other work-related activity "as a condition of ongoing community support." Thus the worthy are to be distinguished from the unworthy. Or more precisely, the homeless, undeserving on the whole, are themselves to be divided into the more and less deserving or undeserving. Provision of the most basic and minimal supports of human life are to be made conditional, and not an obligation of community, while the government of a wealthy community pleads its own poverty. The sheer visual contrast of another categorical distinction, that simply between the haves and have-nots, is particularly striking in the Las Vegas valley, with its gated "communities" containing lavish homes of up to 6,000 square feet of space, equipped with "media rooms" and three- and four-car garages.

In reality, a philosophy of desert leads inevitably to contradictions, inconsistencies, group-frame policies shaped by stereotypes, and highly subjective determinations that raise questions of individual justice, arbitrary exclusion, and discrimination. Although our policies have traditionally proclaimed veterans to be especially deserving, those veterans living in the streets are scorned no less than other homeless people. They are denied the beds, heated shelter, and hot showers provided even to convicted criminals in prison. And despite the task force's pious categorical distinctions, the various government entities in the Las Vegas valley and the state government, as in other parts of the country, have little intention to adequately address the needs of the Have Nots and Can Nots any more so than the Will Nots.

Charity, Justice, and Nondiscrimination

Homeless people have died and continue to die in the streets of Las Vegas. Yet when homeless people die in the streets, few of us would say that they *deserved* to die. We do feel that the community has an obligation to prevent those deaths, and we do so based on a sense of justice derived from the moral value we hold concerning the sanctity of human life. Yet the community, rather than to commit government to the task, takes another way out of this moral dilemma. The obvious shelter needs of homeless people, as well as the care needed by many of them for severe physical and mental health problems, for alcohol and drug abuse problems, for their inability to take care of themselves, and for various other needs, are to be left to the mercies of private charity. But charity selects and chooses whom it wants to help, without obligation to justice, and is driven more by sentiment than justice (although we have seen that many government policies, too, unfortunately, are driven by sentiment), while justice demands that we treat with equal regard those we love and those we despise, those we pity and those we envy, and the wealthy and the poor, without favoring one or the other. These are, at least, the demands of justice in accordance with the principle of life affirmation, and that of nondiscrimination even under the desert frame. Justice is not done through private charity. As private individuals, we tend to help only those who have gained our attention and sympathy, perhaps through appreciative behavior and displays of "innocence." Sympathy is not justice. Giving to those we like and denying assistance to those we despise is not justice.

Many homeless people throughout the nation, rather than being provided with housing, are admitted to shelters in which their stays are subject to arbitrary seven- or thirty-day limitations, or contingent upon job-seeking or goal-oriented behavior. They are evicted from early morning to early evening. Admission is denied to some not only on the reasonable grounds of safety precautions necessary in congregate sleeping facilities (although if people were provided separate housing units, there would be no necessity for such discretion), but often on arbitrary grounds irrelevant to the need to be sheltered. Every year, like clockwork, local television news programs religiously cover the feeding of homeless people queued up in shelters to receive donated Thanksgiving dinners, as viewers get teary-eyed over the community's goodness. One wonders if charity indeed is not merely a token to make the givers feel good—do not homeless people have to eat the rest of the year, too? In any event, we have in charity the triumph of sentiment over principle and community (see also Wagner, 2000).

A special irony in all of this is that many of the charitable organizations today are, to a considerable extent, funded by government. But the rightful role of government is to fund justice, not charity. Even with government funding of charity, we witness what must be called morally ludicrous through the lens of the life-affirmation frame, such as homeless people living in cardboard boxes, or a family in need of tremendously expensive medical treatment for a child having to turn to truly private charity and plead for donations to cover medical bills, leading to the specter of special charity drives set up by neighbors.

We must acknowledge that nondiscrimination does not require the equal distribution of resources to everyone, regardless of the object at hand, but equal treatment of everyone in consideration of them in terms of factors that are relevant to the object at hand. Chief among these objects are those concerning survival of each human life itself, and respect and support for the potential of that life to grow and flourish. Under a universal health care policy, a person with a catastrophic illness will probably receive far more provision of health care, in terms of both treatment and its costs, than a generally healthy person. Yet both are given equal consideration under the policy with respect to the object, health. Likewise, a policy meant to address dire need through cash benefits may distribute those benefits only to those in dire need, yet everyone must be given equal consideration with respect to the object of the policy, dire need. No one can be excluded from consideration on the basis of irrelevant factors, such as race, gender, or age, or for that matter, personal fault.

One can argue that such policies can be grounded in a contractual insurance concept of justice. As with car insurance, we pay into a common pot with the agreement that only those unfortunate people who are involved in an accident will have the right to draw resources out of that pot. The rest of us will feel fortunate not to have had an accident, and will consider the money to have been well spent against the possibility of great loss of personal wealth if we had indeed suffered an accident. Yet the concept does not hold as a basis of justice. Individuals, such as children, newly arrived immigrants, or people who have been poor all their lives, and who may not have paid into the common treasury, draw the community's obligation to address their need. Based on the life-affirmation frame, the addressing of their need is a matter of justice, and thus an obligation of government, which is to draw upon its treasury in order to do justice, and not merely a matter for charitable gestures by individual citizens.

Under the scrutiny of the life-affirmation frame, our current priorities that leave some of the most crucial life and death issues to charity and "humanitarianism" while providing Social Security benefits to even the wealthy, would be viewed as immoral and unjust. David Miller (1999a, p. 228), in contrast, reasoning from a philosophy of desert, seems to suggest that some homeless people are to be distinguished from others in having no claim on justice, but merely on our benevolence: "We should help the homeless person who has lost his home through reckless behavior, but solely on humanitarian grounds: he cannot demand to be helped as a matter of justice." Aside from the "demands" of homeless people or the far louder ones of the retired elderly, determinations of "reckless behavior" will depend on who is doing the judging, and judgments of desert will often favor those who are doing the judging.

The community gives charity, and we refer to it as a "caring community." Sentiment is exuded. But a truly caring community would be a just one, and would have a government that addresses need through predetermined principles of justice and nondiscrimination pertaining to particular objects, such as human survival. Support of human life would be aggressively pursued without exception. Under the life-affirmation frame, the moral obligation of a community cannot be distinguished from government obligation and justice. The state, as representative of the people, has moral obligations.

Valuing Life Unconditionally

A just government is one that benefits everyone in the community, including the poor and the stranger, as well as the criminal. Only government, representing the entire community, can do justice, even though it often does not. When we succumb to our private sentiments even in the making of social policy, we abrogate the *absolute* value of the sanctity of human life and sink into a moral relativism that presumes us fit to judge whose lives are more valuable than others'. In the end, our policies proclaim that the homeless deserve and yet do not deserve to suffer and die, because the valuing of life comes into conflict with the valuing of desert when it comes to matters of life and death.

After more than two decades, the strategy of conditional temporary shelter for homeless people has proved to be a failure. The homeless have not disappeared, nor have they been properly housed. If we really wished to do justice, housing would be made available to everyone currently living in the streets. Their physical and mental health needs would be attended to. Those who present danger to their own lives would be given appropriate care and services. Individual plans would be devised for the care and nurturing of each homeless person, leaving no one neglected. The minimal housing of the homeless would be regarded as an entitlement. Through these actions, we would proclaim to the world that our community values human life unconditionally, and that it recognizes and protects the dignity and sanctity of human life without condition, exception, or exclusion.

Many homeless people work, but do not earn enough to afford housing for themselves. Many homeless people receive (or are eligible for) government benefits, such as veteran's, disability, or Social Security, or have some other source of small income. The problem is that, for many, any available housing would require such a large proportion of their income as to make its rental unfeasible. The flat income tax/social dividend plan proposed in chapter 5 would go a long way in preventing homelessness. But in some parts of the country, depending on how large a social dividend we decide upon, rental housing still might not be affordable to those for whom the social dividend is the sole source of income (with affordable rent estimated at no more than 30 percent of income). In order to house these people, low-rent apartments would have to be built or subsidized for extremely low-income individuals and families. Of course, the object of the community is to ensure that the essential survival needs of everyone are met. The object is not cash redistribution per se. Hence the community, as alluded to in chapter 5, is not obliged to subsidize any individual's squandering of money on liquor, gambling, or other nonessential items. But since it is obliged to protect human life, protective voucher payments of rent would be appropriate in cases in which individual mismanagement of social dividends contributes to homelessness.

Even if a flat income tax/social dividend policy is not accepted, the life-affirmation frame obliges that some floor must be placed above dire need in means-tested programs, without categorization, social engineering, punitive and discriminatory regulations (such as in TANF), or time limits. Currently, in many states, if not all, the TANF benefits to single mothers with children are so low that they do not meet the program's own need standards, and payment of even the lowest rentals available leaves the families with pitifully little money to pay for food, clothing, and utilities. In Nevada, in 2003, a single mother on TANF with two children, if receiving the maximum allowance and paying only $300 per month in rent, would have had $48 per month left over for everything else.

It is evident that such an unequivocal pro-life position that is obliged by the principle of life affirmation cannot condone capital punishment, euthanasia, assisted suicide, or abortion. That is to say, the principle considers such acts to be morally wrong, and if morally wrong, then always so without exception. In my discussion of the philosophy of nonviolence in chapter 2, I pointed out that while Gandhi viewed violence as morally wrong, he thought it sometimes to be necessitated by our ignorance, even if no less morally wrong for that. He had faith, however, in human reason to create and discover new ways of confirming life within the means, even if the ideal of nonviolence could never be perfectly achieved. It is paradoxical, of course, to posit an ideal or principle to contain no exception and yet to admit of its occasional necessity, but the principle itself then presses us to find the means to resolve this contradiction in areas in which exceptions were previously deemed necessities in our prior ignorance. Principles, even if admitting of no exception, are (as discussed in chapter 3) ideals that we may merely aspire to, but never perfectly attain or achieve, thus always leaving exceptions. Yet, as I have insisted, what principles we choose to aspire to are of the utmost practical significance.

The sentiment that draws us to violate the principle of life affirmation in cases in which an individual, even if near the end of his or her life, is suffering severe and unrelenting pain, must be resisted, if principle is to be upheld. Principle is to be upheld because we consider human life to be the most sacred and important value in our world, or otherwise we would not have formulated it into principle in the first place. We do not deem ourselves fit to judge or preside over the matter of its cessation. With euthanasia, the goal is the cessation of pain (or in some instances, of life that cannot be recovered from a vegetative state). But euthanasia requires our complicity in ending life, much less pain.

Moreover, we set ourselves the difficult task of assuring against the possibility of our own selfish motives influencing the decision—the suffering caused to us as lovers and caretakers. We can argue that we are respecting life by complying with the wishes, expressed with free choice, of the patient, but we are also ending freedom by ending life. We can and indeed must say that the act is morally wrong or regrettable, even if we sympathize with the actor. Our sense of justice in accordance with the life-affirmation principle presses us to find new alternatives, perhaps through further advances in medical technology or pharmacology.

Abortion, too, must be seen as morally wrong and regrettable. Although great debates have addressed the question of whether or not the embryo and/or fetus (and in various stages of development) is human life, there can be little disagreement that in both is potential human life. Yet the pregnancy is part of a woman's body, whose own life we must respect, and the pregnancy may even have been forced upon her (through rape). We may allow by law the abortion of pregnancy due to rape, of pregnancy that endangers the woman's own life, or in other exceptional circumstances (although we are still left with the dilemma as to how far into a pregnancy abortion should be allowed), and yet proclaim as unlawful the abortion of pregnancy more generally. More can be accomplished, however, in terms of actually reducing abortions, and without violation of women, through the enlistment of government in the promotion and enhancement of actual life itself, and in the addressing of the social and economic circumstances that may give rise to women's choice of abortion. Moreover, government-backed campaigns could advocate against the use of abortion as simply a matter of convenience or substitute for contraception, or for that matter, any other reason (see also Pelton, 1999a, pp. 105-106).

Life Affirmation in the Criminal Justice System

As I have argued briefly in chapter 1 and more extensively elsewhere (Pelton, 1999a, pp. 125-163), the criminal justice system itself could be geared toward prevention and public safety, and less toward the retribution of a desert orientation. The consequence for a serious crime against persons, such as killing or maiming, would be incapacitation in the form of imprisonment, if there was less than reasonable certainty that the criminal could be constrained from committing a similar crime again through less drastic measures. Incapacitation is the physical restraint of the criminal's freedom to commit criminal acts within the larger community. The responsibility of the individual (as a causal agent in the event) would have to be determined in criminal court, but punishment in terms of notions of desert need not follow unless justice itself is defined in terms of individual desert. Even in the current desert-oriented criminal justice system, we do also aim at prevention of recurrence through deterrence and rehabilitation, as well as incapacitation. But imprisonment for the sake of deterrence (i.e., through punishment, such as imprisonment, instilling the fear in the criminal that if a future crime is committed, punishment will again follow) has little proven effectiveness as used within the current criminal justice system. Moreover, rehabilitation programs (i.e., programs aimed at changing the individual, in terms of his attitudes, beliefs, values, etc., rather than merely suppressing his or her outer behavior under threat of punishment) can only provide moderate statistical success, and can provide no reasonable assurance that any particular individual has been rehabilitated.

Incapacitation might look and feel like retribution to the criminal, but the rules in a system more oriented toward prevention, public safety, and life affirmation would be different from the present system. For one thing, many killers and rapists would probably get longer sentences than they do now. On the other hand, imprisonment would not be considered except in regard to the most severe crimes. Theft, for example, would not be grounds for imprisonment, and the thief might be sentenced to payment of some manner of restitution (taking a page, one might say, from the individual desert frame of justice itself). With the abolition of drug prohibition laws, suggested earlier, or at least the deprisonment of sentences for drug offenses, the prison population in the United States would be far smaller than it is today. Moreover, capital punishment, aside from violating the principle of life affirmation, is of no conceivable necessity in prevention, and would be abolished. I have suggested that such a system, although somewhat satisfying even the desire for retribution, is more life affirming than a system grounded in retribution and merely tinged with a preventive orientation.

Thus I have proposed here some policies that reach for the ideal of life affirmation and that, I claim, are suggested by the life-affirmation frame of justice. But even charity and sympathy promote life-affirming acts. The *principle* of life affirmation, qua principle, requires universality of application, without exception. In reality, we were not able to overcome Kant's contradiction. That is, in *actuality*, the criminal justice system, proposed here to be oriented more toward prevention than retribution, would nonetheless resort to coercion in the form of restriction of freedom (incapacitation), even if only as a last resort, for the purpose of enhancing the well-being and freedom of others, in violation of the means-ends principle and its inherent requirement of the universality of nonexception. From the outset, however, it was the *theoretical* contradiction that I focused upon, in the form of Kant's claim that such coercion (and even physical violence, for that matter) would carry "authorization" connected with "right." I opposed the claim of justice made for an action that violates the means-ends principle. In our continuing ignorance, we resort to coercion in order to protect our interests, but by recognizing its injustice in the context of the means-ends principle, we maintain no contradiction in theory, while pressed to resolve the contradiction in reality and aspiring toward the theoretical ideal by continually seeking nonviolent alternatives.

Nondiscrimination is inherent in the universality without exception of the principle of life affirmation, with the object at hand being life itself. It is in this sense that imprisonment violates the principle of nondiscrimination. Yet when we move to narrower objects, such as the addressing of criminal responsibility with the object of preventing criminal recurrence (see Pelton, 1999a, pp. 141-142), it could be said that there is no discrimination. Yet at the same time, if the object is addressed through imprisonment, then the principle of life affirmation is violated, although less severely so than if the object were to be addressed through capital punishment.

Administering Life Affirmation

Affirmative action policies and their controversies have masked the continuing failure of our national community to even approximate equal educational opportunity for all children at the primary and secondary school levels. All children are similarly situated in regard to the need for educational opportunity. Yet, as already discussed in chapter 5, they are afforded grossly different educational opportunity based on geographic location. In particular, children living in impoverished areas still tend to have less adequately funded schools (meaning, e.g., less adequate school buildings, lower paid and less qualified teachers, fewer and/or outdated books, and shoddy equipment). This amounts to discrimination, of a type that violates the principle of life affirmation in a very severe way. Historically, this discrimination has stemmed from the concept of local funding of primary and secondary schools through property taxes, thus ensuring less adequately funded schools in impoverished areas. Considerable progress has been made in recent years through increased state funding disproportionately targeting the poorest districts, but such discrimination still exists.

Although it has become fashionable for modern liberals as well as conservatives to favor decentralized government, and decisions being made at the "lowest governmental levels," the national community has become rather homogeneous in regard to the needs of individuals in different geographical regions, and this strategy often promotes discrimination. The federal funding of primary and secondary schools would more likely ensure nondiscrimination in regard to educational opportunity. In the current TANF program that leaves much policy as well as funding to the states, a single mother with a child will have quite different rules applied to her, and receive hugely discrepant welfare benefits, depending upon which state she is residing in. With regard to the issue of homelessness, advocates on the state and local levels are often confronted with the contention, not entirely without validity, that a local community that provides adequately for homeless people might act as a "magnet" in attracting homeless people from other areas of the country in which homeless people are relatively neglected and abused. The local community, attempting to act morally and justly, might thereby draw upon itself an unfair burden to shoulder relative to other cities. Ideally, homelessness, seen as the national problem that it is, would be addressed through a more expanded and centralized role of the federal government in providing funding and policy direction, ensuring that the entire national community would share equitably in the housing and care of the homeless.

Thus, the life-affirmation frame would encourage us to ferret out all types of discrimination, not limited to race, ethnicity, gender, age, or sexual orientation. The replacement of one form of discrimination with another merely perpetuates discrimination. We should not use discrimination of the past and present as an excuse to continue discrimination or create new forms of it. Rather, we should work to end all forms of discrimination. Our sentiment toward particular individuals or groups could be used to generate principles concerning all (see chapter 3). On the one hand, we would not have affirmative action policies, but on the other we would have adequately funded schools throughout the country. On the one hand, we would have a flat tax for all, but on the other, we would not have myriad tax breaks.

The flat tax/social dividend proposal described in the previous chapter would elegantly address financial need by replacing the alphabet soup of current social welfare policies, as well as all tax breaks, by allocating a common dividend to everyone (adjusted only for household size). Large segments of the population already receive such social dividends: they are called Social Security benefits for the elderly, and tax breaks. However, many policies governing the distribution of cash benefits are based on highly contestable claims concerning why members of certain groups of needy or even nonneedy people are supposedly "deserving" of such benefits while others are not. A truly universal social dividend system would take the same monies that are currently being redistributed through a plethora of programs, but would simply allocate them in a fairer manner, to everyone. The question of which groups are deserving would not be raised, because the proposed policy would regard everyone as deserving of benefit at least at a level to ensure that no one would go hungry, homeless, or unclothed.

Life Affirmation in Foreign Policy

In chapters 2 and 5, I claimed that since government is a form of collective behavior, it has moral obligations similar to those of individuals. We can thus talk about the rightful conduct of a national community not only toward the individuals within it, but also toward the nations and individuals outside of it. It has a moral responsibility for the survival of others. Yet the policies I have proposed thus far in this chapter, based on the life-affirmation frame, depend upon citizenship (or at least residence) within a national community in possession of a common treasury. The social dividends proposed here would be distributed from the collectively owned national treasury, formed from the taxing of excess wealth that has accrued to members of the community. It was argued that this excess wealth is a product of the establishment and existence of the community itself. Justice within this community requires that the community benefit everyone within it, without discrimination, and hence that its treasury be used to promote nondiscrimination, and the good of all of the individuals within it in a nondiscriminatory manner. A just community is required not only to distribute benefits in a nondiscriminatory manner, but also to collect taxes in the same manner.

I also said in chapter 5 that it is possible to additionally maintain that our community's excess wealth (which is taxed and redistributed) is partially a product of the existence and labors of the world outside of our community. On this basis it could be argued that there is also an implicit contractual obligation (in addition to the moral ones) that its national treasury be used to benefit the world in a nondiscriminatory manner, not only the immediate members of its national community. But many members of the outside world have excess wealth produced by their own national communities, and besides, they do not pay taxes into our own national community.

Moreover, as a national community, we do not have the ability to support life throughout the world in terms of education, health care, and so on, and certainly not in a nondiscriminatory manner. In our foreign aid policies, for example, we favor people in some nations and parts of the world over others. We do so in accordance with criteria unrelated to justice, but do not even have the ability to do it in accordance with justice. We necessarily prioritize, and we do this picking and choosing even in regard to humanitarian interventions to stop extreme human rights abuses, such as genocide. We do this in accordance with the wrong selection criteria, perhaps, but out of inability to help without selection, certainly. In truth, then, as a national community vis-à-vis the rest of the world, we are in a position analogous to that of a private charity in relation to the individuals it seeks to help. Like a charity, the national community may be motivated by and recognize its moral obligation, but it does not even have the capacity to help in a universal and nondiscriminatory manner. We tend to rely on sentiment, national interest, and other motives, but not on criteria of justice. Moreover, there is a further analogy. When charity is called upon to address the problem of homelessness within a national community, some citizens will be unfairly burdened, namely, those citizens who are most sympathetic to the plight of the homeless or who most experience the pangs of moral obligation, for they are the ones who will make contributions. But when government fulfills its moral obligation by addressing the problem itself, the burden on the contribution side is shouldered in a just and nondiscriminatory manner through taxes (assuming a fair tax system). Likewise, a national community acts as a charity unfairly burdening its own members—even when it determines to proceed, as it should, out of moral obligation—in addressing dire socioeconomic deficits in other parts of the world on a unilateral basis. In sum, on both accounts, only through the people of the world acting together as a world community will global justice be done.

A global treasury, even if limited to specific functions, such as food distribution, education, and environmental concerns, must be envisioned, under united global representative control, if global justice is to be meaningfully pursued. Such a scenario in accordance with the life-affirmation frame of justice is likely to emerge only when a point of perceived necessity is reached through a gradual recognition of the pervasive interdependence of the world community. Miller (1999a, pp. 19-20; 1999b) thinks that global justice requirements are limited to the protection of basic rights ("understood as the conditions that are universally necessary to allow men and women to lead minimally adequate lives" [1999a, p.319, n. 25]) and the prevention of exploitation. But the proper and just pursuit of global justice even as so defined would require the pooling of some resources in a global treasury.

But even before that point of global cooperation is reached, it is appropriate to ask what form of foreign policy a nation could unilaterally pursue if guided by the valuing of human life, the principle of life affirmation, and nondiscrimination, in accordance with the life-affirmation frame of justice. I have proposed that such a foreign policy would be means-oriented, would be directed toward enhancing the individual lives of all human beings, and would be directed toward people more so than nations. Moreover, it would be guided by the nonviolent strategies of noncooperation with injustice and evil and cooperation with good, rather than by the reward/punishment strategies of the desert frame (see chapter 2 for a description of nonviolent noncooperation and its contrast with the concept of reward/punishment).

The essence of the proposed policy (see Pelton, 1999a, pp. 185-212, for a fuller description) is to initiate as well as to support more and more actions and enterprises that are intrinsically life-affirming, and to shun and noncooperate with actions that are intrinsically destructive (disregarding reference to the supposed ultimate goals and ideals that those who engage in destructive actions claim to be seeking). The proposed policy would call for the systematic withdrawal of contributions to collective violence and violent enterprises and the transfer and conversion of resources and contributions to actions and enterprises, and means of waging conflict, that are intrinsically life-supporting. The step-by-step process would begin with the withdrawal of weapons supply programs whose intended functions can most easily be served by other means, and whose withdrawal, given the current violent framework of international relations, entails the least risk potential to all concerned parties. Those weapons supply programs intended to "make friends" of other nations can most readily be replaced by trade and aid programs that exchange life-supporting essentials, such as food, or sanitation and health projects, or other products or services constructive to life, that better serve the intention. Such constructive programs might be initiated in a way that would bypass the governments, if necessary, in the countries for which the programs are intended, if that is what is needed to give constructive support to the people. For example, aid might be channeled through nongovernmental organizations operating in such countries.

By the same token, the proposed policy would not be based upon a traditional perspective that divides the nations of the world into friends and adversaries. Nations are not individuals. They contain many individuals who are discriminated against through such a perspective. Moreover, nations and governments are complex social entities, and engage in myriad activities, some life supporting and some destructive, some just and some unjust. The proposed policy would embody the concept of nondiscrimination by directing actions toward actions and enterprises, and not toward nations and governments.

Indeed, such a policy would be aimed at individuals, and not groups we call nations, even though we must often deal with national governments as the presumed representatives of individuals. Such a policy would be modeled, in part, upon policies of such organizations as Amnesty International, that focus on human rights violations impartially without regard to which nation they are occurring in or under what form of government they are occurring; and of such organizations as the American Friends Service Committee, that focus on meeting the needs of individuals in distress without regard to what nation or party to a conflict the individuals belong.

The concept of "linkage" would have no place in the proposed policy, nor would economic aid be used as a "carrot." The policy would call for noncooperation with destructive acts, such as human rights violations, but not necessarily with the nations that perform such acts. Under the proposed policy, opposition and resistance would be limited to specific issues, and noncooperation with certain actions and enterprises would be carried out within an overall context of active cooperation with all nations and peoples in life-supporting endeavors. Traditional American foreign policy has emphasized, aside from outright violent confrontation in some conflict situations, the principles (whether articulated or not) of reward and punishment of nations and governments in the presumed service of national interests. The principle of punishment, in action, has often taken the form of political and economic sanctions against other countries, together with rewards for and cooperation with allied countries. But it also has taken the form of violence, contributions to violence, and threats of violence against other countries. Rather than employing reward or punishment of nations for past actions, or even positive and negative incentives for future ones, the proposed policy would focus on the issue of support or nonsupport for present actions and enterprises.

The life-affirmation frame of justice obliges us to continue to seek and develop creative alternatives to violence in the matter of the *waging* of conflict. Conflict is not synonymous with violence. Conflict has its root in issues, often of a social, economic, or political nature. Such factors as conflicting interests, territorial disputes, economic goals, and social discontents can be said to directly cause conflict, but not war. Violence is simply a means people sometimes resort to, with which to wage conflict. War can be "justified" only within a group justice frame, even if regrets are expressed over "collateral damage." Violence against only those presumed guilty of violence, such as individual terrorists, can be justified within the desert frame of justice, and we often find it consistent with our feelings at the time, but only the life-affirmation frame obliges us to view even such violence as morally regrettable.

Justification for application of the group frame in the form of war in Iraq in 2003 was offered by the American and British governments in terms of the necessity of ridding Iraq of weapons of mass destruction. At the same time, a clear intention was expressed, and efforts made, to limit the loss of life not only among coalition combatants, but also among the Iraqi people, both civilians and soldiers. While the group frame was shown, in actions as well as words, to be regarded as necessary but regrettable, the justice of the desert frame in regard to the Iraqi government's leaders, with the desert that of death, was assumed without discussion. But the zeal of righteousness can overwhelm us, once we embark on the group frame. In early April, I listened with interest to television accounts of the second attempt of the American forces to kill Saddam Hussein, this time in a restaurant in a residential neighborhood of Baghdad. There was much speculation as to whether he was dead or still alive, yet no discussion of whether bystanders were killed in the process. Yet the rationale of necessity for this group justice went by the boards when American government officials claimed that the personal fate of Hussein was irrelevant to our goals, which were being achieved in any case.

If war is the practice of the group frame in its most systematic and deadly form, then terrorism is the practice of the group frame in its most indiscriminate and deadly form. The very purpose of terrorism is the indiscriminate destruction of human life, even though, as with all violence, some ulterior purpose is also claimed. But Al Qaeda terrorists have proffered their unique justification for mass killing to be that the people they killed, even the janitors within the World Trade Center, were in some way responsible for the wrongs they claim to have been done to the people they imagine themselves to represent. Hence, in the agile minds of these terrorists, the group frame is seemingly absorbed into the individual-desert frame, yet everyone is subject to their violence. Perhaps they justify the killing of fellow Muslims in the attacks on the United States embassies in Kenya and Tanzania and the World Trade Center as collateral damage, but this is yet another indication of their astounding group-frame mentality and their imagined "right" to kill anyone for their cause.

The issue for the rest of the world, then, is not these terrorists' conceptions of justice, but how to reduce their capacity for terrorism, and stop their terrorism, as immediately and effectively as possible. However, even in pursuing this goal, we are morally obliged to consider what necessity calls for in light of our sense of justice. It is possible to adhere to the life-affirmation frame of justice as the ideal to strive for, even within the range of strategies presently conceivable to us, rather than to submit to the group or even individual-desert frames of justice in our own actions.

Pacifists are motivated against war largely through concern over group justice. Yet even many nonpacifists, motivated by the desert frame, have advocated that our "war against terrorism" be pursued by hunting down and apprehending individual terrorists, putting them on trial, and giving them their desert, rather than through massive military interventions into, or waging war in, other countries. The principle of life affirmation would recommend, at the least, that the goal should be stopping terrorism and preventing future terrorism, more so than the administration of desert; that capital punishment not be applied; and that the terrorism not deter us from pursuing global justice in accordance with the principle of life affirmation.

Weapons of mass destruction—nuclear, radiological, chemical, and biological—are, of course, the ultimate group-frame weapons. But the ongoing slaughter of human beings in our world proceeds even without their use. Such weapons have not changed the moral issues (see Pelton, 1999a, pp. 165-171, for a discussion), even though they do permit the group frame to potentially be carried out on a far greater scale than ever before. One goal must be to set the world on the road to the destruction of all weapons of mass destruction, and to the reduction to the greatest possible extent as becomes feasible, of conventional weaponry.

Both the group and individual-desert frames, unfortunately, have prevailed thus far in the long-standing Israeli-Palestinian conflict. The group frame has been carried out in the form of terrorism and warfare. Both sides, in some aspects of their conflict, can be said to have valued land over human life—the Israelis in insisting on building settlements in the West Bank, claiming the land as theirs, and the Palestinians in insisting on reclaiming all of Israel, insisting the land of Israel is theirs. They seem intent on not only negotiating a Palestinian state, but also insisting upon the right of return. Individual claims for property should be honored if established in courts of law, but compensation (a form of desert) can take other forms than the transfer of land. In my earlier discussion of compensation, the question of what forms compensation should take was not explored. The life-affirmation frame would dictate that the form should not disrupt life, but support it. Compensation for land can be financial, and hence much less disruptive to any human life. But far more than any compensation, an Israeli-Palestinian mutual resolve to build enterprises and structures, economies and infrastructures, operating both unilaterally and jointly, designed to promote the well-being of every individual within the region, would be the most just resolution of the conflict in terms of the life-affirmation frame of justice. In the modern world economy, groups of individuals can develop a flourishing life-supporting state, no matter how tiny, inhospitable, or devoid of natural resources that territory may be, as several nations, including Israel, have proved within the past half century. It is high time that a Palestinian state, with the aid of Israel if not also other nations in the region, get on with it, with both groups placing human welfare over religious meanings of land and exact quantities of land, and leaving the members of both groups better off than they were before, in terms of security, prosperity, and human decency.

If it were a straightforward and unambiguous matter to divine just policies from the original position, the desert frame, or the life-affirmation frame, we would have no need for further debate, and we could leave policy development to technicians. However, not everyone will agree upon exactly which policies "logically" flow from one or another frame. Moreover, even justice in accordance with a life-affirmation frame orientation is not without its own problems, contradictions, and inconsistencies. Taken to its logical extremes, would we propose laws against killing animals? Some such laws do exist, but would we propose equality of treatment with human beings? Should the life of an animal, even an insect, be considered of the same value as that of a human life? Even confining ourselves to the human realm, is the faith we must place in the ability of human reason to create further alternatives to violence, even when dealing with violent others, warranted?

There are inconsistencies in any system of justice, and so each system must be weighed (in regard to both its moral intrinsic worth and its utility) in comparison to each other, and not in isolation. Yet the value we place on human life is indisputable, and the emphasis that the life-affirmation frame places on valuing human life even within the means, and universally, logically follows from that value. We do aspire toward the life-affirmation ideal within liberal societies, but reasonable disputes arise not only over the occasional necessity of the group frame (as in war), but also over its desirability (such as in debates concerning affirmative action policies). The individual-desert frame is most firmly entrenched in liberal society, and I have criticized it mostly indirectly, in terms of the group-frame social policies that it typically (and perhaps it can be said, inadvertently) yields, and also in terms of its extreme forms, such as capital punishment. As I previously acknowledged, the concept of desert seems to be so entrenched in our sense of justice, and so supported by powerful feelings of sympathy and revenge, that a politics that directly confronts it, rather than criticizing many of the inconsistent policies that ensue from it, is not likely to succeed.

7

Frame Politics

Politicians have not only catered to but also nurtured narrow individual and group interest, along with sentiment and false senses of desert, in public attitudes toward government and public policy.

Of course, in a democracy, a strategy that did not appeal to the self-interests of people would not be viable. People expect to benefit from community, and that is their reason for wanting to be part of it. But they also have a sense of justice, and this can be appealed to not only because they believe that justice will benefit them, but also because they believe in justice for its own sake. The initial successes of the civil rights movement led by Martin Luther King, Jr. were largely due to its compelling appeal to most Americans' sense of justice. At the same time that people want their interests to be served, they want the society they live in to deal justly with all people, in accordance with principle. They support fairness, respect human life, and intuitively understand the concept of nondiscrimination as fundamental to a just society. Yet many people also have a strong sense of justice as desert, and in accordance with that sense, there is much room for disagreement as to who is due what. When politicians and others accept uncritically and unreflectively various claims of desert, they broach the danger of allowing interest and sentiment to prevail over principle and justice in the formation of law and policy.

The Politics of Group Interests and Desert

The politics of desert does not proceed without the politics of group interests. People, such as the elderly, start to organize to defend their perceived collective desert, as is their right. But when politicians respond in categorized kind instead of extracting and promoting principles of justice to be applied to all, they develop policies that favor some groups' interests over others, and groups always remain excluded. Moreover, such group-oriented policies, as we have seen, invariably fail to fully conform to the ostensible principles of desert these policies are purportedly to serve, in that some individuals who are "deserving" are invariably excluded, while "undeserving" others are invariably included. Yet these very same politicians would agree that justice pertains to

138   Frames of Justice

individuals, not to groups. In any event, it is clear that even till today, there is hardly a politician in the United States who has put forth the philosophical grounds and the possibilities for the development of a noncategorical approach to social policies.

At least since the 1930s, Democratic liberalism gained great popularity by extending rights and benefits to more and more groups of people. To be sure, justice was advanced through accommodation to group interests. But each has been mistaken for the other. As James Patterson (1996, p. 638) points out, the civil rights movement "had drawn on one of the most enduring elements of the American creed: belief in the equal opportunity of individuals. As passage of the civil rights laws had suggested, large majorities of people supported this ideal, and they persisted in doing so amid the backlash that ensued: the laws continued to matter. As events after 1965 showed, however, Americans were much less sympathetic when people demanded the 'right' to *social* equality or special entitlements for *groups*" (italics in original). I take "social equality" to mean here equality of individual or group results or outcomes.

Indeed, favorable public opinion among white Americans toward racial integration of schools, public transportation, and housing rose steeply from the 1940s into the 1960s, with substantial majorities achieved by 1963 (Sheatsley, 1966). But some time during the 1960s, as Thomas and Mary Edsall (1991) note, a turning point occurred in that the general public began to perceive a violation of its own sense of fairness. A 1995 *Newsweek* survey, with results consistent with those of previous years, indicated that 79 percent of white Americans opposed racial preferences (Fineman, 1995). So did almost half (46 percent) of African Americans, despite an understandable temptation to support policies that might benefit oneself, regardless of fairness.

A poll conducted in early 2003—while two cases against the University of Michigan's use of racial preferences in its admissions policies were still pending before the U.S. Supreme Court—reminded respondents that "the Supreme Court will be deciding whether public universities can use race as one of the factors in admissions to increase diversity in the student body," and asked if they favor or oppose this practice. Sixty-seven percent said that they oppose the practice, including 50 percent of the black and 51 percent of the Hispanic respondents.[1]

Yet when a Gallup poll asked, several days before the June Supreme Court decision, "Do you generally favor or oppose affirmative action programs for racial minorities?" the public was divided, with 49 percent favoring and 43 percent opposing.[2] (All of the survey results cited in this chapter are based on national adult samples). A Pew Research Center report, based on a survey conducted in early May 2003, concluded that while there is support for the *rationale* of affirmative action (such as overcoming past discrimination or increasing student diversity), Americans question the *fairness* of such programs, "the rationale notwithstanding" (Pew Research Center, 2003). In fact, when a desert argument is embedded in the question, positive sentiment toward affirmative action is successfully invoked. Thus, 63 percent responded favorably (and only 29 percent unfavorably) to the question: "*In order to overcome past discrimination*, do you favor or oppose affirmative action programs designed to help blacks, women, and other minorities get better jobs and education?" (italics added).[3] But even coming after this question, with its narrow-reasoning rationale, when asked, "All in all, do you think affirmative action programs designed to increase the number of black and minority students on college campuses are fair, or unfair?" 42 percent said that they are unfair.

In truth, survey results concerning the issue of affirmative action have ranged all over the boards, in partial indication of the fact that public opinion poll results on many issues are highly sensitive to the exact nature of the wording of the questions. An Associated Press poll conducted early in 2003 found that when asked if they thought that "affirmative action programs that provide advantages or preferences for blacks, Hispanics and other minorities in hiring, promoting and college admissions" should be continued or abolished, 53 percent responded that they should be continued, and 35 percent that they should be abolished.[4] Another survey in February 2003 found 49 percent disapproving of "affirmative action admissions programs at colleges and law schools that give racial preferences to minority applicants."[5] A month earlier, when the same question was asked, 54 percent were found to be disapproving.[6] Another poll, in 2002, found 55 percent to oppose "affirmative action programs that give preferences to blacks and other minorities."[7] Yet a Gallup poll in 2001 found 56 percent to favor "affirmative action programs for minorities and women for admission to colleges and universities," and 58 percent to favor "affirmative action programs for minorities and women for job hiring in the workplace."[8] But a poll conducted by the *Chronicle of Higher Education* before the June 2003 Supreme Court decision (Selingo, 2003; of people aged twenty-five to sixty-five, from every state except Alaska and Hawaii) found that while 78 percent said that it was important or very important to prepare students from minority groups to become successful (and another 17 percent said that it was somewhat important), 64 percent disagreed or strongly disagreed that colleges and universities should admit students from racial minority groups even if they have lower high school grade-point averages and standardized test scores than other students. Even among black and Hispanic respondents, only 24 percent and 8 percent, respectively, strongly agreed with the use of racial preferences in college admissions.

Surely, many politicians have persisted in appealing to a presumed group-frame mentality among their constituents, thereby fostering the dynamics of group politics in which politics as a matter of contending group interests is encouraged rather than politics as the pursuit of policies that promote individual justice for all. And the Supreme Court, in its landmark decision on June 23, 2003, upheld consideration of race and ethnicity in the University of

Michigan's Law School admissions policies, thus countering the principle embedded in the Fourteenth Amendment, and reifying "diversity" as a "compelling state interest" in the composition of student bodies. Hence it is claimed that the "interest" of diversity trumps the principle of nondiscrimination. And thus justice is defined in terms of aggregate results rather than in terms of violation or nonviolation of individuals. Surely, sentiment has triumphed over principle.

During the 2000 presidential primary campaign, one reporter (Holmes, 2000) noted that strategists were "frantically trying to cobble together winning strategies" to appeal to a diverse electorate looking "more than ever like an indistinct montage of contending groups." Political consultants were busy dissecting the results of public opinion polls, on various issues, by race, ethnicity, gender, age, soccer moms, waitress (single) moms, married men, and unmarried men. The "contending groups," however, were in the eye of the beholder, constructed by the pollsters themselves. In this manner, politics comes to be construed as a matter of patching together appeals to the interests of enough (and large enough) "groups" to win a majority of the vote, and therefore politics becomes a matter of appeals to various group interests, and not to principles of justice. Al Gore, in his 2000 campaign for the presidency, followed a strategy consistent with that suggested by pollster Stan Greenberg and his colleagues, who proposed (after examining the polls, of course) that the group that now needed to be appealed to in order to win the election is "working families"—a large group (thus the reason to appeal to it) but just one group nonetheless. Hence politics is reduced to brazen calculated appeals to group interests.

Through group-frame policies and politics, we create a community of (clashing) interests, but not of individual justice. In order to convince groups that they are on their "side," politicians foster a spirit of entitlement among the various groups they are attempting to attract, by telling them what they want to hear, namely, why they deserve the special favorable treatment offered to them for their votes. This is couched in terms of justice—the justice of desert. Once the categories become entrenched, politicians dare not speak out against them for fear of alienating the "entitled." This is one reason why affirmative action policies, once envisioned as a temporary measure, are so difficult to abolish after more than three decades.

The political architects of the Social Security Act and our modern welfare state had, unfortunately, contributed to such perceptions of desert through the deceptions of a separate payroll tax specified for the payment of old-age Social Security benefits. Workers are led to believe that they are paying into a "trust fund" from which they will draw upon in later years. But Milton Friedman's comments made over thirty years ago still hold true today: "The impression is given that a worker's 'benefits' are financed by his 'contributions.' The fact is that taxes currently being collected from current workers are being used to pay benefits to persons who have retired or to their dependents and survivors. No trust fund in any meaningful sense is being accumulated" (Cohen and Friedman, 1972, p. 24). Friedman recommended that the payroll tax be repealed, any further accumulation of benefits be terminated, a new tax-and-distribution structure be enacted (he had recommended a negative income tax system), and all existing beneficiaries as well as current workers be paid the amounts they are entitled to under present law (pp. 44-49).

As Friedman (p. 44-45) pointed out, "the major defect of our current arrangements is the proliferation of special programs either for special groups or special commodities." Such programs, he said, "tend to become the preserve of special vested interests." He advocated "a single program designed to give assistance to persons with low incomes, regardless of the reason why their incomes are low." Such a program, he said, "would cost far less each year than the present ragbag of programs. Yet it would come far closer to alleviating true distress."

As Lester Thurow (1996) claimed, an enormous transfer of resources to the elderly have made them "into one-issue voters who exercise a disproportionate impact on the political process" and who "are so powerful that no political party wants to tangle with them." He pointed out that excluding interest on the national debt, half of the federal budget goes to the elderly. Yet the spirit of entitlement, once nurtured, is difficult to counteract. People develop a strong sense of deserving the particular benefits reserved for them, and come to think of them as their due. To take it away invokes a strong sense of being treated unfairly.

The downside of democracy (although still the best political system yet devised) is its tendency to be group oriented in its politics and policy development. Tempted by the prospect of appealing to enough group interests to win a majority of the votes, and taking the winning of elections and maintaining public office as ends in themselves, politicians often fail to champion individual justice. Although they may privately believe that justice is not being done, they have not the courage to confront their constituencies by challenging the politics of interests as opposed to justice. Having appealed to group interests, our politicians have become beholden to such interests, and have failed to develop the conceptual formulations with which they could successfully rally the public's support by appealing to its sense of justice.

Proposals that help some groups but not others, and that tax some groups and not others (whether it be selective taxes for the "gaming industry," cigarette taxes, alcohol taxes, and even more selectively, beer taxes) serve to drive wedges through the community, splinter it, and provoke questioning of the value of community itself. In Nevada, some citizens have begun to ask why they should pay for others' education (why not oblige the family of each Clark County K-12 student to make a special payment of 40 dollars per month, asks one recent letter to the editor in a Las Vegas newspaper). Why not have everyone out for themselves? Yet the same people who suggest these go-it-alone schemes have profited handsomely from past and ongoing welfare benefits, including the schooling of their own now-grown children, and their current monthly Social Security checks and part of their Medicare coverage. A disturbing trend is currently evident in America, and it is being reinforced and fostered rather than combated by both Republican and Democratic politicians: others should be taxed for my benefit, but selected others should not benefit at all. Although posing a breach in the contract formulation of community and government, it is at the same time fostered by that formulation. The same can be said of the desert formulation of justice. While the trend violates notions of desert, it is justified by merely claiming (and believing) that I deserve to benefit, while others (because of their shiftlessness, idleness, personal shortcomings, and so on) do not.

When politicians continue to appeal to narrow group interests, they reinforce the idea that politics is nothing more than group interests and group struggle, a matter of "power," not justice. It is not so much that politicians as leaders then serve as a model for such behavior, to be emulated by example, but that they set up the dynamic by which politics does become mere power struggle, and one's group better join the fray or lose out. Once that dynamic dominates, only the naive would fail to see that politics has little to do with justice and fail to develop their own group strategies and put forth their own narrow-reasoning rationales to promote their own group interests. The politics of the day thus promotes selfishness rather than justice.

The Enduring Myth of Self-Made Wealth

In chapter 5 I suggested that we share in a *communal* wealth that is far in excess of what would accrue to individuals, despite their efforts, in absence of community. The community has produced and redistributed wealth that is not earned in any real sense by most, if any, individuals within it. Yet people in our community feel entitled to the benefits they have gained merely from having the good fortune to have been born into or to reside within our national community. In fact, most of us have benefited from inventions, discoveries, and innovations in which we have played no role whatsoever.

Many of those who did play a role in innovations that have greatly increased the overall wealth of our nation first benefited and survived because of American welfare programs that were already in place. They came from poverty, and if not aided by public assistance programs, they were helped by having the opportunity to attend public universities, or were supported by public monies (the GI Bill being one example) in attending private universities. The payoff to the community has been enormous. Yet the payoff was also unforeseen. It was not a matter of calculation that led to such supports with such payoffs, but of our ideas of justice. These people had been afforded reasonable opportunity, despite their personal or group histories and backgrounds of poverty and disadvantage.

Many people are supported in whole or part by Social Security and other government benefits, and by subsidized college tuition. Many people have inheritances, earned by their parents or grandparents, with the same help from the community, or enriched by the structures of liberal community. My point is not to begrudge them their good fortune but to rid us of the delusion that we are all making it on our own. Students at public universities may work hard to pay for part of their tuition, but they do not pay anywhere near the full cost of their government-supported education. Some of my students understandably bristle at my suggestion that they are on welfare. Since they have to hold jobs while attending school in order to pay for tuition and other costs, some of them believe that they deserve everything they have. Indeed, one of the consequences of the partial privatization of public universities over the past few decades is the nurturing of some students' false perceptions that they are not reliant upon the community as a whole, permitting them to be resentful of "others" who "feed at the public trough," and to have no difficulty in favoring harsh "welfare" laws aimed at, say, poor single mothers or homeless people.

This spirit of entitlement is understandable, since many people *have* worked hard, but what is difficult for us to realize is that as hard as we have worked, the *extent* of our individual wealth and welfare has not been earned, and can only be attributable to the community as a whole. In a significant sense, then, we are all on welfare. We are all dependent on others and on each other. We are dependent upon our community. Only a fool would believe that his wealth is derived solely from his own efforts. The truth is that we are all getting "something for nothing." That is in the nature of a viable and successful community.

The illusion of individual self-sufficiency is strong and is fostered by the very same structures of liberal community that allow the potential for individual effort to reap its own rewards in the marketplace. There would be nothing wrong with this spirit of entitlement if it were not for the fact that it encourages us to belittle and judge others, and begrudge them even governmental attention to their minimal survival needs. We convince ourselves that while we are deserving of everything we get, there are some individuals within our midst who are deserving of nothing at all. At this point, a sense of deservingness slides into greed and self-righteousness, to be nourished and rationalized through prejudice, stereotype, narrow reasoning, arbitrary distinctions between "us" and "them," and active derogation of those we learn to despise as we pursue the process of suspecting *their* desert.

Not atypically, in a letter to the editor of the largest-circulation Las Vegas newspaper, the *Review-Journal*, one resentful citizen states that people who "work hard and play by the rules" should not have to "pony up money for those who don't want to change their circumstances in life." It is usual for conservative radio talk show hosts and their callers to decry "big government" that forces one to fork over "my" money to others, usually assumed to be "undeserving." Yet if they were to live in a land of anarchy where they could pay no taxes and get to keep all of their income, their same individual efforts would yield little gain, and they would be worse off in every way imaginable, including having far less money to worry about.

On the John David Wells talk radio program in Las Vegas, a caller expresses his hatred toward "illegal aliens"—a code word, one suspects, for all recent Mexican immigrants—in the valley. Why not, the caller asks, charge them a price of $10,000 to become citizens? Why pay to send their children to school or to buy textbooks for them since, he brazenly opines, this would be wasted on them anyway? One caller to another talk show, indignant over proposals for a state income tax in Nevada, proclaims that he paid his taxes back in Indiana, where his children went to school. But he came to Nevada to retire, because it has no income tax. He has already paid his dues (or in his mind, his fair share)—why should he have to pay for the schooling of "illegal immigrants"? Never mind that the parents of those children from Mexico built his new house for him in Las Vegas, with their labor bought cheaply enough to make his new residence extremely affordable for him, another reason why he chose Nevada as his place for "retirement." Another caller claims to have a new idea in regard to the homeless—let's deprive able-bodied people who won't work of the right to vote. The talk show host responds with enthusiastic endorsement. She thinks this is a wonderful idea. Never mind that such a law would deprive most of the large "retirement community" in Las Vegas of the right to vote—rather, it is to be assumed that the law would be written to exclude able-bodied people over sixty-five from it, on the grounds of desert.

The folly of this approach would become apparent if people were to separate themselves into their own group-interested enclaves. Hence "retired" people would move to Nevada to avoid state income taxes, and vote against adequately funding public education, a process that has already begun. Parents with school-age children would begin to congregate in other areas of the country, where interest in public education is mutual. But then the service industry that caters to the elderly in Las Vegas would dry up, and the young parents may even begin to balk at supporting the elderly through payroll ("Social Security") taxes. Thus begins the devolution of community, and it may then be necessary to go a considerable way down that road before people are awakened to the benefits of a just community.

While those radio talk show hosts and their callers enjoy their own unearned fruits of community (and thus do not call for anarchy) they wish to deny benefits to others whom they sit in judgment of as unworthy. Exactly who "don't want to change their circumstances in life," the justice status of "illegal immigrants," the moral status of having reached a certain age, on what grounds some people who don't work are to be favored over others who don't work, or who should be charged for certain government services while others are not charged for different government services, are highly debatable judgment calls, to say the least. It is clear, however, that the "deserving" always turn out to be those doing the judging (and those that the judges have sympathy with), while the "undeserving" are never those doing the judging. If the judges fall into poverty or homelessness we can be certain that they will perceive it as due to circumstances beyond their control, and if they cannot lift themselves from it, this will not be due in their eyes to their lack of will to change their circumstances. And if they are beset with catastrophic illness whose treatment they do not have the means to pay for, they will certainly desire help from government, and will find reason to believe that they, if not others in similar circumstances, deserve it. People are adept at devising reasons for why they are deserving of certain benefits while others are not.

If we really wished to pursue fairness in government policy on the basis of desert, we would have to distinguish between people who slacked off on their jobs through much of their careers, and those who worked hard, or between those veterans who saw combat and those who did not, and so on. As I suggest to my students, there are many people in the large service industry in the Las Vegas valley who work harder, in many senses of that word, than I do, and yet receive far less financial remuneration and other benefits. Are they getting what they "deserve"? Since the marketplace is not really private, and its success is in great part due to the community through the actions of its government, the government has the obligation to ensure that the marketplace does not practice discrimination in employment and toward consumers. But should government be in the business of rewarding work, and of attempting to judge who is worthy of what?

It is good that in the marketplace, people often get well rewarded for their efforts, and many can negotiate their desert in terms of their salary levels. But even in the marketplace, we cannot say that people always get what they deserve and deserve what they get. Yet as imperfect as the marketplace is in terms of fulfilling justice conceived of in terms of desert, government, as we have seen, is even worse. Moreover, as argued here, it is not government's role. Its role is to ensure that the community benefits everyone, that physical survival is assured for everyone unconditionally, and that it affirms life in a nondiscriminatory manner, not allowing discrimination even in the marketplace. To be sure, there are other ways in which government must regulate the marketplace, such as through environmental regulations to prevent injury to people. But that some people profit far more than others in the marketplace is not government's concern, so long as everyone has reasonable opportunity, their survival needs are met, and they are accorded the same procedural rights—such as not to be discriminated against—as all other members of the community.

Hence, in broader terms than those proposed by Locke (see chapter 5), we can say that individuals come together to form a community in order to benefit from it. But we realize that if only some individuals were to benefit from this union and not others, or at the expense of others, then we would have a situation that all of the members of the community could not have agreed to in coming together to form the community in the first place, and the implicit contract would be broken. Thus the contract formulation of community itself requires the principle of nondiscrimination. We could also say, however, from this contract perspective, that membership in the community incurs obligations, as does a contract. And therefore, even while holding to nondiscrimination as a contractual principle, we may find reason to exclude. Perhaps some people have not contributed to the community, and thus have not lived up to their implicit contractual agreement. Perhaps others are not really members of the community, to which the implicit contract applies, but are intruders who have entered our midst only to partake of our communal wealth.

Hence we find reason to exclude on the basis of desert. Others have not fulfilled their contractual obligations, have not contributed to our society, and so are undeserving of sharing in the wealth. But we include and exclude on the basis of group generalizations and stereotypes. Moreover, we overlook any contractual obligation to address need itself. And yet, stemming from our sense of justice that precedes contracts, we do have a sense that need should be addressed. Our way out is to leave it to charity, because we rely on our contract formulation to say that it is not required under the terms of the contract if the individuals did not fulfill their obligations under that contract. And the proof that they did not is their poverty itself. They must have deserved what they got.

The question is whether the community as a whole has an obligation, based on justice, to address dire need without judgment, or whether it is justified in trying to distinguish between the "deserving" and "undeserving," and in finding reason to leave some individuals to continue unfed, unhoused, or unclothed. In the Torah, it is written that we must leave the gleanings of our harvest for the poor and the stranger (Leviticus 19:9-10). Jesus said, "Judge not" (Matthew 7:1), although these two words are apparently a real puzzlement to many Christians, including our political leaders. Perhaps, they think, Jesus didn't say it, didn't mean it, or didn't mean it to apply to government. But if we use government to help ourselves while denying it to others, we as a community mock religious and moral teachings, as well as justice.

Political Strategies toward Life Affirmation

Yet despite the apparent selfishness expressed in abundant anecdotal evidence, people *do* have a sense of justice, and that sense tends toward individual justice, although it often favors the desert frame. The attitudes illustrated above are supported by the myth of self-reliance as well as by a sense of justice expressed as individual desert. Yet the life-affirmation frame of justice also manifests itself in public opinion, as will be shown, and is not entirely obscured by the politics of the day. Here I will attempt to explore the possibilities, and the practical political strategies that would need to be developed, for moving from our current network of social policies more toward the vision of a liberal society based on the life-affirmation frame, if we wished to do so.

Public Opinion

As I argued in a previous book, there are grounds for believing that American opinion toward "welfare" recipients has been misread and misled (Pelton, 1999a, pp. 52-55). A 1986 national telephone survey conducted by Cook and Barrett (1992) found that majorities of 85 percent or more believed that individual benefits in the AFDC and Medicaid programs, as well as the SSI program, should either be increased or maintained at their current levels (keeping up with inflation), and 76 percent wished to see benefits in the Food Stamps program increased or maintained. But politicians' rhetoric affects public opinion as much as the reverse. During a time of public debate over "welfare" in which both Democratic and Republican politicians were deriding the AFDC program, a 1994 survey found that only 42 percent wanted "the amount of tax money now being spent for welfare programs to help low-income families" to be increased or maintained at the present level (Gallup, 1995, pp. 85-89). Yet, even in that survey, majorities of at least 90 percent believed that government should provide job training and childcare for welfare recipients, and 60 percent even believed that government-paid jobs should be provided to welfare recipients when not enough private-sector jobs are available.

There is no doubt, however, that while many Americans maintain supportive attitudes toward poor people, they are highly scornful toward those perceived as trying to get "something for nothing." Thus they are very concerned with distinguishing between the "deserving" and "undeserving" poor. This concern, historically, and surely at the present time, has focused upon the unemployed, the homeless, and most particularly, poor single women with children. The work ethic is strong in America, and people who are viewed as willing to help themselves are admired, while those who are not are scorned, even despised, and perceived as undeserving. Large categories of people are excluded from this wrath, such as people who are elderly and retired from work, and the disabled. They are exempted from the scrutiny that might find many of the retired elderly to be able-bodied or not to have worked very much at all in the past, or many of the disabled to be able to work. Sympathy is engendered by "old age," or "disability." A summary of polls from 1988 through 1991 indicated that 82 percent favored the proposition that people should be required to work in order to receive "welfare."[9] An Associated Press poll conducted in January 1997, a few months after the law was passed that replaced the AFDC program with TANF, found that 75 percent of the American public favored the new time limits on public assistance.[10] However, that same poll showed that 61 percent believed that government should provide enough aid to keep the family fed and sheltered, to a welfare recipient having a "young child" to support, who "either won't work or simply can't hold a job."

Moreover, a composite of polls from 1983 through 1987 showed that more than 42 percent responded either that they "strongly agree," "agree," "neither agree nor disagree," or "can't choose," in regard to the statement that "the government should provide everyone with a guaranteed basic income."[11] In response to the same question in a 1992 poll, the total was 52 percent.[12]

In a May 1990 poll, 67 percent said that they would like to see federal spending on programs for the homeless increased, with 25 percent saying that it should be kept the same.[13] A 1996 poll found that 61 percent believed (either "definitely" or "probably") that it should be government's responsibility to provide decent housing for those who can't afford it.[14] Only 30 percent thought that it should probably or definitely not be. A *Washington Post* poll in 1990 found that 58 percent said that they would be willing to pay more in taxes "if the money went to providing shelter for homeless people in your community."[15] Earlier that year, in a *Washington Post* poll, 62 percent indicated that if the military budget were to be reduced, they would strongly favor using this money to help the homeless, and another 28 percent said that they would somewhat favor it.[16] In a December 1990 Associated Press poll, 75 percent responded "yes" when asked if they would be willing to pay more taxes for federal spending for the homeless.[17] In that same poll (somewhat inconsistently), 58 percent indicated that they think federal spending on helping the homeless should be increased, while another 23 percent said it should remain the same.

A CBS poll conducted in 1991 showed that 62 percent would be willing "to pay $100 a year more in (federal) taxes in order to increase spending on helping homeless people."[18] Another poll that year indicated that 68 percent would agree to pay higher federal taxes if guaranteed that the additional tax money would be used for "housing the homeless."[19] A 1992 poll determined that 68 percent thought that "federal spending on helping homeless people" should be increased, and another 26 percent that it should remain the same.[20] However, in 1994 and again in 1997, the Pew Research Center found that only 53 percent would increase spending for "programs for the homeless" if "you were making up the budget this year."[21] But another 34 percent in 1994 and 31 percent in 1997 would keep it the same.

In 1996, another poll found 79 percent to approve "of having your tax dollars used to help pay for housing for the homeless."[22] And a 1996 Harris poll revealed that 65 percent agreed that "we should be willing to spend our tax dollars to provide inexpensive shelter for all homeless people who want it."[23] Finally, in a 2002 survey, 57 percent agreed (either strongly or somewhat) with the statement: "As long as so many Americans are poor or homeless, our nation has failed to live up to its ideals."[24]

Back in 1994, when America was debating health care reform, a *New York Times* poll found that 82 percent thought it "very important" that in any health care reform plan, "every American receives health insurance coverage."[25] In that same year, a Harris poll indicated that 77 percent believed that "ensuring that everyone has health insurance" was either "absolutely essential" or "very important."[26] When another poll that year asked, "would you prefer a health care reform plan that raises taxes in order to provide health insurance to all Americans, or a plan that does not provide health insurance to all Americans but keeps taxes at current levels," the response was evenly split.[27]

In 2003, one poll found that 74 percent of Americans said that it is "very important" for the President and Congress to deal with the issue of "increasing the number of Americans covered by health insurance" and another 18 percent said that it was "somewhat important."[28] A later poll that year asking the same question yielded nearly identical results (73 percent and 20 percent, respectively).[29] Still later in 2003, a *Washington Post*—ABC News poll showed that 80 percent think that it is more important to provide health care coverage for all Americans, even if it means raising taxes, than to hold down taxes, leaving some Americans uncovered.[30]

Support for a "single payer" plan did not fare well in surveys conducted by Princeton Survey Research Associates for the Harvard School of Public Health in 1994. Another survey, in 2003, showed that the public is about evenly split in favoring and opposing "a national health plan, financed by taxpayers, in which all Americans would get their insurance from a single government plan."[31] Yet the 2003 *Washington Post*—ABC News poll indicated that 62 percent prefer "a universal health insurance program, in which everyone is covered under a program like Medicare that's run by the government and financed by taxpayers" to the current health insurance system in the United States.[32] The poll showed that support plummets, however, if the program would limit one's choice of doctors or entail waiting lists for some nonemergency treatments.

On the other hand, a poll in 1994 found that 61 percent thought that "the federal government should guarantee health care for all Americans."[33] A Gallup poll in September 2000 found that 64 percent of the American public thought that "it is the responsibility of the federal government to make sure that all Americans have health care coverage" (Gallup, 2001, pp. 321-322). Still later, in mid-2003, 72 percent agreed (38 percent "completely" and 34 percent "mostly") that "the government should guarantee health insurance for all citizens, even if it means repealing most of the tax cuts passed under President Bush." Moreover, 63 percent saw this as a "moral issue" as well as a "political issue."[34]

What are we to make of a confusing array of survey findings? It would not be difficult to swing public opinion through political leadership on matters of providing minimal assistance to ensure the necessities of survival for everyone. And although the concept of desert is deeply held, most Americans understand the difficulty of its application.

It will be recalled that when the goal of overcoming past discrimination is invoked, public opinion poll findings can be shifted to favor affirmative action. A similar phenomenon is apparent in regard to questions concerning programs aimed at assisting poor women with children. When the term "welfare" is employed, negative poll findings are common, perhaps because the term invokes the negative stereotype of "welfare" mothers as undeserving (see Cook and Barrett, 1992). From this interesting characteristic of survey research, it can be inferred that the salience of the desert frame is malleable to a considerable extent. If so, it would not be far-fetched to infer that political leadership can exert considerable influence, through emphasizing desert arguments or eschewing them, over the political viability of policy proposals stemming from one frame or another. As we have seen, at the same time that opinion polls indicate the sway of the desert frame in public opinion, they also reveal many strong findings consistent with the life-affirmation frame. There is the question of in which direction politicians concerned with justice wish to lead.

In 1999, when asked if they would prefer using the budget surplus (which existed at that time) to cut taxes or "to pay for social programs such as education and welfare," 58 percent of the American public chose the latter, and only 28 percent went with cutting taxes.[35] In 2003, a huge new tax cut bill proposed by the Bush administration—even in the face of tremendous new homeland security costs in the wake of the September 11, 2001 terrorist attacks, the costs of the war in Iraq, and a growing deficit—was not met with favor by the public. Opinion polls (in 2003), with their results so sensitive to the precise wording of questions, at best found lukewarm support for tax cuts, and when questions juxtaposed tax cuts with spending on domestic programs such as education, health care, and Social Security, the public overwhelmingly chose spending over tax cuts.[36]

While overwhelming majorities have favored the death penalty for a person convicted of murder since the mid-1970s, peaking at 80 percent in 1994, and as high as 67 percent in 2001, smaller majorities were seen from the 1950s into the early 1970s. In 1966, more were against it (47 percent) than for it (42 percent). Moreover, when presented with a choice between the death penalty and life imprisonment "with absolutely no possibility of parole," although majorities still favor the death penalty, the margins are slim. At one point in 2000, 50 percent favored the death penalty, while 47 percent favored life imprisonment instead (Gallup, 2002, pp. 50-52). However, in 2001, the vast majority of Americans supported the death penalty (although no choice was given) for Timothy McVeigh, who at the time had already been sentenced to death for the murder of 168 people in the 1995 bombing attack on a federal office building in Oklahoma City (Gallup, 2002, p. 110).

A poll taken in 2003 found that 64 percent favor "the death penalty for persons convicted of murder" while only 29 percent oppose it. But when asked if they prefer "the death penalty or life in prison with no chance of parole," opinion was split, with 46 percent preferring the death penalty and 47 percent preferring the latter.[37] When the same questions were again asked a few months later, the results were similar: 65 percent favored the death penalty and 25 percent opposed it, but when presented with an alternative, 45 percent preferred life in prison with no chance of parole, while 44 percent preferred the death penalty.[38]

Framing the Issues

One political strategy is to portray, with positive rather than negative stereotypes—but stereotypes nonetheless—the populations we wish to see targeted with supportive rather than punitive policies. The object is to gain sympathy rather than disdain for, say, poor single mothers. This is what some communications consultants, such as FrameWorks Institute, advise "progressive groups" (Mooney, 2003). But such "reframing" misses the mark of the life-affirmation frame of justice as much as negative stereotypes. The mothers are to be helped because they are individual members of our community, not because we like them or don't like them. Politicians have not fostered acceptance of, nor have led from, a coherent and aggressive formulation of the implications of the *principle* of life affirmation. As Gilens (1999, p. 216) concludes, if government fails "to respond in a meaningful way to the growing needs of the poor," as "the history of the American welfare state suggests," then "the blame will lie in a failure of political leadership, not in a lack of concern for the poor among the American people."

It is not so much the micro-reframing through positive imagery that is needed—a strategy that itself plays on sentiment and generalization—but rather, a philosophical reframing. A courageous political and philosophical reframing of issues in American politics would begin with and focus upon the principle of life affirmation by emphasizing that respect and support for the individual has always been the source of our ideals, if not always put into practice. But the emphasis on the individual means that everyone must be valued equally. Support must be directed at individuals, not groups. Policies favoring some individuals over others, and some groups over others, are discriminatory, while the first principle of a just society, as is clear to everyone, and as is embodied in the principle of life affirmation derived from the fundamental value we place on human life, is nondiscrimination. No individual must be favored over another. This indeed means that if government is to provide health care coverage to some individuals, no matter how they might be characterized as different from others, it must provide it to all. If people are to pay taxes, then all are to be taxed in the same manner. Americans can easily relate to this principle of nondiscrimination as a principle of fairness, but they do not abide hypocrisy. But to abandon hypocrisy would mean that discrimination would have to be abolished in all corners of government policy. Politicians emphasizing nondiscrimination must be consistent. They must renounce all forms of affirmative action policies. They must work against the cynical views of government that citizens have formed of it: that industries and businesses can buy special favors and attention from government officials, and that other groups can successfully threaten to withdraw their voting blocs if their special interests are not catered to in policies shaped to favor their interests over those of others. Such politicians must be mindful to appeal to justice rather than to mere group interests.

It must be emphasized, in such reframing, that America is great not only because the individual has been the focus of our ideals, but also that because of those ideals, people are left entirely free to seek what they think they deserve economically—in the marketplace. It is important, contrary to Rawls, to place no limits on what one can gain in the marketplace, so that people may be left free to seek what they think they deserve. But they should not be enabled to seek their imagined desert from government. A system of desert and entitlement is a system of competing interests, not a system of justice. To be sure, some people have been left to achieve fabulous wealth many times that of the average person. We may hold private opinions as to whether they deserve it or not, but that has been irrelevant. People have been free to try to accumulate as much wealth as they can or want. But if government is not to favor one individual over another, it must strive to have nondiscrimination pervade all of its policies and dealings, not desert.

Put another way, everyone is deserving of having their minimal survival needs met, and it is the obligation of the community as a whole, represented by government, to ensure that everyone is fed, sheltered, and clothed. Polls show that the vast majority of Americans are in fact in agreement with this. No one should be left to die. Our policies must ensure this. Above this affirmation of life itself, all other programs must either be aimed at promoting nondiscrimination by ensuring opportunity for everyone (thus it is not difficult to convince the American public that if children from impoverished families must attend inadequate schools, they are being treated in a discriminatory manner), or provide whatever benefits they do in a nondiscriminatory manner. Hence if parks and libraries are to be built with public monies, they must be equally open and accessible to everyone.

Everyone has an obligation to promote and support life. When government is formed, as the representative and instrument of the people, it too incurs that obligation. It is not a contractual obligation, but a moral one. Liberalism took to specifying what rights individuals have, thus by implication opening the door to nonrights. Therefore, for example, we could debate whether people should have economic rights, such as the right to a job, housing, or a decent standard of living. The principle of life affirmation is not about rights, but about the support of all individuals without discrimination. Unless we talk in the sense of universal human rights, the concept of rights becomes co-opted by the concepts of desert and entitlement. The language of "women's rights," "gay rights," "black rights," and so on, is the language of desert and entitlement, necessary for playing the game of group interests that is set up when the desert frame dominates politics, but which can be transcended, with appropriate political leadership and framing, by the concepts of universal human rights, nondiscrimination, and life affirmation.

For example, government engages in discrimination when, on the basis of marital status, it provides benefits, or allows them to be provided, to some individuals but not others equally in need of them. Marriage (which is merely a word that, like all words, is subject to arbitrary definition) is not the issue; the benefits are. In order to address injustice to gays and lesbians, we must unravel or identify the various benefits provided on the basis of marital status. For example, married people are often covered by the health care insurance of their spouses. But if we had a truly universal health care insurance system, every individual would be covered, and discrimination against gays and lesbians in this regard, or against any unmarried individuals, would become a non-issue. There is no question of group rights for gays and lesbians here. On the contrary, justice is promoted by reexamining policies to ensure that they do not respect group membership, such as membership in the ranks of married people. Benefits should be tied to individuals, not groups.

Politics stemming from and promoting the life-affirmation frame of justice would constantly stress that the community exists to benefit everyone. No one has a right to protections and supports that are not accessible to everyone. Such a politics would constantly seek to transcend categorical policies and articulate opposition to them at every opportunity. When debate arises over the extension of Medicare policy to take into account the high costs of drugs to senior citizens, the life-affirmation-frame politician will ask why policy does not address the high costs to all citizens. The selective favoring of some groups of citizens, and their grounds in desert, will be challenged at every turn. Different programs, with different levels of benefits and different eligibility rules, but addressing the same object, such as need, will be challenged as discriminatory. One program, addressing all in need without discrimination, will be advocated.

When desert sets the rules of the game, everyone must become a player for his or her own interests. We have quite an advocacy industry built up in our country, each group being expert at formulating persuasive arguments of desert for its own group, thus pitting the needs and interests of children against elderly people, wealthy against poor against middle class, single against married people, blacks against whites against Hispanics against Asians. Woe to the group that lacks such unique expertise, the power to purchase it, or the power in numbers, or in potential for disruption. The game carries its own internal logic, whose understanding by the public is revealed in the public opinion poll findings, even though those same polls also reveal indications of the life-affirmation frame. The work of life-affirmation politics is to change the game, or the frame, if you will. When the rules are those of nondiscrimination (as Buchanan and Congleton, 1998, advocate), and we have confidence that the rules will be followed and played by, then we need not be desert-conscious in order to defend our own interests. Justice becomes a matter of supporting life rather than resolving disputes between, or reconciling, competing interests, as in Rawls' and other liberal-contractual conceptions. (It will be recalled, yet again, that

Rawls claimed that principles of justice are those that "free and rational persons concerned to further their own interests" would choose in the original position.) Thus justice becomes a matter of principle, not interest, and politicians can appeal to people's sense of justice rather than merely to their interests.

Politicians promoting the life-affirmation frame of justice should say: "Let's stop telling each other stories about what we deserve and others don't. Whether you are young or old, black or white, rich or poor, your income will be taxed at the same rate. Whether you drink or smoke, are male or female, married or unmarried, or engage in one business or another, you will not be favored nor discriminated against, but treated the same as everyone else. Black or white, rich or poor, your children will be provided with the same opportunity for quality education as everyone else."

The very nature of our national community, and whether it is to be a community, is at stake. The very nature of justice, or a just society must be debated. Politicians wishing to promote the life-affirmation frame must be brave enough to confront these issues and lead a national debate. Are we to be concerned with groups, or individuals? Who is deserving of what? What are the myths and realities of "big government"? What principles should guide us? How shall we address homelessness and poverty? Are we all to be out for ourselves? Does this appeal to your sense of justice?

A politics of life affirmation must first point out how myriad social policies aimed at desert actually violate desert for many people through their group orientation. Second, it must expose narrow reasoning wherever it occurs. Third, it must point out the functional desirability of the policy implications of the life-affirmation frame as contrasted with the desert- and group-frame policies.

The Lure of the Half-a-Loaf Strategy

Even for politicians inclined toward the life-affirmation frame of justice, there is an understandable temptation to support partial measures that extend certain benefits to more people than before, but not to all. For example, Senator Edward Kennedy has made admirable efforts over many years to initiate and support policy proposals that would extend health care insurance coverage to greater segments of the population, even though he no doubt favors universal coverage. If universal health plans have not been politically viable, then half a loaf is better than none, even from the perspective of life affirmation, because it supports more human lives, even while it unfortunately continues discrimination among lives. Leading Democratic candidates for the 2004 presidential election proposed patchwork health care insurance policies that would extend coverage to as much as 95 percent of the population, through some combinations of extension of employment-related coverage to employees of small businesses, extension of Medicare coverage through a modest lowering of the age qualification, and extension of Medicaid coverage through raising its means-tested eligibility limits.

But although political expedience in getting anything for anyone may sometimes dictate such strategies, there are dangers in this approach. So long as health care insurance is not truly universal, people will be discriminated against. Government policies will continue to address only certain groups of citizens, such as older people through Medicare. People at high risk for serious illness, perhaps detected through genetic screening, will be discriminated against in employment by employers who wish to avoid high insurance costs. And these same people seeking private insurance on their own will be shunned by companies who want to avoid high risk. Moreover, in promoting such half-a-loaf proposals, politicians implicitly appeal to the desert of constructed groups, even if not intending to do so. The premise that some people are more deserving of health insurance coverage than others continues unchallenged. Finally, the system based on this premise, such as the patchwork combinations noted above, becomes more entrenched than ever, despite its inherent flaw of never being capable of closing all gaps in coverage. In other words, the possibility of a single-payer national governmental health care coverage system becomes even more remote.

Likewise, in regard to homelessness, when some politicians and advocates try to gain housing and other supports for some segments of the homeless population—such as the mentally ill, children, those who have lost their jobs and are looking for work, and those who are paid too little to afford housing—by appealing to sympathy for them, they reinforce the desert frame of justice, the premise that there are other homeless individuals who are not deserving of support, and the belief that the community does not have the obligation to house all of the homeless within it. Advocates against the death penalty, understandably and practically, have initiated and supported recent changes in state laws that abolish the death penalty for children under a certain age, and mentally retarded people. But such measures may serve to "justify" the death penalty for others, even though this would be contrary to the intentions of the advocates.

Hence the dilemma from the perspective of the life-affirmation frame pits the immorality of not promoting life when the possibilities to do so are in reach, against complicity in schemes that serve to continue discrimination between the supposed deserving and undeserving, and to deny the universality of the sanctity of human life. The only way out is to resolve to use the opportunity to support limited measures as a platform for espousing the life-frame perspective. Even in the midst of supporting the limited proposal, the advocate or politician would freely admit that he or she does so in the awareness that it appeals to the desert perceptions of large segments of the public, with which he or she does not agree, and would admonish that justice will not be served until policies are achieved that support human life within the community absolutely, and without exception.

Narrow Reasoning

We must combat scientism in public policy, which often rationalizes discrimination. The temptation is great and the reasoning seemingly compelling, but it is reasoning of the narrow sort, stemming from sentiment, however good it might look when wrapped in scientific dressing. For example, in a tour de force of "scientific" extrapolation, the Centers for Disease Control and Prevention recently concluded that each pack of cigarettes sold in the United States costs the nation seven dollars, with about half of that amount due to smoking-related medical costs, and the other half due to lost job productivity caused by premature death from smoking (Associated Press, 2002). The Centers' Dr. Terry Pechacek was quoted as saying: "There's a big difference in the cost to society and what society is getting back in tax. We believe that society is bearing a burden for the individual behavioral choices of the smokers."

The logical conclusion, compellingly left for the politicians to infer, is that at least seven dollars in taxes should be placed on the sale of every pack of cigarettes. But although Dr. Pechacek refers to individual choices, the statistics derived from the studies are generalizations applicable to groups (in this case, smokers), not individuals. Since African Americans (and poor people) die, statistically speaking, younger than other Americans, why not tax them for lost productivity? After all, one of the causes of this statistic might be the greater frequency of cigarette smoking among African Americans, not to mention the "individual choices" of many of them to live in dangerous ghettos.

For every social phenomenon, there is multiple causation and multiple responsibility. Even if we were to link smoking to the ascribed negative fiscal impacts on society on an individual basis, the issue of narrow reasoning remains: Why select smokers for discriminatory taxation, and not tax people who overeat themselves into obesity, or choose to participate in dangerous sports or occupations, or on and on? After all, the results might be even more impressive than the decline in lung cancer rates in California claimed to be due to a voter-approved measure in 1988 that added a 25-cent-per-pack tax on tobacco products, which was used to pay for anti-smoking and education programs (and to laws restricting smoking in public buildings and workplaces) (Coleman, 2000). I do not object to public health educational campaigns (or to laws restricting smoking in public places), but why not target, in addition, all equivalent health and safety hazards? And if the professed benefit is a societal one (in terms of reduced costs to society), then why not have the community pay for it as a whole, from its common treasury, contributed to, in turn, through the taxes paid by everyone?

In all of this, discriminatory process is involved. In February 2001, surgeons in Melbourne, Australia allegedly refused to provide heart and lung transplants, and coronary-bypass and lung-reduction surgery, to smokers. Why should taxpayers pay for it, one surgeon asked. But the Australian Medical Association objected that it was unconscionable for a surgeon to take a moral stand on treating a patient, and "ethicists said it was discriminatory because lifestyle could be blamed for many illnesses, including obesity and certain types of cancer" (Jauhar, 2003).

Indeed, during the recent wave of selective taxation proposals to make up for state budgetary shortfalls throughout the country, in addition to "sin" taxes targeting cigarettes, beer, and gambling, one innovative New York State legislator proposed the taxing of junk food, video games, and television commercials—which he blames for New York's growing obesity problem—to pay for an obesity prevention program (Associated Press, 2003). The identification of "risk factors," when used for the purpose of individual and group blame, accusation, and discriminatory tax policy is an endless game based on sentiment, simplistic statistical generalizations and correlations, the concepts of group "justice" and desert, and a form of narrow reasoning that, in the name of "fairness," seeks to shift the burdens of community from "us" to "them."

Functional Desirability

As I noted in chapter 1, justice frequently serves practical purposes, and new circumstances sometimes promote the feasibility of new expressions of the sense of justice without the cost that previously would have been entailed. To couch this functional-desirability hypothesis in stronger terms, it can be said that the policy expressions of one frame of justice will most readily win acceptance when circumstances arise that render the policy expressions of the other frames more costly, and less advantageous than previously perceived. Shifts in policy frames are facilitated by the declining necessity, profitability, or desirability of previous arrangements, and the increased feasibility of new ones.

Everyone living in the United States is on welfare of one form of another—usually several forms—in that they receive benefits from government that must be paid for by the community as a whole. In December 2002, nearly 51 million people, or almost 18 percent of the total U.S. population, were receiving OASDI and/or SSI benefits (Social Security Administration, 2003). More than half of all households in America contain at least one member receiving such benefits, and/or veterans' pensions and unemployment insurance (Longman, 1996, p. 3). Millions of other individuals and their households receive benefits from the TANF and Food Stamp programs. But, aside from such direct-benefit programs, far greater numbers of individuals and households receive indirect benefits through so-called tax expenditures, "expressly designed to subsidize some favored group such as homeowners, farmers, or senior citizens" (Longman, 1996, p. 3). At least one tax expenditure program, the Earned Income Tax Credit, is means-tested, up to a point (the point being that if you have no earned income, you get nothing), but most are not, and even favor the wealthy. One of the largest of these is the tax deduction granted to homeowners on their mortgage interest payments. Such tax breaks constitute welfare benefits in that they must be paid for or compensated for by the community as a whole. When some segments of the community are exempted from paying certain taxes into the national communal treasury, then other segments of the community must compensate for these shortfalls in terms of greater taxation for them. In the case of the homeowners' tax exemptions, the burden shifts most obviously to renters, many of whom cannot afford to buy houses.

There are many other benefits, as I have already noted, such as roads, bridges, and water and sewer systems, and the democratic structures of government, that we receive from the community. In that they too must be paid for by the community as a whole, they constitute another way in which we are all on welfare. The question is not whether individuals should receive benefits from government—the rationale for having a community is to benefit the people within it—but whether the benefits are being paid for and distributed in a fair and just manner.

The homeowner's tax break can be rationalized on the basis of a vaguely-defined social engineering merit entailed in providing incentives for people to own their own homes, but from the perspective of justice, the distinction drawn, in effect, between the treatment of homeowners as opposed to renters, seems arbitrary and unjust. Moreover, the sum total of the direct-benefit and tax expenditure programs mentioned above overwhelmingly favors economically advantaged groups, and pays relatively little to address poverty and economic need (Abramovitz, 2001). Up until now, this state of affairs has been supported by our willingness to accept and participate in the politics of group interest and desert to the detriment of justice, at least as reflected in the life-affirmation frame that directs us to support human life without discrimination, and thus to ensure that at the very least, the basic survival needs of all members of the community are ensured before all else. In fact, although I have claimed that we are all on welfare, there are currently tens if not hundreds of thousands of the homeless people among us who are literally living in the streets while being denied even the benefit of congregate shelter.

The politics of group interest and desert, however, eventually reaches a point of impending crisis. Tax expenditure programs grow in number and expense. The costs of Social Security keep rising as the over-sixty-five population as a percentage of the entire population grows rapidly. Federal income tax cuts, as those enacted in 2003, favor the wealthy. Proposals such as California's Proposition 13, approved in 1979, freeze current homeowners' property taxes at low levels while taxing new homeowners at increasing rates. In 2003, that state along with many others faced huge budgetary shortfalls. Even Republican governors, as in Nevada and Alabama, saw it as their obligation to press for new and increased taxes. True, as reflected in comments by Nevadans cited earlier in this chapter, much resentment is expressed by some who, while wishing to continue to collect their own benefits from government, angrily wonder why they should have to share in the costs of benefits to other segments of the population, such as the education of children. And true, many of the taxes eventually enacted in Nevada targeted politically weak minorities, such as smokers, in a discriminatory manner, continuing the politics of group interest and desert (although the revenues raised by such taxes will prove to be insufficient in the long run). However, as also seen earlier, polls indicate that large majorities of the American public want the poor to be helped and the homeless to be sheltered, and want the federal government to ensure that all Americans receive health care insurance coverage. They also want to maintain or raise spending on domestic social programs, such as education. Moreover, perhaps up to half or more are not fundamentally opposed to the idea that government should provide everyone with a guaranteed basic income.

Where there is a will, there is a way, as the saying goes. But caution should be raised here about interpreting evidence of the public's will too strongly. Public survey methodologies are seriously and deeply flawed. For example, nonresponse rates (such as people hanging up the phone on interviewers) are extremely high, and therefore introduce potential bias into the results, and, as already noted, results are extremely sensitive to the exact wording of questions. Thus I wish to interpret the findings quite conservatively, by saying that there is no evidence that majorities of the American public are *against* helping the poor and sheltering the homeless, and so on. Yet there is little evidence of political leaders' will to lead in the directions indicated by the polls. However, there are indications of small and isolated awakenings. In 2003, Governor Bob Riley of Alabama called the current tax system in his state "immoral" (Potter, 2003). (Recall that in this same year, one poll indicated that 63 percent of the American public viewed the proposition that the "government should guarantee health insurance for all citizens, even if it means repealing most of the tax cuts passed under President Bush" as a "moral" as well as a "political" issue.) Indeed, the wealthiest 1 percent of Alabama taxpayers pay only 3.8 percent of their incomes in state and local taxes, while the poorest 40 percent pay more than 10 percent (Potter, 2003). Although Governor Riley's plan for changing the entire tax system—which included a $1.2 billion increase in total tax revenue—met with stiff resistance, and was overwhelmingly defeated by Alabama voters in a September 2003 referendum, perhaps his efforts should be viewed as part of the educational functions of leadership, and of a long-term process.

Eventually, it can be conjectured, the necessity caused by continuing and deepening budgetary crisis acting as the primary stimulus, combined with lesser but important roles of political leadership and persuasive and educational appeals to people's sense of justice, can contribute to a rethinking of public policies consistent with the life-affirmation frame of justice. Prodded by budgetary, and therefore community, crisis, people begin to think about whether taxes are being paid in a manner fair to all, and whether benefits are being distributed fairly. They are forced to reevaluate the meanings of community and justice. They already favor, in belief, fairness in contributing to and benefiting from the community, justice and moral collective behavior in the sense of affirming human life for all and not wishing to see anyone die for lack of care, and reasonable opportunity for all. But if changes to current policies are compelled by economic necessity, then what changes should be made that will be fair and just in their minds?

The universal social dividend and taxation system proposed in chapter 5 may then become more attractive and politically viable. Everyone's income would be taxed at the same rate. There would be no tax breaks that, through narrow reasoning or no reasoning at all, favor arbitrarily constructed groups and the wealthy. Dire need, potential dire need, and even lesser levels of need, would be addressed far more adequately than with the current patchwork and unfair network of programs in which some means-tested programs pay higher benefits than others, and many people in dire need get no benefits at all. The same universal social dividend would be allocated to all (adjusted only for household size). A large part of government bureaucracy, previously necessary for determining eligibility (ostensibly, desert) for a variety of programs such as OASDI, SSI, and TANF, would be eliminated, hence saving the huge administrative costs needed to operate the current judgmental processes of government, which are based on highly contestable claims concerning why members of certain groups of needy or even nonneedy people are supposedly more deserving of such benefits than other individuals.

It is growing necessity that drives current debates about our health care system, too. This issue, however, is a prime example of a social policy area in which policy has been inconsistent with, or even contrary to, existing evidence of the public will for quite a while. Polls, if they are to be taken at face value, have shown that large majorities of Americans believe that increasing the number of Americans covered by health insurance is a very important goal, and even that health insurance should be guaranteed for all citizens. Some incremental policy approaches have been attempted in recent years, such as the State Children's Health Insurance Plan, but they have failed to make much change in the number of uninsured Americans, which had remained at roughly 41 million for more than a decade (Bindman and Haggstrom, 2003). In fact, the number of uninsured shot up to 43.6 million in 2002 (Pear, 2003). (Yet in 2003, leading Democratic presidential candidates, as well as the Republican Bush administration, continued to propose incremental change.) Moreover, Bindman and Haggstrom (2003) suggest that there is the risk that incremental approaches, such as extending Medicare availability to the category of adults aged fifty-five to sixty-four, "could ultimately make it more difficult for all uninsured persons to receive health insurance," in that the "political arguments used to expand insurance coverage to the uninsured who are regarded as deserving might be used as a justification for not addressing the needs of those uninsured who are deemed less deserving."

To be sure, there are additional reasons for reorganizational rather than incremental change. Our current patchwork system of public and private insurers inflates bureaucracy, paperwork, and costs, while creating frustration and confusion for both physicians and patients. The Physicians' Working Group for Single-Payer National Health Insurance (2003) has pointed out that private health insurers and health maintenance organizations consume 12 percent of premiums for overhead, almost four times the proportion needed for overhead costs in the Medicare program and in the Canadian national health insurance program. (The group notes that Blue Cross in Massachusetts employs more people to cover 2.5 million citizens than Canada does to cover 27 million citizens.) Further, because of a multiplicity of insurers, American hospitals are forced to spend more than twice as much as Canadian hospitals on billing and administration. Physicians in private practice must spend excessive time and money on the same. This system converts health care into a business, subject to the demands of profit rather than medical need, necessitating the enlistment of satellite consulting firms and marketing companies that consume and divert additional portions of the health care dollar, leaving less of it to pay for actual health care.

Under the current system, uninsured persons still receive treatment, but at later points of illness and greater expense to everyone. The Physicians' Working Group (2003) has proposed a single-payer national health insurance program that would essentially constitute an extension and modification of Medicare to cover all citizens for all necessary medical care. The group claims that such a system would generate enough savings in administrative expenses (as indicated by several separate analyses by independent investigators and government agencies; the group estimates that these savings would amount to $200 billion dollars per year) to expand health care insurance to everyone while not increasing total health care costs, and that covering the uninsured would save thousands of lives annually. Single-source payment through public insurance administration, the group argues, is the key to both equal access and cost control.

Complexity in policy leads to unfairness in policy, as well as greater expense. A single-payer federally funded truly universal health care insurance program would be consistent with the life-affirmation frame of justice, would entail smaller bureaucracy and simpler policy, and would address medical need without judgment of desert. Strong political leadership, if the will were there, has the opportunity and factual ammunition to overcome resistance to single-payer plans through education and persuasion.

Of course, the universal social dividend and taxation system, combined with a single-payer federal health insurance program, would entail a drastic revision of funding mechanisms. Rescindment of homeowners' tax breaks on the interest they pay on their mortgage loans, for example, would be offset, in part, by lower property taxes (no longer to be used for school funding), the universal social dividend, and saving (due to an extremely simplified tax form) of the few hundred dollars many people pay each year to tax accountants. Separate payroll taxes for Social Security and Medicare would be eliminated, as would insurance premiums and out-of-pocket expenses for necessary medical care, but the amount that many pay in income taxes would be increased. It is difficult to predict, under such a dramatic reorganization, who would get to hold on to a little more of their income and who a little less, but people must be convinced that what they will definitely gain are far simpler, fairer, and less bureaucratic taxation and distribution and health care systems that will benefit everyone in a nondiscriminatory manner, and thereby engender the benefits of justice in the form of a more tranquil society.

Fiscal necessity may be currently on the verge of driving policy reform in other areas as well, which in turn, may actually reduce the costs to the community as a whole. The total prison (federal and state) and jail population on a single day in the United States reached a record high of over 2 million prisoners in 2002, for a rate of 701 prisoners per 100,000 U.S. residents at the end of that year (Harrison and Beck, 2003). This rate is higher than that of all other nations, even surpassing that of Russia, the former world leader in this regard, and higher than that of South Africa. It is more than seven times the rate of Italy, Netherlands, Germany, or France, and more than thirteen times the rate of Japan (The Sentencing Project, 2003a).

With most states facing severe budgetary crises, and with the current annual cost of maintaining a person in prison at approximately $20,000 per year and the cost of construction about $100,000 per prison cell, government officials are being forced to reconsider imprisonment policies (The Sentencing Project, 2003b). Reform of harsh drug offender imprisonment policies in some states in 2001 and 2002 may have already led to the recent modest decline in the number of drug offenders in state prisons, most of whom have no history of violence (The Sentencing Project, 2003b). Yet drug offenders constituted 24 percent of the combined federal and state prison population in 2001 (Harrison and Beck, 2003).

Thus, on the punitive side of desert, no more accurately targeted than the "reward" side, our "war on drugs" has contributed to the largest prison population in the world. The sale, possession, and use of certain drugs, arbitrarily selected for prohibition from among a wider array of drugs, involve no violation of others in itself, and involve no "crime" except its arbitrary designation as such. However, drug prohibition laws have inflated the costs of drugs to users, thereby contributing to increased rates of crime to obtain the money to buy drugs, and have also contributed to a violent underground economy in which drug-dealing gangs battle over turf. Thereby, drug prohibition laws have contributed significantly not only to the drug-offender segment of the prison population, but also to its property-offender and violent-offender segments. The costs and ineffectiveness of the "war on drugs" and drug prohibition laws must be aggressively pointed out to the American public, along with their discriminatory nature. Noncoercive approaches to reducing harm directly caused by drugs, as well as sentencing alternatives to incarceration for crimes not involving violence or the threat of violence, must be more seriously considered.

The rising costs and failure of the present orientation of the public child welfare system, too, with a national foster care population that has reached an all-time high of well over a half million children, may also finally force reconsideration. With its insistence on punishing impoverished parents in the name of child protection, by forcibly removing their children and placing them in foster care, children are being no better "protected" today than when the foster care population was far smaller. The arbitrary and discriminatory nature of the child welfare system's current interventions should be publicly questioned, and noncoercive systemic approaches seriously considered (Pelton, 1999a, pp. 65-94). Both our prison and foster care systems have become major gateways to homelessness, unemployment, crime, and the return to poverty.

The fiscal as well as moral bankruptcy of such punitive policies present the opportunity for successful persuasive and educational leadership in the direction of life-supportive approaches to such problems as drugs and child endangerment, rather than coercive ones.

Shifting Frames

The "big government" we have is due, in large part, to the costly, labor-intensive, and ineffective policies of both inappropriate punitive desert and inappropriate group-specific beneficial desert. Both violate any just notions of desert by arbitrarily punishing and rewarding select groups of people, while sustaining large bureaucracies. Politicians must foster open debate in regard to these costly travesties of justice, and be prepared and willing to offer alternatives.

Many people will still balk at government treating all human life equally, without judgment. They will still resent the prospect that some homeless people who don't want to work would be housed, or receive a government benefit, without conditions attached. They will still cling to the conviction that poor single mothers are not deserving of government benefits without time limits, and that older or retired people deserve greater benefits than other people, in the form of government pensions and special health care arrangements, such as Medicare. They will still insist that they deserve to be benefited by government while others do not. While these beliefs should be challenged in open public debate in a manner that they have never been before, the costs of their beliefs should also be exposed. These costs include unnecessarily large and expensive government bureaucracies, inefficient and unnecessarily cumbersome health care systems, and a costly yet ineffective "war on drugs." In human terms, they include a prison system bloated with inmates who have committed non-violent drug offenses, people living in the streets in conditions worse than those in prison, and sometimes dying there. They even include many people whom these people would consider as the deserving poor falling through the cracks of our social policies that fail to distinguish between the "deserving" and "undeserving" even though they are ostensibly designed to do so.

The shift to a greater leaning on the life-affirmation frame cannot be piecemeal, but must be presented as an entire overhaul of social policy, and on broader philosophical grounds. The idea that government should be in the desert business must be assailed. People who have sought in the marketplace, through their ingenuity, talents, and acquired education and skills, to obtain all that they think they deserve, would be taxed proportionately to the benefits they have obtained in these efforts from the assistance of the community as a whole, merely by dint of being situated within the community. The taxes would be used to support human life without discrimination, and so everyone would be assured of an ongoing social safety net that would ensure that no one goes without health care, or minimal provision of food, shelter, and clothing. Beyond that, the taxes would be used to support programs that enable all individuals, including those that are disabled in some manner, reside in impoverished neighborhoods, have childcare responsibilities, etc., to gain the education and skills they are capable of achieving, in order to pursue whatever level of wealth they wish, or believe they are deserving of, in the marketplace. In other words, the taxes would be used to support nondiscrimination in the sense often referred to as "equal opportunity."

Government would also be responsible for enforcing nondiscrimination *within* the marketplace. Even beyond this, policies, programs, and measures intended to even more greatly enhance human life through enhancing the community as a whole, but without discrimination to any person, and not catering to mere preferences of some, would be instituted to the extent that the community as a whole consents and allows. Such would include the care and expansion of parks and playgrounds, arts programs, and public libraries. Protection and conservation of the environment, of course, to the extent that failure to do so would be harmful to individuals currently living as well as to future generations, would be high up on this list of priorities. The politics of life affirmation would advocate a revamping of priorities toward the most life-supporting measures. The housing of everyone must take precedence over the expansion of school athletic and music programs. Health care for everyone must take precedence over the building of parks and monuments.

The entire concept that is expressed here—taken as a whole and not piecemeal—can, I think, be regarded as potentially viable within the political realm, and certainly not dead on arrival. The mixture of results of public opinion polls does not rule out its viability. But the key is reconceptualizing, or reframing, if you will, a vision of the purpose of community and government. This vision is one that makes appeal to people's sense of justice as being grounded in reverence for life, at the same time that it strives to reorient their notions of desert as a viable pursuit of government. The concept would be advocated as one that is fairer to everyone than present arrangements, fairer to all current generations, and fairer to future generations.

The political strategy proposed here would constantly stress the moral worth of each and every human life. We wish to establish the position that the goal of social policies and programs is not to selectively punish or reward individuals for past behavior or supposed differential worth, but to enable everyone, by addressing unmet survival needs and removing barriers to life-functioning (such as those posed by disabilities or racial discrimination), to fulfill their life potential, and to become all they are capable of being.

Notes

1. Quinnipiac University Poll, February 26-March 3, 2003.
2. Poll conducted by the Gallup Organization, June 12-18, 2003. Data provided by the Roper Center for Public Opinion Research, University of Connecticut.
3. Poll conducted for the Pew Research Center by Princeton Survey Research Associates, April 30-May 4, 2003.
4. Poll conducted by the Associated Press, February 28-March 4, 2003. Data provided
5. *Time*/CNN/Harris Interactive poll, February 19-20, 2003. Data provided by the Roper Center for Public Opinion Research, University of Connecticut.
6. *Time*/CNN/Harris Interactive poll, January 15-16, 2003. Data provided by the Roper Center for Public Opinion Research, University of Connecticut.
7. Survey conducted for the *Washington Post* and Henry J. Kaiser Family Foundation, by Princeton Survey Research Associates, August 2-September 1, 2002. Data provided by the Roper Center for Public Opinion Research, University of Connecticut.
8. Survey conducted for CNN and *USA Today*, by the Gallup Organization, August 3-5, 2001. Data provided by the Roper Center for Public Opinion Research, University of Connecticut.
9. General Social Surveys, 1972-1996: Cumulative Codebook, November 1996. National Opinion Research Center, University of Chicago. Data distributed by the Roper Center for Public Opinion Research, University of Connecticut. Q391A.
10. Survey conducted by the Associated Press, January 24-28, 1997. Data provided by the Roper Center for Public Opinion Research, University of Connecticut.
11. General Social Surveys, 1972-1996: Cumulative Codebook, November 1996. National Opinion Research Center, University of Chicago. Data distributed by the Roper Center for Public Opinion Research, University of Connecticut. Q723G.
12. Survey conducted by National Opinion Research Center, University of Chicago, February 1992. Data provided by the Roper Center for Public Opinion Research, University of Connecticut.
13. Survey conducted by Times Mirror/Princeton Survey Research Associates, May 1-31, 1990. Data provided by the Roper Center for Public Opinion Research, University of Connecticut.
14. General Social Surveys, 1972-1996: Cumulative Codebook, November 1996. National Opinion Research Center, University of Chicago. Data distributed by the Roper Center for Public Opinion Research, University of Connecticut. Q688I.

166   Frames of Justice

15. Poll conducted by the *Washington Post*, April 27-May 1, 1990. Data provided by the Roper Center for Public Opinion Research, University of Connecticut.
16. Poll conducted by the *Washington Post*, January 12-16, 1990. Data provided by the Roper Center for Public Opinion Research, University of Connecticut.
17. Poll conducted by the Associated Press, December 5-7, 1990. Data provided by the Roper Center for Public Opinion Research, University of Connecticut.
18. Poll conducted by CBS News, March 17-19, 1991. Data provided by the Roper Center for Public Opinion Research, University of Connecticut.
19. *Money Magazine* survey conducted by Willard & Shullman, October 22-30, 1991. Based on a national sample of "household financial decision makers." Data provided by the Roper Center for Public Opinion Research, University of Connecticut.
20. Poll conducted by CBS News/*New York Times*, January 22-25, 1992. Data provided by the Roper Center for Public Opinion Research, University of Connecticut.
21. Surveys conducted for the Pew Research Center for the People and the Press, by Princeton Survey Research Associates, December 1994, and May 15-18, 1997.
22. Survey conducted for Knight-Ridder by Princeton Survey Research Associates, January 5-15, 1996. Data provided by the Roper Center for Public Opinion Research, University of Connecticut.
23. Poll conducted by Louis Harris & Associates, April 25-29, 1996. Data provided by the Roper Center for Public Opinion Research, University of Connecticut.
24. Survey conducted by Public Agenda, for the National Constitution Center, July 10-24, 2002.
25. Poll conducted by the *New York Times*, March 8-11, 1994. Data provided by the Roper Center for Public Opinion Research, University of Connecticut.
26. Poll conducted by Louis Harris & Associates, May 23-26, 1994. Data provided by the Roper Center for Public Opinion Research, University of Connecticut.
27. Survey for *Time* and CNN conducted by Yankelovich Partners, June 15-16, 1994. Data provided by the Roper Center for Public Opinion Research, University of Connecticut.
28. Survey conducted for the Henry J. Kaiser Family Foundation and the Harvard Law School by Princeton Survey Research Associates, April 3-6, 2003. Data provided by the Roper Center for Public Opinion Research, University of Connecticut.
29. Survey conducted for the Henry J. Kaiser Family Foundation and the Harvard Law School by Princeton Survey Research Associates, June 5-8, 2003. Data provided by the Roper Center for Public Opinion Research, University of Connecticut.
30. *Washington Post*—ABC News poll conducted October 9-13, 2003.
31. Survey conducted for the Henry J. Kaiser Family Foundation and the Harvard School of Public Health, by ICR-International Communications Research, February 26-March 2, 2003.
32. *Washington Post*—ABC News poll conducted October 9-13, 2003.
33. Survey conducted for *Time* and CNN by Yankelovich Partners, July 13-14, 1994. Data provided by the Roper Center for Public Opinion Research, University of Connecticut.
34. Survey conducted for the Pew Research Center for the People and the Press, by Princeton Survey Research Associates, June 24-July 8, 2003.
35. Survey conducted by CBS News, September 14-18, 1999. Data provided by the Roper Center for Public Opinion Research, University of Connecticut.
36. See survey by the Gallup Organization, May 19-21, 2003; survey conducted for CNN and *USA Today* by the Gallup Organization, May 30-June 1, 2003; survey conducted by ABC News/*Washington Post*, January 30-February 1, 2003; survey conducted for National Public Radio, Henry J. Kaiser Family Foundation, and the

Kennedy School of Government, Harvard University, by ICR-International Communications Research, February 5-March 17, 2003 (for the foregoing surveys, data provided by the Roper Center for Public Opinion Research, University of Connecticut); Quinnipiac University Poll, April 10-14, 2003; and poll conducted by the Stony Brook University Center for Survey Research, May 1-20, 2003.

37. Quinnipiac University Poll, February 26-March 3, 2003.
38. Quinnipiac University Poll, June 4-9, 2003.

8

Faith and Reason

War, mass slaughter, and genocide have afflicted humankind throughout history, culminating with the tens of millions killed in the twentieth century alone. That this is a matter of concern to us must be because we hold a common belief in the value of human life. Yet it can be said that neither religion nor reason has hindered the advances of mass slaughter at best, and that they have facilitated them at worst. But both faith (religious or otherwise) and reason proceed from perceptual and cognitive constructs. The individual constructs his or her world and is, as Merleau-Ponty (1962) claimed, a meaning-giving existence. Our constructs, including values, principles, beliefs, stereotypes, and theories, are part and parcel of the human thought processes that allow us to grasp the world around us, relate aspects of it to each other and to ourselves, and to subjectively organize it.

This book began with an inquiry into the frames of justice reflected in the Bible. They, too, are cognitive constructs, common to the human mind, reflected, not surprisingly, in the Koran as well. It is from such constructs that we reason, for the purpose of adapting to and ordering our world, controlling it insofar as possible, understanding it and imbuing it with meaning, solving problems both personal and social, making policies to live by, and coming to terms with our existence. In the matter of frames of justice and their policy implications—even policies of genocide—we must examine the roles of faith and reason. Lastly, we must examine the ways in which the sanctity of human life may be upheld.

Faith in God

It is easy to understand the belief in God, as a prime mover, since we cannot imagine how something could have been created out of nothing. The belief is even reasonable, given the nature and capacity of our reasoning abilities, since our experience in the temporal dimension is that everything has a beginning as well as an end. We are stumped not only in regard to the creation of something from nothing but, despite Darwin's theory of evolution, in regard to a universe containing life, and such high-order complexity as displayed in the functional capacity of human beings. Of course, God as creator of the universe does not solve the problem as presented to reason, because, given the nature of our reason, it compels us to ask how God was created. Yet that infinitely regressive puzzle is what spurs us to refer to the prime mover as God in the first place. And although reasonable as a conjecture, we have no evidence to support it (the conjecture of God) other than our perception of ourselves and the universe around us, which is the same evidence, then, that we have circularly reasoned from in the first place. Hence, although reason is involved, the belief is ultimately based on faith. God is a mystery personified.

But the veracity of our beliefs (unless they come into conflict with the physical world) matters less to how we will relate to the world and each other than the beliefs themselves. The belief in God as caring about, and as a caregiver of, life in the universe, and particularly human life; as concerned with the fate and moral conduct of human beings; as concerned with justice among human beings and their doing of justice; and further, as intervener to do justice—this, although the professed belief of most of humanity, has no grounds of reason to recommend it, as well as no evidence to support it. Of course, that is why we call it faith, and say that it is based on faith and not reason.

God, Desert, and the Hereafter

Yet we assume that if God *does* care about us, then He will ensure that we get what we deserve. Wherefrom does such a belief arise? And what is it that we deserve, or what makes us deserving? We observe that our fragile lives, which we wish to preserve and enhance, are subject to the whims of nature and other human beings. We observe, too, that our actions have consequences, that there is cause and effect not only in the natural world, but with us as causative agents. Yet we are often not powerful enough to protect ourselves from the seemingly random occurrence of natural dangers, such as floods, or the more deliberate efforts of invading armies even if we band together, not to mention the occurrence of individual misfortune at the hands of nature or others. Reasoning from our observations that we are causative agents, yet not powerful enough to protect ourselves from all of the potential dangers that beset us, we hope that we can cause or influence a higher power, perhaps the prime mover Himself, to intervene as an intermediary on our behalf.

We have here a problem to solve. What will cause the desired effect? What do we think would favor God toward us? We can praise God, worship Him, sacrifice to Him, pledge complete obedience to Him, and plead our case to Him. But what case is there to plead, and what does God want? We claim our innocence, our "good" deeds to others, and repentance for past "bad" deeds, while we promise to do "good" deeds to others in the future. How we come to surmise what is good and bad in God's eyes is a mystery in itself, but we seem to believe that it has something to do with justice, and we project our own sense of justice onto God. It must have something to do with what we would want others to do, or not do, to us, and thus stems from egoism, as does this entire problem-solving project.

Although all of this is a manifestation of our recognition of the limits of our own power, it is nonetheless also an attempt to control our world and our own fates. We are reminded of the famous cartoon illustrating two rats in a Skinner box in a psychology laboratory. One turns to the other and says: "Boy, I sure have this guy conditioned. Every time I press the lever, he delivers a food pellet." Even ritualistic behavior becomes reinforced when we observe that no ill befalls us each day after we perform it.

If people get what they deserve, then there must be certain ways in which I can conduct myself that will allow me to control my future, or at least protect it from negative outcomes. Ritualistic behavior, prayer, obedience to God, and belief in an intervening God have the same origins, and that is why they are embedded in religions as much as is the concept of justice as desert. But what are we to do when confronted with the evidence from our experience and knowledge that there are times, at least, when one does not get what he or she deserves, and that not everyone gets what he or she deserves, and not merely in trivial ways? Even in Ecclesiastes it is acknowledged that "sometimes a good man perishes in spite of his goodness, and sometimes a wicked one endures in spite of his wickedness" (7:15). Surely, many people, in an apparently random and undeserving manner, are struck with fatal illness, or become subject to being in the wrong place at the wrong time, and become arbitrary victims of violence and natural disasters.

Starting with their assumption of a just world regulated by God, in which people get what they deserve and deserve what they get, Job's onlookers reasoned that Job must have deserved his misfortunes. They had no evidence for this, but they believed so strongly in their assumption that they could not reason or conclude otherwise. This belief could not be shaken even by Job's presentation of evidence to the contrary.

These beliefs may seem innocuous enough, yet there is a downside. As Rabbi Harold Kushner suggested in his book, *When Bad Things Happen to Good People* (1981), the belief in an *all-powerful* just God tempts us to blame the victim. "Blaming the victim is a way of reassuring ourselves...that there are good reasons for people's suffering. It helps fortunate people believe that their good fortune is deserved, rather than being a matter of luck. It makes everyone feel better—except the victim..." (p. 39). Blaming the victim, we might add, tempts and encourages us to stand by rather than intervene while the victim suffers, and helps us to rationalize our decision to do nothing.

Kushner's solution, in terms of maintaining his own faith in a just God, is to reject the belief that God is all-powerful. He is not *able* to intervene in a manner that would ensure justice (or, as Kushner conjectures later in his book, "God has set Himself the limit that He will not intervene to take away our freedom" [p.

81], hence leaving human beings with free will, even to harm each other). Kushner concludes: "If God is a God of justice but not of power, then He can still be on our side when bad things happen to us.... Our misfortunes are none of His doing, and so we can turn to Him for help.... We will turn to God, not to be judged or forgiven, not to be rewarded or punished, but to be strengthened and comforted" (p. 44). But we are left with a God that cannot intervene to prevent injustice, nor even to correct, compensate for, or counter injustice once it has occurred. He can only help us, it seems, by "strengthening and comforting" us. This is of little value, however, to murdered victims of injustice. And this limited intervention, if we can call it that, would seem to depend upon our belief and faith in God, rather than on God Himself.

The concept of justice as desert requires human enforcers of desert, at least insofar as humans can control desert, and requires the intervention of God, if not evident in this world, then in the next. Thus we may be driven to a belief in a hereafter, in a heaven and a hell, in which people will finally get what they deserve, with those who conduct themselves appropriately even acquiring everlasting life, surely as a matter of desert. Of course, there is no evidence for this either, and that is why we call such beliefs a matter of faith, and not reason and evidence, in the first place. Yet recent surveys have found that not only do 92 percent of American adults believe in God,[1] but as many as 74 percent believe in life after death,[2] 76 percent or more in a heaven,[3] and 74 percent in hell.[4]

In the Book of Daniel (12:2), it is written: "Many of those that sleep in the dust of the earth will awake, some to eternal life, others to reproaches, to everlasting abhorrence." There is hardly any other unambiguous reference to a hereafter in the Jewish Bible (the Tanakh), particularly one in which judgment is envisioned to be executed in terms of reward and punishment. But such references are plentiful in the New Testament, and in the Koran which, according to the Muslim religion, was revealed to Muhammad, a messenger of God sent forth to confirm previous scriptures revealed to the Jews and Christians through previous messengers, including Abraham, Moses, and Jesus (Dawood, 1999, p. 2).

John the Baptist preached that people should repent, "for the kingdom of heaven is at hand" (Matthew 3:2), and Jesus frequently refers to this kingdom. Jesus says of the persecuted, "great is your reward in heaven" (Matthew 5:12). He speaks of certain people as being "in danger of hell fire" (5:22), as being "cast into hell" (5:29), and as not being forgiven "in the world to come" (12:32). He says that at the end of the world, the angels shall "sever the wicked from among the just, And shall cast them into the furnace of fire..." (13:49-50). But those who follow Jesus "shall inherit everlasting life" (19:29). Jesus says that "the hour is coming" in which "all that are in the graves...shall come forth; they that have done good, unto the resurrection of life; and they that have done evil, unto the resurrection of damnation" (John 5:28-29). In the exceedingly strange Book of Revelation, there is much commotion, destruction, bizarre imagery, and what appears to be group justice. ("Thus with violence shall that great city Babylon be thrown down, and shall be found no more at all" [18:21]) in the time of God's judgment.) But in Revelation it is also written, "I saw the dead, small and great, stand before God...and the dead were judged...according to their works" (20:12), and "whosoever was not found written in the book of life was cast into the lake of fire" (20:15).

The desert frame is emphasized throughout the Koran, but particularly in regard to a hereafter: Those that commit evil "shall be the inmates of the Fire" and will abide there forever, while "those that have faith and do good works are the heirs of Paradise; there shall they abide forever" (Koran, as translated by Dawood, 1999; Surah 2:81-82).[5] It is said: "The life of this world is but a sport and a diversion. Surely better is the life to come for those that fear God" (Surah 6:32). And: "Good is the reward of those that do good works in this present life: but far better is the abode of the life to come" (Surah 16:30).

As Rabbi Kushner said, by believing that God is a righteous judge who gives people exactly what they deserve, "we keep the world orderly and understandable" (1981, p. 9). Yet, as he observed, this belief does not fit the facts, and we have no evidence of a hereafter. Furthermore, he comments, while it is tempting and comforting to believe that an individual's innocent and undeserved suffering is a contribution to God's greater design, why "should we excuse God for causing such undeserved pain, no matter how wonderful the ultimate result may be?" As he suggests, this would violate our commitment to "the supreme value of an individual life" (p. 19). Indeed, if God had a greater purpose or design, unfathomable to us, that would "justify" the suffering of innocent people, and even if those people had a reward waiting for them in the hereafter, then He would be using individuals as a means toward an end, as mere instruments rather than ends in themselves.

In commenting on Albert Camus' novel, *The Plague*, Richard Rubenstein (1966, pp. 203-204) states: "Because Father Paneloux believes God to be the omnipotent Lord of history, he must see the plague as an expression of God's primitive retribution. He interprets the disaster, as the Prophets and teachers of Israel and the theologians of the Church have interpreted similar disasters for millennia, as God's chastisement of a sinful world." But: "Father Paneloux's theology breaks down as he watches a small boy die horribly of the plague. According to his theology, the child must be a sinner, but every human instinct within the priest rejects this. In the presence of the real suffering and death of a child, Father Paneloux's whole attempt to construct a theological interpretation of history disintegrates."

God and the Group Frame

Natural catastrophes, violence, conquest, and even enslavement often befell *groups* in ancient times. How to explain this, except in group terms, and especially group desert? Hence to God are attributed actions toward groups, and group desert. It was noted in chapter 1 that many of the stories in the Bible may represent a quest to understand events after they had occurred, and many of these events concerned group history. Thus the exile of the Jews from their land to Assyria is understood in the Tanakh as the result of God's discontent with "the Israelites" as a group to follow His commandments, or to behave righteously. This perspective is continued in the Koran, where God says that He "destroyed generations before your time on account of the wrongs they did..." (Surah 10:14). God afflicted Mecca "with famine and fear as punishment for what its people did" (Surah 16:112). Nations are acted upon: "Nor would the Lord destroy the nations without just cause and due warning. They shall be rewarded according to their deeds" (Surah 6:131-133). God has "destroyed many a sinful nation and replaced them by other men" (Surah 21:11).

This quest for meaning and understanding has led to an interpretation of the Holocaust as due to God's will, and as punishment for some presumed previous sins, or a straying from God on the part of "the Jews." God as represented in the Bible delivers group justice in the name of desert. If we were to follow the logic of the Tanakh, we might come to the bizarre conclusion reached by some fundamentalists, reminiscent of Job's onlookers, that the Holocaust was God's punishment of "the Jews" for not obeying all of His hundreds of commands more diligently, and that they must surely have not, since the Holocaust did occur. On the other hand, in some Christian circles the "sin" for which they were punished was their failure to accept Jesus as their Lord and Savior, or even to have killed Christ.

In either case, we are to accept the specter of God being responsible for the mass slaughter of a group, including infants and children, for "sins" that "they" have presumably committed, or else we must accept that the interpretations are human-made myths. In the Tanakh, there are instances in which the meting out of "group justice" seems to ensue from God's anger rather than from His sense of justice, and yet there are other indications, such as in some of the commandments themselves, and in the blessings and curses that are part of the Covenant, that the "group justice" frame is embedded in God's thinking. We are reminded that it takes Abraham and then Moses to confront God about His reliance on this frame, and to appeal to His sense of justice by pressing other frames, in the process suggesting to us that God's sense of justice is a projection of man's sense of justice, including the group frame. In the end, it is man proclaiming, from his own sentiment, a value extended from himself to others, and made into principle through reason, that individual human life itself is sacred.

There is also the possibility of an intervening God who fails to intervene. At best, we can speak of a God who knows what is just, but does not act on that knowledge. In the Tanakh it is said: "If you refrained from rescuing those taken off to death, those condemned to slaughter—if you say, 'We knew nothing of it,' surely He who fathoms hearts will discern the truth, He who watches over your life will know it, and He will pay each man as he deserves" (Proverbs 24:11-12). But what of He who fathoms hearts? What if *He* refrains from rescuing those taken off to death? Either God administers group "justice," using victims and perpetrators as mere instruments, or He stands by while the innocent suffer.

Other than that, we are left with the alternatives of not to believe in God at all, or to believe in God as the prime mover, who perhaps has created beings with their own free will, but since the creation itself, has not intervened at all, is a non-intervening God, or is dead. Giving praise to a prime-moving non-intervening God, rather than to an intervening one, would actually be a more genuine expression of appreciation, since nothing could be expected in return for the praise. We are also left with the possibility that even if there is or was a God, the Bible is a false representation of God. But then God is not a source of justice, except perhaps in the giving of commandments incorporating principles pertaining to justice, and the administration of justice cannot be left to God, even though leaving it in the hands of human beings is also problematic.

Justice is left to us, and only we can uphold the sanctity of human life. How to defend that sanctity without contradicting it in violence is the question not only for Jewish ideology, but for all of humankind.

Selection and Exclusion

Since social organization is a fact of human behavior, and since events befall groups, there is the desire to believe that one's group is favored, through its special relationship with God, through the deeds and beliefs of the group and its members, or through some natural goodness or superiority of the group and its members. Not surprisingly, then, these tendencies, too, are reflected in the Bible and the Koran. God's desert or other consequences accrue to a group as a whole, as well as to individuals, and one wishes, or hopes, to be part of a favored group.

In the Torah, God makes a covenant with Abraham, assigning land to him and his offspring, and pledging to be their God (Genesis 15:18; 17:1-21). But Abraham and his offspring must "keep the way of the Lord by doing what is just and right" (18:19). Later, having shown his willingness to make a sacrifice of his son Isaac to God, Abraham is told that his descendants "shall seize the gates of their foes" (22:17). On Mount Sinai, God instructs Moses to convey to the children of Israel, "if you will obey Me faithfully and keep My covenant, you shall be My treasured possession among all the peoples" (Exodus 19:5). God then proceeds to give Israel the Ten Commandments, and many other laws. The group-oriented blessings for keeping this contract, and curses for breaking it, all as forms of desert, are enumerated in Leviticus and Deuteronomy, and have already been referred to in chapter 1. This covenant is at once exclusionary, a promise of divine protection of the group, and a warning that if the individuals within the group do not obey God, follow the prescribed rituals, and pursue justice, then ill fate will befall the group as a whole. Yet it is this very groupthink, itself a projection of human thought processes, that is also challenged by Abraham and Moses' sense of justice.

In the New Testament, as alluded to in chapter 1, a cult of Jesus arises, and group inclusion and exclusion are made voluntary. Christ died for all of us, and through his grace we may be saved, but only those who believe in Jesus will be saved. Those who follow Jesus "shall inherit everlasting life" (Matthew 19:29). One must believe in God's "only begotten Son" in order to have eternal life, or otherwise be condemned to suffer the wrath of God (John 3:13-18, 36). John portrays "the Jews" as the enemies of Jesus, and while Peter portrays "all the people of Israel" as the killers of Jesus (Acts 4:10), he allows for their "sins" to be blotted out if they repent and be baptized in the name of Jesus (Acts 2:38; 3:19). One's fate is tied to the group, but group membership is open. Yet Jesus' precepts of justice, by their very nature, extend to all without condition. Perhaps, then, only divine justice is conditioned on belief in Jesus as divine. But if nonbelievers shall suffer the wrath of God, they must be deserving of punishment, and hence worthy of worldly attack, too.

In the Koran, the "unbelievers" are equated with the evildoers (Surah 2:1-16), but in this case the believers are those who follow Muhammad and his teachings. "The only true faith in God's sight is Islam" (Surah 3:19). "The unbelievers shall be sternly punished, but those that accept the true Faith and do good works shall be forgiven and richly recompensed" (Surah 35:7). Of "the People of the Book" (which in the Koran includes Christians as well as Jews) it is said: "Some are true believers, but most of them are evil-doers" (Surah 3:110). Of the Israelites it is said: "You will ever find them deceitful, except for a few of them" (Surah 5:13). "Believers, take neither the Jews nor the Christians for your friends" (Surah 5:51). Yet it is also said that if the People of the Book "observe the Torah and the Gospel and what has been revealed to them from their Lord, they shall enjoy abundance from above and from beneath" (Surah 5:65).

Thus it is the unbelievers who are doomed, while Jews and Christians occupy ambiguous ground: those who believe in the God of the Bible believe in the God of Islam, since they are one and the same, but many Jews and Christians are thought to be unbelievers. According to the Koran, Noah said: "'Lord, do not leave a single unbeliever on the earth. If you spare them, they will mislead Your servants and beget none but sinners and unbelievers'" (Surah 71:26-27). Moreover, it is said in the Koran that "those who deny the life to come are doomed, for they have strayed far into error" (Surah 34:8).

As in the New Testament, beliefs as to who is graced and who is not—beliefs that are readily tolerable to those who do not hold the same beliefs—devolve into derogation and accusation, such as the claim that most Christians and Jews are evildoers. Exhortations within religious institutions for human-initiated counteractions are never far behind. In the Koran it is said: "Idolatry is more grievous than bloodshed" (Surah 2:191). As in the Tanakh, although killing is forbidden, qualifications are made, in that it is said that "you shall not kill—for that is forbidden by God—except for a just cause" (Surah 6:152).

Thus the door is opened a crack. "Let those who would exchange the life of this world for the hereafter, fight for the cause of God." On whoever does so, God "shall bestow a rich recompense" (Surah 4:74). Those "who are slain in the cause of God" will be admitted to Paradise (Surah 47:4-6). Believers are exhorted to "slay the idolaters wherever you find them" (Surah 9:5) and make war on the unbelievers (Surah 9:12-14). "Believers, make war on the infidels who dwell around you. Deal firmly with them" (Surah 9:123). "Prophet, make war on the unbelievers and the hypocrites, and deal sternly with them. Hell shall be their home, evil their fate" (Surah 66:9). God will sternly punish believers who do not go to war (Surah 9:39). It is also said: "Those who follow him [Muhammad] are ruthless to the unbelievers but merciful to one another" (Surah 48:29).

It is true that it is also said: "Fight for the sake of God those that fight against you, but do not attack them first. God does not love aggressors" (Surah 2:190). But it is commonplace in the history of warfare that each side believes its own violence to be defensive, and the other's aggressive. Often the same premises that led the leaders of a group to war also led them to believe that their side of the war was defensive. And each side derives its interpretation of the other's violence as aggressive from its original premises. Violence is hardly ever committed in the name of aggression, although the victims are no less dead on that account.

The Hebrew and New Testaments, as well as the Koran, contain concepts of selectivity and exclusion that potentially justify violence against other groups. Yet similarly as in regard to the sense of justice and the frames of justice, selection and exclusion are manifestations of human cognition in interaction with reality. They do not originate in the Bible and the Koran, but are merely reflected there, and religion is not responsible for them.

Reason in the Service of War and Group Destruction

As we have seen, human reasoning can proceed from many premises, including hypotheses and theories about aspects of the world, and those that stem from faith, wishful thinking, fear, self-interest, group interest, a sense of justice, and a belief in the sanctity of human life. Above all, it is placed in the service of problem solving, from whatever perceptions and constructions of reality the problems that we wish to solve might arise. The reasoning process itself, however, is amoral. Practicality, necessity, and problem solving do not necessarily coincide with morality and individual justice. What is perceived as practical and necessary to solve a problem may not be just. We have seen (in chapter 1) that in biblical times, while individual justice was predominantly applied within the society, the group frame predominated in regard to the enemy societies, and both choices may have been driven by perceived necessity. Reasoning is merely a servant of premises.

Indeed, there is nothing rational about the valuing of human life. The valuing itself is nonrational. It is merely one of the many premises from which reasoning may proceed. Reason has often been placed in the service of the destruction of human life, whether starting from premises that devalue human life, from the perception of the existence of a problem that can be solved only through the use of violence as a tool, or a combination of both. Social systems may be set up in which rationality conflicts with morality. War, for example, is a social system in which it becomes rational to kill others of a different group in order to prevent them from killing you. Yet from the perspective of the principle of life affirmation, the act of killing, which the system promotes, is immoral, and hence we must conclude that the system itself is immoral, if we do in fact hold the sanctity of human life as a moral value.

Social conflict can be viewed as a problem for its participants, whether they be nations, groups, or individuals. Each of the two participants has certain goals it wants to achieve, and believes that the other participant is setting obstacles in its path. The problem is how to overcome the obstacles and achieve the goals. One attempt at solution, often seen as a "last resort" by leaders who could not conceive of viable alternatives, has been the use of violence. Parties to a conflict make the decision to employ violence when they see no other way of confronting their problems. Violence is in this sense a tool.

Although many factors contribute to violence at some point and in some way, what is fundamental to the organized violence that is responsible for the overwhelming proportion of violent deaths is that it is rationally planned and obediently executed. These are the minimal factors needed to describe modern war. Deliberated, calmly and rationally planned violence, which often relies on the obedience of others, marks organized, instrumental violence as opposed to impulsive violence. Emotions are not significant contributors to the planning of organized violence. When people are faced with a problem that they find no other means of confronting except by violence, their lack of anger will matter little. National leaders do not declare war on the spur of an angry moment. Rather, the decision to go to war is often the outcome of months of deliberation, involving many people in discussion and even deep reflective thought. The violence responsible for the greater parts of the slaughter of our times is more closely associated with the cognitive, rational, and calculating side of human beings, than with their emotional, irrational, passionate, and impulsive side. It is not reflexive violence that has destroyed the most human life, but reflective violence, planned and organized.

But rational thinking must proceed from certain premises. If one does not accept the premises, he or she is not likely to accept the conclusions, even if compelled to admit that these conclusions were rationally arrived at from the premises. When I speak of violence as rationally planned, I refer to the process that proceeds from certain already-accepted assumptions.

David Halberstam (1972) took pains to emphasize that the men who made the policy decisions in regard to the Vietnam War were above all intelligent and rational individuals, looked upon as "the best and the brightest" of their generation. Yet, according to Halberstam (1972, p. 371), they "were tied to a policy of deep irrationality, layer and layer of clear rationality based upon several great false assumptions."

Such premises or assumptions may, first of all, concern the construal of the problem itself that is to be resolved. In regard to the Vietnam War, for example, the much disputed premises of the American decision makers included the belief that communism was a monolithic bloc that kept expanding and had to be contained; the famous domino theory; the assumption that the North Vietnamese were aggressors in South Vietnam; and the belief that the fall of the South Vietnamese government would threaten the security of the free world, and of the United States itself. More recently, in regard to the American invasion of Iraq in 2003, American leaders came to the conclusion that Saddam Hussein possessed weapons of mass destruction that were an imminent threat to the Western world, and to the United States itself. What we have here is reasoning from group interests to be defended, not from justice even as desert, although group defense is couched in terms of justice.

Secondly, such premises or assumptions may pertain to how the perceived problem should or could be solved, or how the perceived conflict should be waged. Leaders may believe that all possible means of resolving the problem have been attempted and exhausted, leaving only organized violence as the tool of "last resort."

A third set of premises, not held by American decision makers in regard to the above-mentioned military ventures, may pertain to the nature of the group itself, and thus its entire membership, with which we perceive ourselves to be in conflict. The group itself is the problem, and the solution must then be to isolate all members of that group, to exclude them from all interaction with us, cleanse certain territory of them and, if we perceive them to have evil attributes and characteristics that might infect members of our own group, to exterminate them, thus solving the problem. Here we are talking about assumptions we call stereotypes and prejudice that slide into what Daniel Goldhagen (1996) has characterized as an eliminationist mentality.

Selection and Exclusion in Nazi Germany

Goldhagen (1996) attributes the sole motivational cause (both necessary and sufficient) of the planning, implementation, and manner of implementation of the Holocaust to the "cognitive model" of Jews, which has deep roots in European history but was especially nurtured, inculcated, and widespread in its most virulent form within German society, beginning in the nineteenth century and into the 1930s, and thus even before the Nazi rise to power. This cognitive model, which had early roots in the stereotyping of "the Jews" as "Christ-killers" and guilty of "blood libel," and animosity toward them for obstinately refusing to accept Jesus as their savior, evolved over centuries to include attributions of responsibility for the Black Death, and evil conspiracies to gain power over the broader community through Bolshevism and capitalism. In Germany, "the Jews" came to be accused of responsibility for that country's defeat in World War I, its economic collapse, the humiliating conditions of the Versailles treaty, and every imaginable ill that befell the German community. The Jews themselves, in Germany, came to be imagined and depicted as a morally depraved and subhuman "race," whose very presence infected and corrupted the body politic, the economy, and the moral righteousness of the wider community. Human cognition, as is its nature, sought rational solutions to this long-emerging "Jewish Problem." The anti-Semitism model in Germany was so virulent as to lead to eliminationist solutions (some already having a European tradition of implementation going back centuries), such as ghettoization, the banning of Jews from certain professions, the stripping away of the rights of citizenship, humiliating measures such as the forced wearing of a yellow star of David in public, forced emigration, institutionalization in the form of concentration camps, and finally, when the power, means, and opportunity were at hand, genocide. The elimination of the Jews and their influence from German society in a manner that they could not infect that society ever again would be assured by their complete annihilation not only in Germany and its conquered territories, but throughout the world. "The Jews are our misfortune" went one Nazi slogan.

Goldhagen (1996, p. 389) argues that Germans treated Jews as they did "because of a set of beliefs that defined the Jews in a way that demanded Jewish suffering as retribution, a set of beliefs which inhered as profound a hatred as one people has likely ever harbored for another." He speaks of "Germans' belief in the justice of the enterprise" (p. 394), that is, the extermination of the Jews. Perhaps, then, it can be asked, what frames of justice were operative?

Hitler believed in the necessity of the annihilation of not only Jews, but of Gypsies, and the mentally incompetent and physically incapacitated, and the subjugation of other groups, for the future well-being of the world. In *Mein Kampf* he wrote: "We all sense that in the distant future problems could approach man for the conquest of which only a highest race, as the master nation, based upon the means and the possibilities of an entire globe, will be called upon" (1939, p. 581). He believed that he was fighting for the preservation of humankind. Of the Social Democratic Party, he said that "mankind must rid the world of her as soon as possible, or otherwise the world might easily be rid of mankind" (p. 52). He spoke similarly of the Jews (p. 84). Hitler imagined many enemy groups within as well as outside German society, and he sought to annihilate many of them out of perceived necessity, as bizarre as his beliefs and assumptions were. Unfortunately, the "problem" that Nazi Germany sought to solve was the mere existence of Jews and other unwanted people.

Zygmunt Bauman (1992, p. 72) states that like the Nazi attempts to exterminate their mentally and physically impaired compatriots, and to breed a superior race, "the murder of Jews was an exercise in the rational management of society." The Nazi project, he suggests, "was an exercise in social engineering on a grandiose scale" (p. 66). "For the Nazi designers of the perfect society, the project they pursued and were determined to implement through social engineering split human life into worthy and unworthy; the first to be lovingly cultivated and given *Lebensraum*, the other to be 'distanced,' or—if the distancing proved unfeasible—exterminated" (pp. 67-68).

Yet this rational design and process was built upon irrational fears and assumptions, not to mention the total disregard of the sanctity of individual human life (or at least of *all* individual human life). The Nazis saw themselves as fit to be judges of who should live and who should die. The Jews were regarded as malignant in intention and hence, as Goldhagen (1996, pp. 469-471) suggests, morally culpable and thus deserving of cruelty and unnecessary suffering even before death. The mentally ill, however, while seen through Nazi eyes as posing a malignant threat to the biological health of the German people, were not seen as having malignant motives or of being responsible for their own condition. They were simply to be removed or destroyed.

Under the so-called "euthanasia program," "handicapped and mentally ill Germans of all ages were condemned as 'life unworthy of life' and 'useless eaters.' They were murdered in hospitals and psychiatric institutions" (Rubenstein and Roth, 2003, p. 152). In fact, "the first Nazi targets of mass destruction were not Jews but Germans who had been certified as 'unfit' for life within Hitler's Reich" (p. 152). What was called "Social Hygiene," as Timm Kunstreich (2003) explains, "was social regulation construed as a purification process through which those deemed to be deviant, inferior, or degenerate must be eliminated from society because they are supposedly contaminating and contagious factors that threaten the well-being of society as a whole." Those who did not fit the group construct of "ideal German"—such as Jews, the Roma and Cinti (both commonly called Gypsies), communists, the "antisocial," homosexuals, the poor, and the "feeble-minded"—were selected for the exclusionary measures of relocation, sterilization, deportation, imprisonment and other forms of institutionalization, and murder.

The tasks of conceptually separating the worthy from the unworthy remain at the base of genocide, of the construction of the "problem," from which the rational processes of "problem solution" will ensue. Bauman (1992, pp. 91-92) speaks of a gardener's vision, in which all of the weeds in the garden must be segregated, prevented from spreading, removed, or destroyed. Although weeds cannot be said to be deserving or undeserving, they are not worthy of being in the garden, insofar as any distinction can be made between the concepts of deserving and worthy.

While such distinctions can be found in the cognition and treatment of various groups and their members, the common denominator underlying these distinctions is selection and exclusion. Based on whatever "reasoning," individuals and groups are cognitively selected for exclusion from the universe of moral obligation. They are then to be treated "as necessary," to protect the group from the imagined threat, with the treatment of exclusion ranging from deportation and institutionalization to death, or they are to be treated according to their supposed just deserts, which might include desert as revenge or even rational balance for imagined wrongs, again with the manner of exclusion holding a range of possibilities.

It is hence the group frame of "justice" that is operative, with actions that violate individuals for the sake of a perceived necessity (with the necessity pertaining to the well-being of one's own group), or common good (with the "common good" not so common as to include all people, but referring only to one's own group, however defined), being viewed as just. Yet the extreme nature of the cognitive constructs themselves, or stereotypes, developed of "the Jews" inspire hatred and desire for revenge that presuppose desert. The venomous cognitive constructs of "the Jews" went beyond mere generalization to the notion of racial inheritance of evil, and conspiracy images of the Jewish "race" as a "corporation," as a whole. Jews are no longer imaged as individuals, but as a whole, an entire undifferentiated entity that is an agent of evil. This image extends desert to the entire group, and therefore justifies actions taken toward each individual Jew in terms of individual desert. Group justice merges with individual justice—through the vehicle of the desert frame. Mass murder then proceeds from one's sense of justice, and not only from perceived necessity—whether in the minds of the leaders alone, members of the establishment institutions also, or indeed everyone. In any event, it is the cognitive construct of the group, as irrational as that construct is, that necessitates the treatment, or in other words, that leads through reason to the "final solution."

Of course, the group frame violates the idea of "each one according to his works or deeds" (the infants and children who were slaughtered could not have done anything relevant to the stereotypes of desert), but the "one" becomes the group, even if requiring another layer of irrationality. It is no longer only necessity that justifies or even drives the slaughter, but also desert. The problem to be solved is merely to punish those deserving punishment, and the desert frame, unlike the group frame alone, not only allows but motivates the brutality as well as the murder.

Both the group frame and the desert frame of justice have the power and propensity to limit the universe of application of the third frame, of the principle of life affirmation, by constricting the universe, even if already limited to human beings and not extended to animals, in a manner that contradicts it. The group frame presupposes that there are certain groups that are to be treated differently in the manner of justice than members of our own community, and excludes certain people from our community. In the most extreme applications of the group frame, members of the excluded groups are cognized as subhuman, even sometimes in an evil rather than animal-like way, deserving of their treatment as nonhuman, and even deserving of cruelty and death. The mass destruction of human life that was the Holocaust was not merely a reasoned solution to a problem in the sense of finding a way to overcome barriers in the way of achieving a goal, but was the goal itself. Means and ends became perfectly indistinguishable, but in the form of the destruction of human life.

This is the dark side of the sense of justice. People suffer from socioeconomic crises, and feel that it's not fair, that they have been wronged. They look to who is to blame and become greatly angered and vengeful, inspired with hatred. This sense of justice is the justice of desert, transformed through generalization to whole groups of people, without further distinction. It is difficult to know where the sense of justice leaves off and naked emotions of vengeance take over. This sense that they deserved better, that the scales have not been and need to be balanced, is based upon and facilitated by the desert frame of justice, either taken to the extent of belief that all Jews are the culprits, or merged through desire for vengeance with the group frame. Only the increased salience of the life-affirmation frame, especially in public policy, could possibly safeguard against this escalation to the extreme consequences of the group and desert frames. The derogation of life is a slippery slope.

Either the sense of justice stands apart from the notion of necessity, or the latter is compatible only with the group frame which, to be sure, places any sense of *individual* justice outside of it. The group frame can be employed in the service of perceived necessity or some ultimate "good." Desert, as we have seen, can be employed in the service of the group frame. On the other hand, only the life-affirmation frame can deny vengeance its justification, and the cognitive processes of selection and exclusion their power. Yet we often succumb to the illusions, realities, and pressures of necessity, usually as defined by others, and surrender to others' definitions of the situation.

Compliance and Complicity

In a survey taken in the aftermath of the Mylai massacre, when asked what they would do "if ordered to shoot all inhabitants of a Vietnamese village suspected of aiding the enemy, including old men, women, and children," 51 percent of the American public said that they would follow orders and shoot (Kelman and Lawrence, 1972).

Once organized violence is rationally planned, it must be obediently executed. Surely the internalization of such attitudes as that one's cause is just, that violence is necessary to uphold it, and that the enemy is evil, along with feelings of anger and hostility toward the enemy, might contribute to the making of a good soldier, and to the obedience process itself. But such factors are beyond the minimal requirements of soldiery. Obedience, for whatever reason, is all that is necessary. The *potential* for obedience to generate violence was demonstrated in Stanley Milgram's (1963, 1974) famous studies, in which a large majority of a representative sample of American citizens inflicted what they believed to be severe pain upon fellow human beings merely because a particular authority figure, who possessed no sanctions, had ordered them to do so.

Milgram (1974, p. 123) spoke of his subjects being seduced into performing harsh acts by their "uncritical acceptance of the experimenter's definition of the situation." The definition that the experimenter provided was to study the effect of punishment on learning. Thus the cause of science was implicitly invoked as a higher good. When subjects hesitated in going on to deliver what they believed to be increasingly higher levels of electric shock, the experimenter would say (p. 21): "It is absolutely essential that you continue." Or: "You have no other choice, you *must* go on."

In Milgram's studies, there was no tangible risk or threat involved in disobedience, but obedience was prevalent nonetheless. To be sure, it is often surprising to observe how slight a risk, how small a reward, and how minimal a threat of punishment, and indeed that fear of the most trivial form of social disapproval, is often enough to gain the compliance of people to do what they otherwise would not have done. It is by now well documented that German soldiers who refused to follow orders to kill unarmed civilians never faced dire punishment, and few received any punishment whatsoever (Browning, 1992, p. 170; Goldhagen, 1996, pp. 379-381). Nor was there much risk to people in Nazi Germany who asked to be transferred from certain jobs that were contributing to the Holocaust (Rubenstein and Roth, 2003, p. 363). Yet few soldiers or others did ask for transfers or refuse to follow orders.

Importantly, those who participate in destructive obedience may often do so partly because of a belief that their acts serve some ultimate noble end. As Milgram (1974, p. 142) said: "Ideological justification is vital in obtaining *willing* obedience, for it permits the person to see his behavior as serving a desirable end" (italics in original). But Milgram speaks of an ideological deference to authority "that constitutes the principal cognitive basis of obedience. If, after all, the world or the situation is as the authority defines it, a certain set of actions follows logically" (p. 145). Authority defines the situation, or a group such as the Jews, in a way, to borrow a phrase from Milgram (p. 181), "that makes cruel and inhumane action seem justified." But the mystery remains why people so readily accept the authority's definition of the situation or ideology, or surrender their own judgment to others' claims of necessity or justice, particularly when the claims, as in Nazi Germany, were bizarre.

One explanation may stem from the realization that a sense of justice is salient not only toward the defined enemy, but toward one's own community or group, and this sensed justice has to do with one's supposed allegiance and obligations to that community, and consequent duty to obey its legitimate and representative authorities. In short, obedience to legitimate authority is seen as a contractual obligation, and one's disobedience as a breach of contract. One has an obligation to the group, to the state. One's compliance is owed to the national community as a contractual obligation in exchange for the benefits derived from being a member of the community. It is what we call patriotism. This contract formulation of justice, as we have already seen, is a manifestation of the desert frame of justice. However, there is always a point at which the authority, or the orders it gives, may come to be seen as illegitimate. Hence there is a delicate balance between the strength of perceived obligation to the state (or of the state deserving our allegiance), on the one hand, and its success in portraying the group whose members are to be violated as the enemy and deserving of the drastic actions ordered, on the other. Acceptance of this portrayal makes the individual's following of orders to participate in brutality and murder, as well as the authority's task of gaining compliance, easier. Milgram paid his subjects for their participation in his experiments, hence invoking a contractual obligation (although there were other implicit contractual obligations present also, such as prior agreement to participate, and allegiance to science as a noble enterprise in itself). One's implicit contract with the community, however, is a far stronger one, and thus capable of eliciting obedience in far more drastic actions, as witnessed when a nation goes to war.

Other factors, too, make compliance and its elicitation easier, and they generally are ones (as also demonstrated in Milgram's studies) that increase the physical and psychological distancing of the perpetrator from the victim. Most acts that contribute to violent destruction are not inherently violent; they are violent due to the social context in which they are performed. The soldier complies with a social system whose product is violence. His daily actions are more likely to be motivated by a desire to do his job well than by an aggressive motive. Ultimately, he contributes to violence by obeying orders. Surely, relatively few of the many people who contribute to organized violence ever perform any skills that can be construed as *specifically* violent, without regard to the social context in which they are performed. Performance of the same skills that allow a pilot to fly his passengers to a Bermuda vacation can contribute significantly to the bombing of a village. Indeed, the same act of dynamiting that opens a copper mine can destroy a crowded building. What is of importance is being influenced to give obedience while ignoring the moral implications of lending one's labors to an enterprise whose purpose is human destruction. Most acts that contribute to organized violence do so at a considerable distance, making the denial of responsibility easier.

Obedience, of course, can serve good as well as evil. Yet the fact is that obedience was necessary for, and did contribute to, much of the massive slaughter of our time. As Rubenstein and Roth (2003, pp. 362-363) explain: "The Reichsbahn's [German National Railway] personnel were respectable citizens. No experts in Jewish affairs, they were merely people doing their jobs. Yet what they did could have been neither a mystery nor a secret to most of them. The German railroads delivered about three million Jews to their deaths" (or about half of the total number of Jews who were slaughtered in the Holocaust). They further state (p. 366): "Whether a person was part of the relatively small cadre who killed firsthand or one of the huge network of desk-bound personnel who destroyed people by composing memoranda, drafting blueprints, signing correspondence, and making telephone calls, he or she frequently took comfort from referring to orders from superiors and the necessity to obey." Moreover, they remind us that many German physicians and lawyers, judges, teachers, university professors and their students, captains of industry, scientists, engineers—in short, "the best and the brightest"—were deeply complicit in the crimes of Nazi Germany.

In fact, those who carried out the so-called "euthanasia program" were highly educated people, including some of Germany's most prominent physicians and psychiatrists who, uncoerced, saw themselves as implementing a special therapy program for the benefit of the German community (Rubenstein and Roth, 2003, p. 155).

The complicity of many social workers and social welfare bureaucrats with the Nazi regime is well documented in Hamburg (Kunstreich, 1997, pp. 175-233; 2003), and is also known to have occurred among social work professors in Germany. The roles of these "helping" professionals involved the formation of group constructs, the development of criteria to govern selection for inclusion and exclusion, and the actual selection of persons for exclusionary purposes. These crucial roles, as Timm Kunstreich explains, were an extension of long-standing social welfare practices of distinguishing the "worthy" from the "unworthy." True, the results were extreme this time, and perhaps unforeseeable by those who took part in the selection processes, yet these processes were instrumental.

Bauman (1992, pp. 13-30) speaks of the necessity of advanced forms of bureaucracy for mass murder on the scale of the Holocaust. Bureaucratic organization turns killing into an abstraction, and detaches the participants from the "product," hence allowing the killing to proceed as a "rational" process devoid of sentiment, of contact with the victims as human beings, and thus of moral repulsion. Moreover, bureaucracy and technology may provide the more efficient means for group extermination.

Certainly, the extent of the "success" of the Holocaust in terms of the quantity and proportion of an identified group's members who were murdered was in part attributable to modern technology and bureaucracy. Yet in Rwanda in

1994, mass group slaughter on the scale of hundreds of thousands proceeded with the use of machetes and loose organization. The most important detachments are purely conceptual, and precede the organization of the social machinery. Moreover, while the processes of bureaucracy may facilitate obedience to authority, they are not necessary for it.

Furthermore, obedience alone cannot account for the uncommanded acts of cruelty often witnessed in the context of war and other forms of organized human destruction. Previously developed stereotypical belief systems may generate anger and hostility toward "the enemy," and may further lead to dehumanized images of the enemy, or dehumanization may develop during the course of war to alleviate guilt feelings attending acts of violence already committed through obedience (Pelton, 1974, pp. 199-204). Defining people as subhuman lowers inhibitions against killing them, or bypasses "inhibitions against the taking of human life" (Bernard, Ottenberg, and Redl, 1971, p. 103). Opton (1971) found dehumanization to be very common among American soldiers actually engaged in the fighting in Vietnam. "The Vietnamese are turned into debased abstractions—gooks, slopes, dinks—or are spoken of in zoological terms" (p. 66). Dehumanization developed to allay guilt may, in turn, permit violent behavior to go beyond obedience to be perpetrated through uncommanded acts. Sergeant Michael Bernhardt, the man who refused to fire at Mylai, reported that in one village, an old Vietnamese man was dropped into a well, and a hand grenade thrown in; in another, some soldiers were interrupted in the act of attempting to hang a villager for no reason; in another, an old man pleading for the return of some keepsakes taken by soldiers who had just ransacked his hut was gunned down by one of them in exasperation (Lelyveld, 1969). In some incidents, civilians who were shot down seemed to be victims of only a soldier's whim. Dehumanization reduces inhibitions against violence.

Yet even such uncommanded acts, committed by ordinary people who have been drafted into armies without any known extraordinary dispositions toward extreme violence and cruelty, and even if they were previously inculcated with dehumanizing cognitions of "the enemy," would not have occurred outside of the context of a permitting and sanctioning social environment. Whether done within the larger context of obedience to overall and general orders issued from higher authority, which the soldier then takes liberty in carrying out specifically, or in the narrower social environment of group permissiveness and social pressures, at least lowering inhibitions to go along to get along, the social-situational context is needed.

Most people resist the belief that the unfathomable cruelty inflicted upon Jews in the death marches, in the camps, and in the shooting massacres and "Jew hunts" could have been done by normal people. Goldhagen contends that the answer to this puzzle lies in the eliminationist cognitive model of the Jews held by most Germans, which instilled deep hatred toward Jews—a pathological hatred if you will—in "ordinary Germans." He argues that Germans willingly inflicted cruelty and death on Jews even when not ordered to do so. But while Milgram's experiments demonstrated that ordinary people, due only to their obedience to authority, could inflict considerable physical pain on others, a small exploratory experiment provides some suggestive evidence that ordinary people, without a history of pathology, violence, or criminality, or even any previously developed hatred toward their victims, could act with cruelty without being ordered to do so, given certain situations.

The particular situation involved the random assignment of normal university students, who had volunteered to participate in a psychological study of "prison life," to either a "guard" or "prisoner" role in a mock prison constructed in the basement of the psychology building at Stanford University (Haney, Banks, and Zimbardo, 1973). During the six days that the experiment lasted, the experimenters "witnessed a group of prison guards who seemed to derive pleasure from insulting, threatening, humiliating and dehumanising their peers—those who by chance selection had been assigned to the 'prisoner' role." This was due merely to the "conferring of differential power on the status of 'guard' and 'prisoner.'" "Most dramatic and distressing to us was the observation of the ease with which sadistic behaviour could be elicited in individuals who were not 'sadistic types'...." The authors state that the most hostile guards "moved spontaneously into the leadership roles of giving orders and deciding on punishments" and became role models for the other guards. Even those "good" guards who were less drawn into the power dynamic than the others never contradicted or interfered with the actions of more hostile guards. By the end of the experiment, most guards "had become sufficiently involved in their roles so that they now enjoyed the extreme control and power which they exercised and were reluctant to give up."

No doubt prior hateful group stereotypes can interact with situational factors to contribute to particularly cruel behavior toward certain people, but the point is that the power dynamic generated by the situation, with its assigned roles, cannot be ignored. While the above findings are based on the observed behavior of only eleven "guards," compared to the hundreds of participants in the obedience-to-authority experiments, they are suggestive of a power dynamic in human behavior, standing apart from cognitive beliefs and frames of justice, that motivates behavior as much as needs do, and whose mystery warrants far more study than has hitherto been devoted to it.

Goldhagen (1996) has argued that the extreme and unimaginable brutality used by many (indeed, perhaps the vast majority of) members of Hitler's police battalions in the course of murdering Jews, documented beyond doubt, indicates that both the brutality and the murders themselves were "autonomously motivated," far beyond mere obedience to authority. He rejects arguments of coercion, blind obedience to authority, "social psychological pressure engendered by situational factors and their peers" (p. 383), the pursuit of bureaucratic, career, or other individual self-interests, or incomprehension of their actions. Rather, as previously mentioned, he argues that Germans treated Jews as they did because of their profound hatred of them.

There is no doubt that ethnic hatred was a causal factor in the "war" against the Jews, as it has been in many recent group conflicts that have eventuated in wars around the world. But just how widely and deeply this animus toward Jews as a whole was held amongst German people is an issue that will be debated for the foreseeable future. More important, however, is the question of how widely and deeply such cognitions, or any cognitions, need be held before an organized society can institute genocide, and what are the minimal requirements for such institution.

It is well known that Hitler and his Nazi leadership held venomous exclusionary cognitions of the Jews, and that early on, very large percentages of the German people voted for him and supported his leadership, even though his intentions to exclude and degrade the Jews (although not yet his intentions to kill them) were not hidden from view even at that time. But once firmly in power, what inhibits (short of rebellion and revolution) or facilitates the leadership of an organized society in regard to successfully implementing its cognitions and intentions? The moral approbation of its own citizens or of the other nations of the world could possibly inhibit it, but this did not happen. As for facilitation, we must assume that the Nazi regime benefited from the social mechanisms that, in part, regulate all organized societies, including: coercion; reward; perceived "legitimate" power that gains widespread obedience to authority without reference to reward and punishment; positive psychological identification with the leader; and continuing social influence through propaganda.

The enterprise that the Nazi society would undertake was unusual indeed, but there is no reason to believe that the mechanisms that contribute to the leadership achieving its goals in "ordinary" societies were not in operation (some perhaps in heightened form) here. To be sure, owing to the unusual obscenity of Nazi Germany's enterprise, we might expect inner conflicts between "conscience and authority," as Milgram once put it, to be pervasive among its people. But the resolution of such conflicts often favored authority even amongst the "ordinary people" that Milgram had recruited as participants in his experiments. And the extent to which these conflicts existed among the German people is unknown. Most could have adopted the group frame of "justice" toward the Jews, as we do know many Germans did. The point is that while the cognitions and intentions are crucial, they are sufficient within the leadership, and helpful if more widespread. We cannot say with any degree of certainty how widespread they were, and we *do* have evidence of the successful operation of other mechanisms of societal implementation and social control. Looked at in another way, instead of asking what the motivational causes of the Holocaust were, as Goldhagen has done, we can ask under what conditions the murder of millions of Jews as well as others would *not* have taken place, even granted a widespread prejudice and hatred of the German people toward the Jews. There may be many such conditions, but the absence of Hitler's specific policies of extermination—policies for which there is no evidence that the German people widely willed—is surely one of them. Even Goldhagen (1996, pp. 447-448), however begrudgingly, finally admits as much.

Yet the responsibility of all others who were complicit in the Holocaust is not thereby relieved. All acted autonomously, for that is the nature of human functioning. In the kinds of events under discussion, no human being could be likened to an inanimate object, whose behavior is entirely determined by external forces, like a ball upon the ocean waves, such as if he or she were seated in a plane brought down by a missile attack. The individual has causal agency, is a locus of causation. Regardless of the multiple causes that have brought the person to a particular situation, there is a time within that situation when he or she has the power of choice, and can exercise conscious decision-making. At the point of complicity in a crime, both the necessary and sufficient conditions for such complicity reside within the individual. In short, the person can opt not to comply. This is true even if the only alternative would be death. As already mentioned, for most Germans the consequences of noncomplicity—such as members of the police battalions deferring from going on killing missions, or railroad engineers operating trains to death camps asking to be transferred to other jobs—would not have been death or even imprisonment. In fact, there would have been no severe consequences at all, as documented by the cases in which such forms of noncomplicity took place. (Acts of active protest against the ongoing massacre of the Jews, however, were another matter, as documented by specific cases in which harsh penalties were administered.)

In any event, the evidence is overwhelming not only that human beings have demonstrated their capability of participating in—either actively or by remaining silent—the most vile and brutal destruction of human life, but that this is also true of not only an anomalous few but many highly educated people, and of not only a few, but many religious people, even church leaders.

The German churches remained silent—at best—in regard to the slaughter of Jews, and this silence was fostered by their desert images, their own blind obedience to German authority (overcome occasionally in regard to other groups)—no matter that the Nazi leadership was anti-Christian in philosophy—and even their religion-connected beliefs about "the Jews." Much earlier in history, even Protestant reform leader Martin Luther not only expressed his contempt for "the Jews" but advocated specific ways in which Jews should be violated (see Rubenstein and Roth, 2003, pp. 56-65). Between the world wars in Poland, anti-Jewish measures aimed at ridding that country of Jews were actively supported by Poland's Roman Catholic Church, "which regarded the Jews as agents of secularization, liberalism, and Bolshevism" (Rubenstein, 1992, p. 117).

Later, German churches, both Protestant and Catholic, opened their baptismal records to the Nazis in full awareness that by helping to distinguish between "Aryan" and Jew, they were helping to seal the fate of the Jews (Rubenstein and Roth, 2003, p. 255). Army chaplains witnessed mass murder of Jews in silence, giving "spiritual" comfort to the murderers (pp. 257-258). Church leaders throughout Europe, before and during the war, issued statements condemning the Jews as an accursed people for refusing to accept the belief that Jesus is the Lord and for having killed Jesus (p. 274), statements certainly not unhelpful to the successful execution of the Holocaust. The Hungarian Cardinal Justinian Seredi demonstrated the extent of his belief in Christ by issuing a statement in June 1944 endorsing the deportation of Hungarian Jews to Auschwitz (p. 276). It must be concluded that those who scorned the Sermon on the Mount as an appropriate subject for ridicule were not on that account disqualified from appointment to high office within the Catholic Church. Catholic rescuers of Jews were unsuccessful in their attempts to prevail upon Pope Pius XII to speak out against extermination (p. 278).

What possible higher authority could many Christian church leaders, either in their silence or in their more active complicity, have imaged themselves to be obeying, or what principles could they have thought themselves to be abiding by? What did their beliefs in God and in Jesus as the son of God amount to? When the time came for active assent or obedience to God, they chose the easier path of utility, and obedience to the Zeitgeist of human destruction.

The Holocaust was the result of *policies* bureaucratically executed. Some carry them out enthusiastically, some without passion, and some reluctantly, but all obey and follow orders. The only way out is to question the goal of the enterprise itself, the system itself, but few do. Indeed, it is not only participation in the bureaucratic machinery of actual killing that must be resisted, but also participation in the processes of selection and exclusion that are part and parcel of the myriad policies of group desert that currently exist even in democratic societies, for these processes are counter to support of the sanctity of human life even on their own account, and even if not serving as merely preliminary stages for the destruction of classes or groups of human beings altogether.

Beyond Reason

The technology of the Holocaust only applied to the means, and the rational planning and obedient implementation may adequately describe the means, but do not begin to explain the ends which, as Emil Fackenheim (1982, p. 182) states, were degradation, torture, and murder having no higher purpose, themselves being the highest purpose. As Fackenheim explains, even when facing crushing defeat, the Nazis found it more important to annihilate the remaining Jews than to save Germans. For example, "Eichmann redirected trains from the collapsing Russian front to Auschwitz" (p. 230). The extermination of the Jewish people "became an end more ultimate than the Third Reich's very survival" (p. 231). Since the means were destructive while the ends were destruction, the means were consistent with the ends in not the valuing but the devaluing of human life.

Rubenstein (1978, p. 89) states: "Outside of the polis there are no inborn restraints on the human exercise of destructive power." He also asserts, in effect, that there can be no justice without desert and the power to inflict penalties (p. 90). With secularization, according to Rubenstein (p. 91), the state "becomes the only true god on earth with the power to define realistically what is good and will be rewarded and what is evil and will be punished; this truly sovereign god also has the ultimate power of divinity, the power to decide who shall live and who shall die." I wish to argue here that, on the contrary, there is a sense of justice that resides in individuals aside from the polis, and that power can ensue from this sense of justice to restrain the human exercise of destructive power. Yet, paradoxically, it is from this same sense of justice, residing in individuals, from which the human exercise of destructive power can ensue. Moreover, although facilitated by social organization, this power not only ensues from the sense of justice, but itself resides within the individual. The only "true god" ultimately resides within the individual, not the state.

Rescue and Resistance

In the face of mass cooperation with evil that was necessary for the total domination achieved over certain groups by the Nazi state, individuals could and some did represent expressions of the "only true god" in their individual acts of defiance and/or life affirmation. But these were expressions of the god of life affirmation, not the god of desert. Moreover, these acts greatly risked the lives of the men and women who performed them, and in some cases assured their deaths. They were life affirming only in the sense that they were acts of defiance of, resistance to, and noncooperation with the murderous processes of a murderous organization. Yet the acts paradoxically included dying or being killed on one's own terms rather than in cooperation with the perpetrators, not very life affirming in itself or when viewed out of context. I do not speak here of violent resistance, but of the refusal to comply with the Nazi process, even to the point of hastening one's own death, and proactively attending to the support of the life of others.

Such resistance embodied the sanctification of life, and selfless action. According to Fackenheim (1982, p. 225): "Many performed the *mitzvah* [commandment] of *kiddush ha-hayyim* [the sanctification of life] by enhancing, defending, or even just barely clinging to life. Some could sanctify life only by choosing death." Fackenheim continues: "There was no purer resistance to the Nazi regime than the handful of Munich students who called themselves the 'White Rose.' They knew that their action—distributing anti-Nazi pamphlets at the late date of 1943—was almost sure to be futile. They knew, too, that they were almost certain to be caught and put to death. They knew it: yet they did it" (p. 267). Thus they acted morally, in the service of life, "without regard to consequences" (p. 275).

We must come to grips, then, with the possibility of the god of life affirmation residing within individual human beings, and furthermore, with the possibility that in certain contexts, dying or killing oneself, or even otherwise not unusual acts, can be expressions of life affirmation. The steps that Oskar Schindler took (hiring people to work in his factory) would have been viewed as having no remarkable life-affirming merit in "normal" times.

What do we take responsibility for, and why? One of the great fascinations of the story of "Schindler's List" is that we do not have a clue as to what led or enabled Schindler to resist evil in a manner that made him stand out uniquely from his compatriots. Just as we do not understand what personal factors contributed to the ability of masses of German people to commit crimes against humanity during the reign of the Nazis, we are baffled by the germane personal factors of the rescuers. If we had tried to predict beforehand which individuals would resist, we might never have chosen Schindler, or for that matter, many of the other individuals who had resisted evil and saved lives during that period. In fact, all the indicators that many people would have used would have misled them—they would have chosen people who were especially good to their neighbors in everyday life, who spoke of love and caring, who were not wheeler-dealers in their work, who were frequent churchgoers, who were not "womanizers," and so on—in short, precisely the people who failed to resist evil in droves, and who were unlike Schindler. Why the moment of truth conclusively proved Schindler, and not others, to be a righteous individual is not yet understandable to us. Social scientists have studied the psychology of social control, but they have not yet studied the psychology of individual resistance.

Moreover, it is not at all clear that many of the rescuers in Nazi Europe acted from an explicitly formulated principle of life affirmation, or the life-affirmation frame of justice, as it has been called here, as the most salient frame. To be sure, studies have revealed a wide range of motivations, with only a portion of the rescuers articulating this principle as a ground for their actions (Fogelman, 1994; Oliner and Oliner, 1988). In many cases, sentiment might have been more salient than principle. However, many may have acted out of a strong moral imperative to help those in need, aided by strong individualistic, independent, and self-reliant inclinations (Tec, 1986).

Belief in the sanctity of human life—or of someone's life—has little to do with rationality, although one can rationally proceed to develop and implement a strategy based on that premise, as Schindler did in saving hundreds of Jews from death. But others, as noted, risked certain death merely to support the *idea* of the sanctity of human life, with little hope of saving even one life. Their acts, we may say, were truly "without regard to consequence," and along with

Schindler's, purely moral. Individual resistance must ultimately stem from conviction, not reason.

It was only through his or her individual defiance of the Nazi death machine that the individual could affirm life in the face of the Holocaust. But to overcome the death machine, the defiance of many individuals must be organized. Gandhi's social invention of the philosophy and strategy of nonviolence—his contribution to the concept of *ahimsa*—included the key idea of the power inherent in organized moral resistance, the extension of one person acting in accordance with moral principle to an organized many doing so, with the ultimate form of resistance taking the form of organized noncooperation. Gandhi had often said that no government, even the most despotic, could exist without the cooperation of the people, and thus as soon as the subject ceases to fear the despot, the latter's power is gone (see Pelton, 1974, p. 175).

But it takes the organization of like-minded individuals to effectively resist. Acts such as that of the "White Rose" were purely moral, but if multiplied by a few hundred thousand other German actors, such acts would also have gained the power to halt mass destruction. Gandhi's idea, ultimately, was an attempt to extend the principle of life affirmation into an area that was previously reserved for war and violence, except for feeble attempts at a "just war" doctrine. Yet although facilitated by social organization, the power of nonviolence resides, in the last analysis, in the individual: each individual must retain his or her own moral compass and the willingness to act upon it in the form of noncooperation.

Terrorism

While Schindler and other individuals risked their lives in the act of saving other lives, suicide bombers have destroyed themselves in the act of destroying others. One act is in the service of life, while the other is in the service of destruction of life. The terrorists and the suicide bombers seemingly kill for the sake of killing. The connection between the means and the vaguely proclaimed distant ends is so tenuous that it must be strongly suspected that destruction of human life is itself the purpose. The means include indiscriminate killing that encompasses not only infants and children in the "enemy" group, and attacks on civilian targets with no strategic value, such as buses taking people to work, but also members of groups not considered to be the "enemy" and even members of one's own group who happen to be on the scene (unfortunately for them), and even, through suicide, the most loyal members of one's own group. The deadly means are ends in themselves no matter what the professed ultimate purpose, and are driven by revenge related to notions of having been wronged. The motive of group-oriented revenge is revealed in the seeming senselessness of the carnage, and the congratulatory mood of the perpetrators and their followers. They celebrate violence and death itself, and the suffering of members of the "enemy" group, for there is certainly no visible advance toward a victory for the perpetrators' version of a utopian society. There is no victory of any sort in sight, except that of revenge.

Moreover, we see once again that, contrary to Rubenstein's suggestion, it is not only the state that has "the power to decide who shall live and who shall die," but also the individual. While the state perhaps has the capacity to kill in greater quantity, we know that modern techniques, although more modest than those in the hands of the state, have increased the quantity of people that individuals can kill. Suicide bombers, acting on their own, have proved this. And with a little organization, now relatively small groups can organize the killing of thousands, as was done in the September 11, 2001 attacks on the United States. The power of life *and* death—or we might say, the gods of both life affirmation and destruction—resides within the individual as well as the state.

According to Jessica Stern (2003, p. 32), "real or perceived national humiliation of the Palestinian people by Israeli policies, and often by Israeli individuals, has given rise to desperation and uncontrollable rage." She points out that "terrorist leaders deliberately inculcate the idea that 'martyrdom' operations are sacred acts, worthy of both earthly and heavenly rewards" (p. 33). The terrorists, in their own eyes, seek retribution against the heathen enemy, an enemy that is decadent, brutal, and arrogant, and has strayed from God. Violence is good when committed in the name of God. "Because they believe their cause is just...they persuade themselves that any action—even a heinous crime—is justified" (p. 282). They believe, Stern suggests, that they are morally as well as politically right, and that God is on their side.

It is righteousness driven by a sense of justice and by the group and desert frames of justice that allows such views to have any credence at all, or to win the sympathy of or be convincing to anyone at all. Without these frames, no adherents could be won. The Islamist terrorists believe that Islam is under attack and must be defended. As Paul Berman (2003, p. 91) suggests, the perceived "attack" may be through the spread of liberal ideology, with its doctrine of religious tolerance and separation of church and state, and not necessarily of a military nature. (However, recent military interventions in response to terrorism can only increase the perceived righteousness of the cause to those dedicated to it.) The enemy deserves what it gets from us, we have a right to defend ourselves and our religion, we are justified in doing what we do—these are arguments from desert and perceived necessity. "Principles" must be defended, through sacrifice and blood, by "suicide operations and martyrdom for Allah," in the words of one of the Islamist terrorist leaders (Berman, 2003, pp. 119-120).

Berman (2003, pp. 121-153) suggests that while many observers tend to seek rational explanations underlying such death-focused political movements, they are best described as "pathological" movements, having no rationality to them. He derides the liberal faith in universal rationality, or the belief that "people are bound to behave in more or less reasonable ways in pursuit of normal and identifiable interests" (p. 153). Unless we wish to conclude with Berman that the terrorist movements are pathological, and the participants insane, we face the paradox that from the sense of justice, evil can ensue. Berman's case can be made—the terrorists are out of touch with reality since their goals are unachievable, they lack the capacity to distinguish between right and wrong, and they exhibit irrational thinking—but then what are we to say of those who give their lives defiantly, in hopeless causes, such as some of the resisters in Nazi Europe? The sense of justice itself is nonrational. It is a sense, not derived from reason, but from sentiment extended from oneself to others, and that in an affirmative manner (for the terrorists, to their own "community"). Yet this sense potentializes the frames of justice, which themselves can actualize evil. Perceived injustice is a dangerous thing. It is, in fact, perceived injustice that invokes our anger like nothing else can, and in turn, may lead to revenge. This fact, I suggest, is available to everyone's own introspection.

Justice and Religion

The Islamist terrorists are no more insane than were the Nazi leadership of Germany and the overwhelming numbers of Germans who participated in the Holocaust. Unlike the Nazi leaders, however, they claim to reason from premises rooted in holy scriptures, in this case, the Koran. The Koran, as well as the Tanakh and the New Testament, provide grounds for all sorts of imaginative inferences, interpretations, and justifications to be applied to current plans, acts, and situations. As we have seen, the human propensities toward selectivity and exclusion are expressed in all three texts, and are consonant with the group frame of "justice" which is reflected in abundance throughout the Bible and Koran.

The Koran, however, also exhibits the same difficulty with the group frame as does the Bible, in this case always qualifying statements about nonbelieving Jews and Christians to stop short of group justice. For example, to the "children of Israel" God says: "Guard yourself against a day on which no soul shall stand for another..." (Surah 2:122-123). It is also said: "Each man shall reap the fruits of his own deeds: no soul shall bear another's burden" (Surah 6:164-165). Although the Koran subscribes to the group justice visited upon the Egyptians by God, according to the Torah, in the form of plagues (Surah 7:130-136), the group frame continues to be troublesome to God, who is defensive about it. Thus He asks, were there among the generations and towns He destroyed, "any upright men who preached against evil," except the few He delivered from among them? (Surah 11:116)

As in the Tanakh and New Testament, justice as an individual matter is acknowledged and promoted. However, it is the desert frame of individual justice that permeates the Koran, as it does the Bible, with promises of reward for those who help others and obey God. Whether in this life or the next: "Whatever good you do shall be recompensed by God" (Surah 2:110). "Whatever alms you give shall rebound to your own advantage" and "shall be repaid to you in full" (Surah 2:272). Although the righteous person "does good works for the sake of the Most High only, seeking no recompense" (Surah 92:17-21), it seems that such a person will gain it in the hereafter.

Yet, again as in the Bible, the other side of the coin of the desert frame is pervasive. As we have already seen, those who do not do good works, but moreover, do not accept certain beliefs, such as belief in God or even in life after death, or in short, do not believe as we do, are deserving of punishment, and should and will be punished. "God is stern in retribution" (Surah 2:211) and "God is capable of revenge" (Surah 3:4). As many times it is said that God is forgiving and merciful, it is also said that He is stern in retribution. "He [God] will requite the evil-doers according to their deeds, and richly recompense those who do good works" (Surah 53:31).

As in the Tanakh, the administration of desert is not left to God alone. Prescription for punishment for crimes appears to go beyond the law of the talion: "As for the man or woman who is guilty of theft, cut off their hands to punish them for their crimes" (Surah 5:38). Yet it is also said: "If you punish, let your punishment be commensurate with the wrong that has been done to you" (Surah 16:126). In truth, many, many times in the Koran it is said that individuals will be dealt with according to their deeds. Be that as it may, as we have seen in the Koran as well as in the Bible, desert for deeds slides into desert for beliefs, and not only God will administer it. It is at this point that religion departs from themes of justice, and its struggles to define justice, to embrace authoritarianism. In addition to their acts being judged, individuals are to be judged, and this on the basis of their beliefs, not their actions (other than their unquestioning obedience to authority). Through this process, the desert frame merges with the group frame, for beliefs become the basis upon which individuals are prejudged and grouped, at least in the minds of the judges, without any individual acts need having been performed. Thus the process is one of selectivity and exclusion, and hence discrimination, since desert no longer need be related to individuals' life-supporting acts or good deeds, on the one hand, or their life-violating acts, on the other. Rather, other factors, arbitrarily designated by the judges, categorize and classify individuals into groups. To be sure, as we have seen, many other factors, too, have been used to select, exclude, categorize, and classify individuals into groups, and neither religion nor beliefs have a monopoly on the grounds on which selectivity and exclusion can be based. We are dealing with inclinations of the structure of the human mind, which can only be overcome by our active promotion of competing inclinations, also rooted in that structure.

It is not only the detachment of desert from deeds that is problematic in the ways noted. Desert implies a consequence, a result, that "ought" to come about as a "just" outcome, as conditional upon a person's actions or conduct, and is thought to rightly accrue to the person as a result of his or her conduct. Desert shifts the focus from the conduct to the person, who is to receive, or is thought to be deserving of, reward or punishment. As such, from the perspective of the life-affirmation frame, the exercise of desert (however judged by a controlling authority) perhaps can be used as a form of social control, but desert has no value as a moral principle, for morality refers to the conduct itself that desert seeks to reward or punish—a conduct that must have intrinsic moral value without reference to desert or consequence, even though it might be performed for that purpose. Most importantly, we can ask whether the conduct intended to deliver desert is itself intrinsically moral. Conceived of in this manner, moral action is not to be evaluated on the basis of the intent that motivated it, or upon the consequences that result from it outside of the action itself, but only upon its own intrinsic merit. The desert frame can be, and often has been, employed in the service of the violation of human life.

I have already said that the logic of justice as desert leads believers in an intervening and just God to the necessity of a belief in a judgmental hereafter. It can then be incorporated into the desert principle, as one form of desert. Yet it is interesting how frequently religious proselytizing, especially by television evangelists, incorporates appeals to one's selfish concerns for one's own happiness and desire for one's own continuation in a comfortable hereafter, with rarely a mention of justice, moral behavior, or the Sermon on the Mount. The hereafter of the Western religions, at least, concerns the fate of the self. Even self-sacrifice for a cause is couched in terms of reward in the hereafter. According to the Koran, it will be recalled, those "who are slain in the cause of God" will be admitted to Paradise (Surah 47:4-6). Ultimately, belief in a hereafter stems from a personal desire for one's own salvation, which one wishfully thinks he or she will have control over through conduct in the present life. It stems from sentiment toward oneself, but I have claimed that the sense of justice, too, stems from such sentiment, and transcends it when formulated into principle. Sentiment toward oneself can lead to sentiment toward others, but only principle can express justice, whether formulated in terms of desert or life affirmation.

When we praise God for saving ourselves or loved ones in a catastrophe that destroyed others, or when we say that there but for the grace of God go we, we are not attending to the injustice done to others. We demonstrate that our faith in God is based in selfish reasons, and that we praise God for selfish reasons, irregardless of the justice of His interventions.

Yet putting egoism aside, it can be said that the prominence that the afterlife attains in the New Testament and Koran, serving as desert, is aimed at resolving the pessimism about justice actually occurring in this world, as expressed in the Book of Job. Of course, the justice implied here is that which is defined by the desert frame, and while we make feeble efforts to enforce this form of justice, ultimately we have little control over it, as attested to by Job's plight. Moreover, persistence in the formulation of justice as desert in this world allows much leeway for human thought and action to facilitate the violation of life, and the ends of desert to determine and overwhelm the means in the name of justice. Yet even an atheist may emphasize the desert frame of justice, believing that justice lies in trying to ensure that people *do* get what they deserve, through human intervention. Justice, from this perspective, even takes on the appearance of rationality and logic, in that actions are followed by reactions that are consistent with them. Judgment as to what the precise reaction should be appears to be made dispassionately. Important distinctions are discerned in deciding that one person shall receive the death penalty, another twenty years in prison, and yet another a five-year prison sentence. Our intellects are pleased by this symmetry of justice in the desert frame, by justice as balance.

Yet this formulation of justice, as desert, allows vengeance to be carried out in the name of justice, even if only to the extent that balance, in the eye of the judge-beholder, is achieved. We have seen God (in people's projections), as well as people, time and again acting out of revenge rather than justice, but in the name of desert. Finally, desert facilitates the ease with which people can be selected for exclusion, along the lines of ostensible desert.

Earlier I referred to a power dynamic in human behavior, standing apart from cognitive beliefs and frames of justice. While the human exercise of destructive power can ensue from our sense of justice, as just noted, it can also be generated by impulses toward domination and control. We have even seen these impulses projected onto God, with the Bible portraying Him as acting out of power and domination. Both the revenge dynamic and the power dynamic can drive policy. Yet from whichever of these two sources the human exercise of destructive power may ensue, it is from the sense of justice that power can ensue to restrain the human exercise of destructive power. Moreover, although residing within the individual, this power to restrain is facilitated by social organization. But since the desire to control and dominate can also be rationalized in the name of desert, it is only social organization in the service of the life-affirmation frame of justice that can counter the human exercise of destructive power from either of these sources.

As we have seen, both the group and individual-desert frames, as well as the selectivity and exclusion that religion promotes, can serve the destruction of human life. Yet we have seen that the life-affirmation frame, as well, is reflected in the Tanakh and New Testament. Likewise, it is reflected in the Koran. Reminiscent of the competition among frames in the Bible, while believers are exhorted not to show kindness to enemies (Surah 60), it is also said that "it shall be best for you to endure your wrongs with patience" (Surah 16:126). Believers are admonished: "Do not allow your hatred for other men to turn you away from justice" (Surah 5:8). At several points it is said: "Requite evil with good" (Surah 23:96; 28:54). "Good deeds and evil deeds are not equal. Requite evil with good, and he who is your enemy will become your dearest friend" (Surah 41:34). Paradoxically, it is said: "Let evil be rewarded with evil. But he that forgives and seeks reconcilement shall be recompensed by God" (Surah 42:40). Believers are told to give their wealth away to kinsfolk, orphans, the destitute, travelers in need, and beggars (Surah 2:177), to render the alms levy, to be charitable, and to do good works. The righteous share their goods "with the beggars and the deprived" (Surah 51:15-19). Thus the sanctity of human life is promoted. And reminiscent of the Talmud, the Koran asserts that "whoever saved a human life shall be regarded as having saved all mankind" (Surah 5:32).

Moreover, religious tolerance is supported. Famously, it is said: "There shall be no compulsion in religion" (Surah 2:256). "You shall not use coercion with them [the unbelievers]" (Surah 50:45). Addressing (apparently) the Jewish, Christian, and Muslim communities at once, the Koran urges: "Vie with each other in good works..." (Surah 5:48). "We have our own works [scriptures] and you have yours; let there be no argument between us. God will bring us all together, for to Him we shall return" (Surah 42:15). To "vie with each other in charitable works: this is the supreme virtue" (Surah 35:32).

It is not sufficient to say that the peoples of these religions, together with their religious leadership and institutions, should stress what they hold in common, while deemphasizing the rest. They hold in common various scriptural pronouncements that sanction group "justice," permit or encourage revenge in the name of desert, emphasize selection and exclusion, and beckon an authoritarian obedience that can serve destruction of human life as well as its support. It is the common ground of the presumption of the sanctity of human life, found in the Tanakh, the New Testament, and the Koran, as well as in the scriptures of other religions, that should be emphasized in religious teachings, if destruction in the name of religion is to be avoided, and if religion is actually to become a force for the promotion of peace and justice. Jews, Muslims, Christians, and others can choose to emphasize the life-affirming aspects of their scriptures as indeed, most already do. But they must join together to ensure that the governments that represent them develop and implement policies that promote the affirmation of every human life to the maximum extent possible.

The Fate of Justice

I have claimed that the principle of life affirmation is rationally derived from sentiment, in that if it is accepted that individual human life is to be valued in itself, for its own sake, then it follows that all and every individual life is to be valued. Kant believed that reason alone is involved, but as Schopenhauer and John Stuart Mill pointed out, Kant's formula of universal law is ultimately connected to utility and interest. One follows principles of justice due to desert, obedience to God (religion), reason grounded in interest, or for its own sake.

Justice based on reason alone, as in Kant, still alludes to outcomes, as does faith in divine desert, and we return to a faith, this time in reason or principles that will yield desert or good outcomes. An alternative is to ignore even the supposed outcomes, at least in the formation of principles. This is to focus on right action involving *ahimsa*, and for its own sake, without prospect of reward or punishment. Even still, it was faith in reason that Gandhi had when he believed that nonviolent alternatives could eventually be found for every situation. The frame of life affirmation proceeds rationally from sentiment to acceptance of the premise of the unconditional sanctity of life as a moral absolute. This is not the rationality of problem solving, although it has rational implications for problem solving, primarily in indicating that means must be sought that converge with ends in the nonviolation of human life.

If unrestrained by the life-affirmation frame, the rationality of problem solving finds dangerous refuge in the group and desert frames, and vice versa. The group and desert frames are routinely used to justify terrorist attacks, suicide bombings, "ethnic cleansing," genocide, and war. Ted Honderich (2003a), for example, speaks of the possibilities of "terrorism for humanity" and "the categories of clear innocents, half-innocents, unengaged combatants, and non-combatants." His proposition that we need "to try to save people from bad lives" is not a moral principle, as he claims (Honderich, 2003b, p. 53), but a goal, akin to Hitler's goal of the preservation of humankind. Moral principle, in contrast, informs behavior or conduct, such as that which we may engage in to get to the goal. This brings us back to the frames of justice. Which frame does Honderich speak from? He seems to endorse group justice, and then he makes the attempt, through his categorizations, to distinguish between the "guilty" and others (2003b, p. 159)—to enlist the desert frame in his group-frame thinking.

Justice in accordance with the life-affirmation frame, on the other hand, is to be found in the support and affirmation of individual human life. Anything that violates that life, even in the name of group justice or desert, is unjust. Support and affirmation of each and every individual is the end in itself. Violence may successfully be used to solve a problem, but it is morally wrong. It may be used to balance accounts or provide desert, but it is morally wrong. If we do not regard violence as morally wrong, then judgments of whose violence is immoral and whose is "moral" will vary widely, and will depend upon who is doing the judging. Unless we are willing to condemn violence absolutely, we implicitly endorse a moral relativism in which violence is considered to be immoral under some conditions and in some situations. If we are to maintain any morality at all, it is that human life is not to be violated. We must regard all violence as morally regrettable and wrong.

The support of human life is an end in itself, and not merely an instrument for the attainment of some other end. The life-affirmation frame is not written in the language of cause and effect, claiming for example, that housing and otherwise helping homeless people is not a successful endeavor unless some other end, such as the "self-sufficiency" of such people is obtained through some change evinced in their behavior or mentality. The scientism of the day, ever ready to measure and assess effects, lends itself to the promotion of this sophistry.

But what motivation is there to pursue justice in accordance with the life-affirmation frame? When we speak of a passion for justice in accordance with the principle of life affirmation, we are not merely referring to fair distribution in accordance with contract, or merely a fair agreement, but passion in support of life. The contractual formulation of justice is purely utilitarian itself, even if for individuals instead of the group as a whole. In modern times, utility has replaced the command of God as rationales for laws. But *ahimsa* does not reference contracts. Nor does it posit a covenant as in the Torah, for a covenant involves desert, with penalties for breaking it and rewards for keeping to it.

Justice may appeal to self-interest, but also may transcend self-interest. What motivation is there to transcend self-interest, other than sentiment? While the sense of justice derives from sentiment, sentiment is transcended by justice only through the rational formulation of principle. To be sure, there are many things that take us beyond self-interest as we become engrossed or obsessed with objects of interest to ourselves, such as invention, discovery, and even forms of recreation and games. Problem solving in itself holds our interest and motivates us, even if the problem to be solved does not pertain to our self-interest. Perhaps a search for meaning, or a need to construct meaning in one's world, is behind such pursuits, but I will propose that it is certainly behind our pursuit of justice for its own sake. We say that it gives us purpose (as we also say of many other activities). Religion, too, must be regarded as a search for meaning. Man faces mortality, and we attempt with religion to instill hope and meaning in the face of mortality. The concern with one's death, of course, is ultimately concern with oneself. It is a selfish concern. Our prospect of death impresses upon us how insignificant we are in the workings of the universe. We will disappear from it without a trace, returning to the nothingness of dust and ashes.

According to Viktor Frankl (1984, p. 104), the striving to find meaning in one's life is the primary motivation of human beings. For this reason, they are able to live and even to die for the sake of their ideals and values. Human beings seek to find a purpose and meaning to their lives, and this includes being responsible to someone or something (p. 114). According to Frankl (p. 115), "being human always points, and is directed, to something, or someone, other than oneself." Frankl suggests, however, that behaving with "responsibleness" is central to finding meaning in one's life (p. 134). Moreover, his philosophy is premised on his belief in "the unconditional value of each and every person" (p. 151).

We know that we are insignificant within the universe; but just as surely, we know that we are not insignificant to others' suffering. And people suffer as individuals. Our actions and inactions can make a difference to others' suffering—we can deepen it or ameliorate it. Our actions or inactions are meaningful in this regard—in regard to others. We can find meaning in either deepening or alleviating others' suffering. Thus the search for meaning alone is not sufficient for the pursuit of justice, and why one chooses to use freedom in a "responsible" manner, guided and aimed at upholding human dignity and the value of human life, is not yet explained. As all too much evidence suggests, man can also search for and find meaning in "ideals and values," as perverted as most of us might view them, that guide people toward destruction, revenge, murder, and celebration of destruction of life, in the name of God, honor, and utopian end states in heaven or on earth. The destroyers even proclaim that they act out of a sense of justice. Indeed, as much as we protest to the contrary that what we have in these destroyers' acts is abundant evidence that man's sense of justice can be overridden, eclipsed, or rationalized in such a bizarre manner as to completely obliterate it, we do know that human beings, and therefore even these destroyers, do have a sense of justice.

But as much as we and the destroyers aim for ends, and rationalize our actions in terms of ends, meaning must be found in the act or process itself. We engage in the acts because we believe them to be "right," independent of the ends or consequences that may or may not ensue. Advocates for policies in regard to homeless people consistent with the life-affirmation frame could often become depressed and declare their actions to be meaningless if they were to look to positive results alone, since their "victories" are often modest and far and few between. We find meaning and satisfaction in the belief that we are doing the right thing, that what we are doing must or ought to be done, regardless of success in terms of outcomes. So too for the destroyers. But since we are sustained by the meaning we find in the process and not in the future outcomes, then our mortality or immortality, or that of humankind, is of no consequence to it.

Paradoxically, while Abraham acknowledged his insignificance as dust and ashes, he exercised his capability to argue with God in order to save other lives. That's all he had. Thus the individual is significant, not in the greater universe to which he is surely insignificant, but to other individuals, over whom he has the power of life and death, whether this significance be demonstrated by those who saved others during the Holocaust, or those whose very objective was to destroy other lives. Hitler had significance to the course of human history in the human destruction that he led, with, of course, the necessary assistance of countless obedient followers who ranged over a broad spectrum of motivation. But each person has, ultimately, the power of choice, and it is the exercise of that choice to support life that most of us consider moral. The only significance we have is to each other, one way or another.

The promotion of justice is the ultimate expression of our concern for others, and ultimately, human life itself, not centered on our own life. It is the way we overcome, or is our response to, our own mortality, or the insignificance of our own life. It is not much, and perhaps doomed to fail, with the knowledge that even the human species may be mortal, and may at some time perish in its totality, to disappear from the universe. Yet it is all we have, and it is an act of defiance in the face of the indifference and neutrality of a universe that contains no meaning and no principles of justice except that which we attempt to infuse. We either conform to its indifference, or strive to overcome it. Everyone does the latter, but the shape this striving takes varies from religious myths, to pleasure seeking, to the quest for justice itself.

But if we grant that even the destroyers have a sense of justice, then we must look at this in another way. I have said that the sense of justice is nonrational and is derived from sentiment extended from oneself to others in an *affirmative* manner. It is because we value the lives not only of ourselves and loved ones, but of those in our community, however defined by us, including those we have never even met, that we and our sense of justice are disturbed when we imagine or perceive that any of these lives, or the community as a whole, is threatened or wronged. Thus our passion for justice may derive from our sense of justice itself. We wish to control the fate of these lives and of the community, and are motivated to act out of perceived necessity and/or through the deliverance of perceived desert. Since these propensities stem from our valuing of life, we are not unaware of the contradiction in reason that action based on these propensities may entail. Yet reason, as we have seen, can also serve perceived necessity and desert. In desert, there is not only the logic of balance, but the assumption of presumed deterrence of future wrongful behavior.

Thus all three frames of justice—group, desert, and life affirmation—are present and in competitive struggle within the human mind. They coexist, moreover, with propensities toward selection and exclusion, vengeance and cruelty, the power dynamic of control and domination, and the dynamics of obedience to authority. If we grant that the motives, propensities, and constructions of the destroyers live within all of us—that the destroyers live within all of us—then we must perceive our task to be to uphold the sanctity of human life beyond the group and desert frames. Beyond the struggles in our own minds, we must do so within the social systems that we are responsible for and within the governments and policies that represent us.

The matter of justice, then, is left to us, to our formulations, our values, and our actions, from wherever their constructions and motivations are ultimately derived. The continuing instances of mass destruction and crimes against humanity in many parts of the world, unfathomable, cry out for our promotion of the life-affirmation frame. You can kill in the name of God, necessity, and even justice (as desert) but you cannot kill in the name of *ahimsa*. In accordance with the life-affirmation frame, morality, and hence justice, has no intention or end, other than that which is implicit in it, that is, *ahimsa* or noninjury. To destroy life and call it justice can only be rationalized within the group and desert frames. Defense through violence may be called self-preservation, but not justice. And until sentiment is transformed into principle, we may even have love, but not justice. In accordance with the life-affirmation frame, whenever individuals are violated, justice is violated.

I have claimed in this book that not only the sense of justice, but the three frames that ensue from them, are part and parcel of all human minds. It is futile to try to *eliminate* one or another of the frames through persuasion, education, or the like; it is only possible to promote greater reliance on one or another in terms of application to the practical world. I maintain, or conclude, that the only or best way to uphold the sanctity of human life in public life is to promote and further the influence and predominance of the life-affirmation frame in the development of public policy. We must advocate for policies that affirm life in every respect. Obedience to authority can serve good rather than evil, and can be so harnessed by instituting policies that stem from the life-affirmation frame.

The government represents us (and this can be said formally for a dictatorship as well as a democracy) and its behavior is our collective behavior. We are responsible for our government, its policies, and its actions. But if we accept this view, as we must if we include among those responsible for the Holocaust those Germans and others who obeyed, complied, and remained silent, we broach a profound dilemma. Terrorists, too, for the injustices they perceive, hold citizens of the "enemy" nations responsible, thereby seeking to justify, through the group and desert frames, what otherwise must be regarded as indiscriminate violence. Only through the lens of the life-affirmation frame is this dilemma resolved: We are all responsible for upholding the sanctity of human life, without condition, judgment, or exception, and not only through our personal behavior, but through our social systems, our governments, and through our social policies from which our collective behavior ensues. But violence is only the extreme form of disrespect for the individual and his or her autonomy and well-being. We must more diligently attempt to apply the moral value of the sanctity of human life, in every sphere of life, to means rather than to ends only. Indeed, when applied to ends only, it paradoxically has the opposite effect of justifying the disparagement of human life.

We are inspired by those who defied evil and who affirmed life even at the risk of death. But as inspired as we may be by individual acts of defiance in the face of organized human destruction, we have seen that the defiance of many individuals must be organized. Although the power of nonviolence resides in the individual, it is facilitated by social organization. Likewise, the organization of like-minded individuals, with a shared belief in the sanctity of human life, is needed to gain the power of people to move governmental policies, through politics, further away from their present over-reliance on and reflections of the desert frame of justice and toward greater manifestations of the principle of life affirmation and thus more consistent revelation of our common belief in the sanctity of human life.

We must organize to promote policies that endorse nondiscrimination, eschew exclusion, address the basic human needs of all individuals, and enhance the well-being of every individual—policies that aspire to uphold the sanctity of human life without condition, judgment, or exception. We must promote the principle of life affirmation, in our own minds as well as others, and more diligently seek alternatives to violence in the waging of social conflict. It is in this sense, devoid of its context of authoritarianism and desert, that we can understand the biblical injunction of Deuteronomy (30:19): "I have put before you life and death... Choose life..."

Notes

1. Survey conducted for Fox News, by Opinion Dynamics, September 23-24, 2003, based on a national sample of registered voters. Also survey conducted by Quinnipiac University Polling Institute, June 4-9, 2003. Data provided by the Roper Center for Public Opinion Research, University of Connecticut.
2. Survey conducted by Quinnipiac University Polling Institute, June 4-9, 2003. Data provided by the Roper Center for Public Opinion Research, University of Connecticut.
3. Survey conducted for *Newsweek*, by Princeton Survey Research Associates, July 11-12, 2002. Also survey conducted for Fox News, by Opinion Dynamics, September 23-24, 2003, based on a national sample of registered voters. Data provided by the Roper Center for Public Opinion Research, University of Connecticut.
4. Survey conducted for Fox News, by Opinion Dynamics, September 23-24, 2003, based on a national sample of registered voters. Data provided by the Roper Center for Public Opinion Research, University of Connecticut.
5. A surah is a chapter in the Koran.

References

Aaron, Henry J. (1978). *Politics and the professors: The Great Society in perspective.* Washington, D.C.: Brookings Institution.
Aaron, Henry J. and Bosworth, Barry P. (1997). Preparing for the baby boomers' retirement. In Robert D. Reischauer (Ed.), *Setting national priorities: Budget choices for the next century* (pp. 263-301). Washington, DC: Brookings Institution.
Abramovitz, Mimi. (2001). Everyone is still on welfare: The role of redistribution in social policy. *Social Work*, 46(4), 297-308.
Allison, Dale C., Jr. (1999). *The Sermon on the Mount: Inspiring the moral imagination.* New York: Crossroad.
Alperovitz, Gar. (2000). On liberty. *Boston Review*, October/November.
Angell, Marcia. (2002). The forgotten domestic crisis. *New York Times*, October 13.
Associated Press. (2002). CDC: Smoking costs society $7 a pack. *Las Vegas Review-Journal*, April 12.
Associated Press. (2003). New York junk food tax faces opposition. *Las Vegas Review-Journal*, June 12, p. 18A.
Atkinson, A. B. (1975). *The economics of inequality.* Oxford, United Kingdom: Oxford University Press.
Atkinson, A. B. (1995). *Public economies in action: The basic income/flat tax proposal.* Oxford, United Kingdom: Oxford University Press.
Axinn, June and Levin, Herman. (1982). *Social welfare: A history of the American response to need.* Second Edition. New York: Harper & Row.
BAG SHI (Bundesarbeitsgemeinschaft der Sozialhilfeinitiativen) (Eds.) (2000). *Existenzgeld für alle: Antworten auf die Krise des Sozialen.* Neu-Ulm, Germany: AG SPAK (Arbeitsgemeinschaft sozialpolitischer Arbeitskreise) Bücher.
Bauman, Zygmunt. (1992). *Modernity and the Holocaust.* Ithaca, NY: Cornell University Press.
Belkin, Lisa. (2002). Just money. *New York Times Magazine*, December 8.
Berkowitz, Edward D. (1988). Disability insurance and the Social Security tradition. In Gerald D. Nash, Noel H. Pugach, and Richard F. Tomasson (Eds.), *Social Security: The first half-century* (pp. 279-298). Albuquerque, NM: University of New Mexico Press.
Berlin, Isaiah. (1951). A letter to George Kennan. In Henry Hardy (Ed.), *Liberty: Isaiah Berlin.* Oxford, United Kingdom: Oxford University Press, 2002.
Berlin, Isaiah. (1969). *Four essays on liberty.* Oxford, United Kingdom: Oxford University Press.
Berman, Paul. (2003). *Terror and liberalism.* New York: W. W. Norton.
Bernard, Viola W., Ottenberg, Perry, and Redl, Fritz. (1971). Dehumanization. In Nevitt Sanford and Craig Comstock (Eds.), *Sanctions for evil* (pp. 102-124). San Francisco: Jossey-Bass.
Bindman, Andrew B. and Haggstrom, David A. (2003). Small steps or a giant leap for the uninsured? *Journal of the American Medical Association*, 290(6), 816-818.

Bobo, Lawrence and Kluegel, James R. (1993). Opposition to race targeting: Self-interest, stratification ideology, or racial attitudes? *American Sociological Review*, 58, 443-464.

Bobo, Lawrence and Smith, Ryan A. (1994). Antipoverty policy, affirmative action, and racial attitudes. In Sheldon H. Danziger, Gary D. Sandefur, and Daniel H. Weinberg (Eds.), *Confronting poverty: Prescriptions for change* (pp. 365-395). Cambridge, MA: Harvard University Press.

Bondurant, Joan V. (1967). *Conquest of violence: The Gandhian philosophy of conflict*. Revised Edition. Berkeley and Los Angeles, CA: University of California Press.

Bowen, William G. and Bok, Derek. (1998). *The shape of the river: Long-term consequences of considering race in college and university admissions*. Princeton, NJ: Princeton University Press.

Brewer, Geoffrey. (2000). Out to pasture, greener pasture. *New York Times*, June 21, p. C1.

Browning, Christopher R. (1992). *Ordinary men: Reserve Police Battalion 101 and the Final Solution in Poland*. New York: HarperCollins.

Buchanan, James M. (1997). Can democracy promote the general welfare? *Social Philosophy and Policy*, 14(2), 165-179.

Buchanan, James M. and Congleton, Roger D. (1998). *Politics by principle, not interest: Toward nondiscriminatory democracy*. Cambridge, United Kingdom: Cambridge University Press.

Burtless, Gary, Weaver, R. Kent, and Wiener, Joshua M. (1997). The future of the social safety net. In Robert D. Reischauer (Ed.), *Setting national priorities: Budget choices for the next century* (pp. 75-122). Washington, DC: Brookings Institution.

Carroll, James. (2001). *Constantine's sword: The Church and the Jews, a history*. Boston, MA: Houghton Mifflin.

Carson, D. A. (1999). *Jesus' Sermon on the Mount—and his confrontation with the world: An exposition of Matthew 5-10*. Toronto, Canada: Global Christian Publishers.

Century Foundation. (2002). *Bad breaks all around: The report of the Century Foundation Working Group on Tax Expenditures*. New York: The Century Foundation Press.

Chapple, Christopher Key. (1993). *Nonviolence to animals, earth, and self in Asian traditions*. Albany, NY: State University of New York Press.

Cohen, Wilbur J. and Friedman, Milton. (1972). *Social Security: Universal or selective?* Washington, DC: American Enterprise Institute for Public Policy Research.

Coleman, James. (1968). The concept of equality of educational opportunity. *Harvard Educational Review*, 38, 7-22.

Coleman, Jennifer. (2000). California sees lung cancer fall. *Las Vegas Review-Journal*, December 1, p. 7A.

Cook, Faye Lomax and Barrett, Edith J. (1992). *Support for the American welfare state: The views of Congress and the public*. New York: Columbia University Press.

Dawood, N.J. (1999). *The Koran*. Translated with notes by N. J. Dawood. London, United Kingdom: Penguin Books.

Dershowitz, Alan M. (1994). *The abuse excuse*. Boston, MA: Little, Brown and Company.

Dershowitz, Alan M. (2000). *The genesis of justice: Ten stories of biblical injustice that led to the Ten Commandments and modern law*. New York: Warner Books.

DeWitt, Larry. (1999, August). The history and development of the social security retirement earnings test. Washington, DC: Social Security Administration, Historian's Office.

D'Souza, Dinesh. (1995). *The end of racism: Principles for a multiracial society*. New York: Free Press.

Edsall, Thomas Byrne and Edsall, Mary D. (1991). *Chain reaction: The impact of race, rights, and taxes on American politics*. New York: W.W. Norton.

Edwards, Chilperic. (1904/1971). *The Hammurabi Code*. Port Washington, NY: Kennikat Press.
Egan, Timothy. (1994). Sunset for the oil boom and Alaska's life style. *New York Times*, April 24, p. E3.
Erikson, Erik H. (1969). *Gandhi's truth: On the origins of militant nonviolence*. New York: W.W. Norton & Company.
Fackenheim, Emil L. (1982). *To mend the world: Foundations of future Jewish thought*. New York: Schocken Books.
Fineman, Howard. (1995). Race and rage. *Newsweek*, April 3, pp. 23-25.
Fish, Stanley. (1994). *There's no such thing as free speech...and it's a good thing, too*. New York: Oxford University Press.
Fogelman, Eva. (1994). *Conscience and courage: Rescuers of Jews during the Holocaust*. New York: Anchor Books.
Fox, Emmet. (1989). *The Sermon on the Mount: The key to success in life*. New York: HarperCollins.
Frankl, Viktor E. (1984). *Man's search for meaning: An introduction to logotherapy*. Third Edition. New York: Simon & Schuster.
Friedman, Milton. (1962). *Capitalism and freedom*. (Reissued in 1982). Chicago, IL: University of Chicago Press.
Funiciello, Theresa. (1993). *Tyranny of kindness: Dismantling the welfare system to end poverty in America*. New York: Atlantic Monthly Press.
Gallup, George, Jr. (1995). *The Gallup poll: Public opinion 1994*. Wilmington, DE: Scholarly Resources Inc.
Gallup, George, Jr. (2001). *The Gallup poll: Public opinion 2000*. Wilmington, DE: Scholarly Resources Inc.
Gallup, George, Jr. (2002). *The Gallup poll: Public opinion 2001*. Wilmington, DE: Scholarly Resources Inc.
Gandhi, Mohandas K. (1941). *Constructive Programme: Its meaning and place*. Ahmedabad, India: Navajivan Press.
Gandhi, Mohandas K. (1954). *Gandhi's autobiography: The story of my experiments with truth*. Washington, DC: Public Affairs Press.
Gandhi, Mohandas K. (1961). *Non-violent resistance*. New York: Schocken Books.
Garfinkel, Irwin and McLanahan, Sara. (1994). Single-mother families, economic insecurity, and government policy. In Sheldon H. Danziger, Gary D. Sandefur, and Daniel H. Weinberg (Eds.), *Confronting poverty: Prescriptions for change* (pp. 205-225). Cambridge, MA: Harvard University Press.
Gates, Henry Louis, Jr. (2001). The future of slavery's past. *New York Times*, July 29.
Gilens, Martin. (1999). *Why Americans hate welfare: Race, media, and the politics of antipoverty policy*. Chicago: University of Chicago Press.
Goldhagen, Daniel Jonah. (1996). *Hitler's willing executioners: Ordinary Germans and the Holocaust*. New York: Alfred A. Knopf.
Graetz, Michael J. and Mashaw, Jerry L. (1999). *True security: Rethinking American social insurance*. New Haven, CT: Yale University Press.
Greenberg, Stanley B. (1997). Popularizing progressive politics. In Stanley B. Greenberg and Theda Skocpol (Eds.), *The new majority: Toward a popular progressive politics* (pp. 279-298). New Haven, CT: Yale University Press.
Gross, Jean-Pierre. (1997). *Fair shares for all: Jacobin egalitarianism in practice*. Cambridge, Great Britain: Cambridge University Press.
Halberstam, David. (1972). *The best and the brightest*. Greenwich, CT: Fawcett.
Haney, Craig, Banks, Curtis, and Zimbardo, Philip. (1973). Interpersonal dynamics in a simulated prison. *International Journal of Criminology and Penology*, 1, 69-97.

Harrison, Paige M. and Beck, Allen J. (2003, July). *Prisoners in 2002*. Washington, DC: Bureau of Justice Statistics, U.S. Department of Justice. Revised August 27.

Hertz, J. H. (1972). *The Pentateuch and Haftorahs: Hebrew text, English translation, and commentary*. Second Edition. London, United Kingdom: Soncino Press.

Hitler, Adolf. (1939). *Mein Kampf*. New York: Reynal & Hitchkock.

Holmes, Steven. (2000). The melting-pot politics of 2000 are truly soupy. *New York Times*, February 13, Section 4, p. 1.

The Holy Bible: King James Version. (1991). New York: Ivy Books (Ballantine).

Honderich, Ted. (2003a). A reply to Richard Wolin on suicide bombings. *The Chronicle of Higher Education*, November 28, p. B17.

Honderich, Ted. (2003b). *After the terror*. Expanded, Revised Edition. Montreal, Canada: McGill-Queen's University Press.

Hume, David. (1740/2000). *A treatise of human nature*. (Book 3: Of Morals). Oxford, United Kingdom: Oxford University Press.

Hume, David. (1751/1975). *Enquiries concerning human understanding and concerning the principles of morals*. Third Edition. London, United Kingdom: Oxford University Press.

Jauhar, Sandeep. (2003). When doctors slam the door. *New York Times Magazine*, March 16.

Jewish Publication Society. (1985). *Tanakh: A new translation of the Holy Scriptures according to the traditional Hebrew text*. Philadelphia: Author.

Jones, Hardy. (1980). A Rawlsian discussion of nondiscrimination. In H. Gene Blocker and Elizabeth H. Smith (Eds.), *John Rawls' theory of social justice: An introduction* (pp. 270-288). Athens, OH: Ohio University Press.

Kant, Immanuel. (1785/1998). *Groundwork of the metaphysics of morals*. Cambridge, United Kingdom: Cambridge University Press.

Kant, Immanuel. (1797/1996). *The metaphysics of morals*. Cambridge, United Kingdom: Cambridge University Press.

Kelman, Herbert C. and Lawrence, L. H. (1972). Assignment of responsibility in the case of Lt. Calley: Preliminary report on a national survey. *Journal of Social Issues*, 28, 177-212.

Kertzer, David I. (2001). *The popes against the Jews: The Vatican's role in the rise of modern anti-Semitism*. New York: Alfred A. Knopf.

Klassen, William. (1984). *Love of enemies: The way to peace*. Philadelphia, PA: Fortress Press.

Kozol, Jonathan. (1992). *Savage inequalities: Children in America's schools*. New York: Harper Perennial.

Krebs, Hans-Peter and Rein, Harald (Eds). (2000). *Existenzgeld: Kontroversen und Positionen*. Münster, Germany: Westfälisches Dampfboot.

Kumarappa, Bharatan. (1961). Editor's note. In Mohandas K. Gandhi, *Non-violent resistance*. New York: Schocken Books.

Kunstreich, Timm. (1997). *Grundkurs Soziale Arbeit: Sieben Blicke auf Geschichte und Gegenwart Sozialer Arbeit*, Band I. Hamburg, Germany: Agentur des Rauhen Hauses Hamburg.

Kunstreich, Timm. (2003). Social welfare in Nazi Germany: Selection and exclusion. *Journal of Progressive Human Services*, 14(2), 23-52.

Kushner, Harold S. (1981). *When bad things happen to good people*. New York: Schocken Books.

Ladd, John. (1999). Translator's introduction. In Immanuel Kant, *Metaphysical elements of justice: Part I of the metaphysics of morals*. Second Edition. Indianapolis, IN: Hackett Publishing Company.

Lagnado, Lucette. (2002). Forgotten survivors, families of past terrorism seek aid. *Las Vegas Review-Journal*, March 15, p. 14A.
Lehman, Jeffrey S. (1994). Updating urban policy. In Sheldon H. Danziger, Gary D. Sandefur, and Daniel H. Weinberg (Eds.), *Confronting poverty: Prescriptions for change* (pp. 226-252). Cambridge, MA: Harvard University Press.
Lelyveld, J. (1969). The story of a soldier who refused to fire at Songmy. *New York Times Magazine*, December 14.
Leonhardt, David. (2002). Out of a job and no longer looking. *New York Times*, September 29, Section 4, p. 1.
Lerner, Melvin J. (1980). *The belief in a just world: A fundamental delusion*. New York: Plenum Press.
Levin, Henry M. (1975). Education, life chances, and the courts: The role of social science evidence. *Law and Contemporary Problems*, 39, 217-240.
Locke, John. (1689/1963). *The works of John Locke*. A New Edition, Corrected. Vol. V. Darmstadt, Germany: Scientia Verlag Aalen.
Longman, Phillip. (1996). *The return of thrift: How the coming collapse of the middle-class welfare state will reawaken values in America*. New York: Free Press.
Merleau-Ponty, Maurice. (1962). *Phenomenology of perception*. (Translated from the French by C. Smith). New York: Humanities Press.
Miles, Jack. (1996). *God: A biography*. New York: Vintage.
Milgram, Stanley. (1963). Behavioral study of obedience. *Journal of Abnormal and Social Psychology*, 67, 371-378.
Milgram, Stanley. (1974). *Obedience to authority: An experimental view*. New York: Harper & Row.
Mill, John Stuart. (1859/1990). On liberty. In Mortimer J. Adler, Editor in Chief, *Great books of the western world*. Vol. 40. Chicago, IL: Encyclopaedia Britannica.
Mill, John Stuart. (1861/1990). Representative government. In Mortimer J. Adler, Editor in Chief, *Great books of the western world*. Vol. 40. Chicago, IL: Encyclopaedia Britannica.
Mill, John Stuart. (1863/1990). Utilitarianism. In Mortimer J. Adler, Editor in Chief, *Great books of the western world*. Vol. 40. Chicago, IL: Encyclopaedia Britannica.
Miller, David. (1999a). *Principles of social justice*. Cambridge, MA: Harvard University Press.
Miller, David. (1999b). Justice and global inequality. In Andrew Hurrell and Ngaire Woods (Eds.), *Inequality, globalization, and world politics* (pp. 187-210). Oxford, United Kingdom: Oxford University Press.
Mooney, Chris. (2003). Breaking the frame. *The American Prospect*, 14(4), April 1.
Murray, Michael L. (1997). *"...And economic justice for all": Welfare reform for the 21st century*. Armonk, NY: M.E. Sharpe.
Musto, David F. (1987). *The American disease: Origins of narcotic control*. Expanded Edition. New York: Oxford University Press.
Nanda, B. R. (1958). *Mahatma Gandhi: A biography*. Boston, MA: Beacon Press.
Oliner, Samuel P. and Oliner, Pearl M. (1988). *The altruistic personality: Rescuers of Jews in Nazi Europe*. New York: Free Press.
Ontario Fair Tax Commission. (1993). *Fair taxation in a changing world: Report of the Ontario Fair Tax Commission*. Toronto, Canada: University of Toronto Press.
Opton, Edward M., Jr. (1971). It never happened and besides they deserved it. In Nevitt Sanford and Craig Comstock (Eds.), *Sanctions for evil* (pp. 49-70). San Francisco: Jossey-Bass.
Parker, Hermione. (1989). *Instead of the dole: An enquiry into integration of the tax and benefit systems*. London, United Kingdom: Routledge.

Patterson, James T. (1996). *Grand expectations: The United States, 1945-1974*. New York: Oxford University Press.
Pear, Robert. (2003). Big increase seen in people lacking health insurance. *New York Times*, September 30.
Pelton, Leroy H. (1974). *The psychology of nonviolence*. Elmsford, NY: Pergamon Press.
Pelton, Leroy H. (1989). *For reasons of poverty: A critical analysis of the public child welfare system in the United States*. Westport, CT: Praeger.
Pelton, Leroy H. (1999a). *Doing Justice: Liberalism, group constructs, and individual realities*. Albany, NY: State University of New York Press.
Pelton, Leroy H. (1999b). Welfare discrimination and child welfare. *Ohio State Law Journal*, 60(4), 1479-1492.
Pew Research Center. (2003, May 14). *Conflicted views of affirmative action*. Washington, DC: The Pew Research Center for the People and the Press.
The Physicians' Working Group for Single-Payer National Health Insurance. (2003). Proposal of the Physicians' Working Group for Single-Payer National Health Insurance. *Journal of the American Medical Association*, 290(6), 798-805.
Posner, Richard. (1999). *The problematics of moral and legal theory*. Cambridge, MA: Belknap Press of Harvard University Press.
Potter, Will. (2003). Alabama voters to decide on scholarship plan tied to tax increase. *The Chronicle of Higher Education*, September 5, p. A29.
Pritchard, James B. (Ed.). (1969). *Ancient Near Eastern texts relating to the Old Testament*. Third Edition with Supplement. Princeton, NJ: Princeton University Press.
Puit, Glenn. (2000a). Ousted Paiutes vow fight. *Las Vegas Review-Journal*, December 31, p. 1B.
Puit, Glenn. (2000b). Paiutes aided by tax code. *Las Vegas Review Journal*, December 31, p. 6B.
Purdum, Todd. (2000). Even beneficiaries oppose plan to reward teachers: California governor stands nearly alone. *New York Times*, June 4, p. 12.
Radhakrishnan, Sarvepalli and Moore, Charles A. (Eds.). (1957). *A source book in Indian philosophy*. Princeton, NJ: Princeton University Press.
Rawls, John. (1971). *A theory of justice*. Cambridge, MA: Harvard University Press.
Rhys Williams, Lady Juliet. (1943). *Something to look forward to: A suggestion for a new social contract*. London, United Kingdom: MacDonald.
Rousseau, Jean-Jacques. (1762/2002). *The social contract and the first and second discourses*. New Haven, CT: Yale University Press.
Rubenstein, Richard L. (1966). *After Auschwitz: Radical theology and contemporary Judaism*. Indianapolis, IN: The Bobbs-Merrill Company, Inc.
Rubenstein, Richard L. (1978). *The cunning of history: The Holocaust and the American future*. New York: Harper Colophon Books.
Rubenstein, Richard L. (1992). *After Auschwitz: History, theology, and contemporary Judaism*. Second Edition. Baltimore, MD: The Johns Hopkins University Press.
Rubenstein, Richard L. and Roth, John K. (2003). *Approaches to Auschwitz: The Holocaust and its legacy*. Revised Edition. Louisville, KY: Westminster John Knox Press.
Schieber, Sylvester J. and Shoven, John B. (1999). *The real deal: The history and future of social security*. New Haven, CT: Yale University Press.
Schmid, Randolph E. (2003). Uninsured strain communities. *Las Vegas Review-Journal*, March 6.
Schmidt, Peter. (1997). Continuing budget cutbacks throw chill over higher education in Alaska. *The Chronicle of Higher Education*, October 31, p. A41.
Schön, Donald A. and Rein, Martin. (1994). *Frame reflection: Toward the resolution of intractable policy controversies*. New York: BasicBooks.

Schopenhauer, Arthur. (1839/1995). *On the basis of morality*. Providence, RI: Berghahn Books.
Selingo, Jeffrey. (2003). A special report: What Americans think about higher education. *The Chronicle of Higher Education*, May 2, p. A11.
The Sentencing Project. (2003a). *U.S. prison populations—trends and implications*. Washington, DC: Author.
The Sentencing Project. (2003b). *New inmate population figures demonstrate need for policy reform*. Washington, DC: Author.
Sharp, Gene. (1960). *Gandhi wields the weapon of moral power*. Ahmedabad, India: Navajivan Press.
Sheatsley, P. B. (1966). White attitudes toward the Negro. *Daedalus*, 95, 217-238.
Shridharani, Krishnalal. (1939). *War without violence*. New York: Harcourt, Brace.
Sivard, Ruth Leger. (1996). *World military and social expenditures 1996*. 16th Ed. Washington, DC: World Priorities.
Slemrod, Joel and Bakija, Jon. (1996). *Taxing ourselves: A citizen's guide to the great debate over tax reform*. Cambridge, MA: MIT Press.
Smart, Ninian. (1993). *Religions of Asia*. Englewood Cliffs, NJ: Prentice Hall.
Smith, Adam. (1759/1966). *The theory of moral sentiments*. New York: A.M. Kelley.
Social Security Administration. (2003, June). *Fast facts and figures about Social Security*. Baltimore, MD: SSA Press Office.
Staples, Brent. (2003). Coming to grips with the unthinkable in Tulsa. *New York Times*, March 16, p. 12.
Starr, Paul. (1997). An emerging Democratic majority. In Stanley B. Greenberg and Theda Skocpol (Eds.), *The new majority: Toward a popular progressive politics* (pp. 221-237). New Haven, CT: Yale University Press.
Stern, Jessica. (2003). *Terror in the name of God: Why religious militants kill*. New York: HarperCollins.
Strauss, David A. (1991). The law and economics of racial discrimination in employment: The case for numerical standards. *Georgetown Law Journal*, 79, 1619-1657.
Sullivan, Roger J. (1996). Introduction. In Immanuel Kant, *The metaphysics of morals*. Cambridge, United Kingdom: Cambridge University Press.
Sun, Lena H., Cohen, Sarah, and Salmon, Jacqueline L. (2002). Survey: Much of Sept. 11 donations remain unspent. *Las Vegas Review-Journal*, June 12, p. 1A.
Sunstein, Cass R. (Ed.). (1990). *Feminism and political theory*. Chicago, IL: University of Chicago Press.
Tec, Nechama. (1986). *When light pierced the darkness: Christian rescue of Jews in Nazi-occupied Poland*. New York: Oxford University Press.
Thurow, Lester C. (1996). The birth of a revolutionary class. *New York Times Magazine*, May 19.
Tolstoy, Leo. (1885). *What I believe*. London, United Kingdom: Elliot Stock.
U.S. Bureau of the Census. (2000, September 20). *Current population survey: Poverty thresholds in 1999, by size of family and number of related children under 18 years*. Revised September 26. Washington, DC: Author.
Van Parijs, Philippe. (2000). A basic income for all. *Boston Review*, October/November.
Wagner, David. (2000). *What's love got to do with it? A critical look at American charity*. New York: The New Press.
Webster's New World Dictionary. (1994). Third College Edition. New York: Prentice Hall.
White, Julie Ann. (2000). *Democracy, justice, and the welfare state: Reconstructing public care*. University Park, PA: Pennsylvania State University Press.
Worth, Roland H., Jr. (1997). *The Sermon on the Mount: Its Old Testament roots*. Mahwah, NJ: Paulist Press.

Name Index

Aaron, 5, 7
Aaron, Henry J., 65, 66, 207
Abel, 13
Abraham, x, 7, 8, 11, 12, 13, 172, 174, 175, 176, 203
Abramovitz, Mimi, 158, 207
Adler, Mortimer J., 211
Agag, King, 1
Ahab, King, 4
Allison, Dale C., Jr., 9, 10, 207
Alperovitz, Gar, 81, 207
Amalek, 1, 103
American Friends Service Committee, 132
Amnesty International, 132
Angell, Marcia, 118, 207
Associated Press, 139, 147, 148, 156, 157, 207
Atkinson, A.B., 88, 89, 207
Axinn, June, 44, 207

Baasha, King, 4
BAG SHI (Bundesarbeitsgemeinschaft der Sozialhilfeinitiativen), 89, 207
Bakija, Jon, 87, 213
Banks, Curtis, 188, 209
Barrett, Edith J., 147, 150, 208
Bauman, Zygmunt, 181, 186, 207
Beck, Allen J., 162, 210
Belkin, Lisa, 110, 111, 207
Berkowitz, Edward D., 51, 207
Berlin, Isaiah, 29, 31, 39, 207
Berman, Paul, 195, 196, 207
Bernard, Viola W., 187, 207
Bernhardt, Sergeant Michael, 187
Bindman, Andrew B., 160, 207
Blocker, H. Gene, 210
Bobo, Lawrence, 69, 208
Bok, Derek, 67, 106, 208
Bondurant, Joan V., 29, 37, 39, 40, 208

Bosworth, Barry P., 65, 207
Bowen, William G., 67, 106, 208
Brewer, Geoffrey, 79, 208
Browning, Christopher R., 184, 208
Buchanan, James M., 102, 153, 208
Burtless, Gary, 61, 64, 208
Bush, President George W., 113, 149, 150, 159, 160

Cain, 13
Camus, Albert, 173
Carroll, James, 16, 208
Carson, D.A., 10, 208
Century Foundation, 104, 208
Chapple, Christopher Key, 11, 208
Cohen, Sarah, 46, 213
Cohen, Wilbur J., 77, 81, 141, 208
Coleman, James, 66, 208
Coleman, Jennifer, 156, 208
Comstock, Craig, 207, 211
Congleton, Roger D., 102, 153, 208
Cook, Faye Lomax, 147, 150, 208

Danziger, Sheldon H., 208, 209, 211
Darwin, Charles, 169
David, King, 2, 6
Davis, Governor Gray, 47, 83
Dawood, N.J., xi, 172, 173, 208
Dershowitz, Alan M., x, 24, 45, 208
DeWitt, Larry, 80, 208
D'Souza, Dinesh, 63, 208

Edsall, Mary D., 138, 208
Edsall, Thomas Byrne, 138, 208
Edwards, Chilperic, 8, 9, 209
Egan, Timothy, 81, 209
Eichmann, Adolf, 191
Erikson, Erik H., 42, 209
Ezekiel, 5

215

Fackenheim, Emil L., 191, 192, 209
Fineman, Howard, 138, 209
Fish, Stanley, 56, 209
Fogelman, Eva, 193, 209
Fox, Emmet, 10, 209
Frankl, Viktor E., 202, 209
Friedman, Milton, 77, 81, 88, 140, 141, 208, 209
Funiciello, Theresa, 89, 91, 209

Gallup, George, Jr., 138, 139, 147, 149, 150, 209
Gandhi, Mohandas K., x, 20, 21, 25, 26, 30, 31, 33, 34, 36, 37, 38, 39, 40, 41, 42, 125, 194, 201, 209, 210
Garfinkel, Irwin, 62, 209
Gates, Henry Louis, Jr., 113, 209
Gilens, Martin, 151, 209
Goldhagen, Daniel Jonah, 179, 180, 181, 184, 187, 188, 189, 190, 209
Gore, Vice President Al, 140
Graetz, Michael J., 77, 209
Greenberg, Stanley B., 70, 140, 209, 213
Gross, Jean-Pierre, 83, 209

Haggstrom, David A., 160, 207
Halberstam, David, 179, 209
Haney, Craig, 188, 209
Hardy, Henry, 207
Harris, Louis, 148
Harrison, Paige M., 162, 210
Hawking, Stephen, 78
Hertz, J.H., 3, 21, 210
Hitler, Adolf, 180, 181, 188, 189, 190, 201, 203, 210
Holmes, Steven, 140, 210
The Holy Bible: King James Version, xi, 9, 210
Honderich, Ted, 201, 210
Hume, David, 53, 210
Hurrell, Andrew, 211
Hussein, Saddam, 133, 179

Isaac, 175

Jauhar, Sandeep, 157, 210
Jeremiah, 5
Jeroboam, 4
Jesus Christ, x, xi, 9, 10, 11, 12, 13, 14, 15, 16, 31, 35, 146, 172, 174, 176, 180, 191
Jewish Publication Society, xi, 1, 210

Job, 4, 105, 120, 171, 174, 199
John, 176
John the Baptist, 172
Jones, Hardy, 102, 210
Joshua, 1, 2

Kant, Immanuel, 26, 27, 28, 31, 32, 33, 36, 38, 42, 53, 54, 57, 99, 101, 127, 200, 201, 210, 213
Kelman, Herbert C., 183, 210
Kennedy, Senator Edward, 154
Kertzer, David I., 16, 210
King, Martin Luther, Jr., 39, 41, 56, 137
Klassen, William, 10, 210
Kluegel, James R., 69, 208
Kozol, Jonathan, 95, 210
Krebs, Hans-Peter, 89, 210
Kumarappa, Bharatan, 34, 36, 210
Kunstreich, Timm, 120, 181, 186, 210
Kushner, Harold S., 171, 173, 210

Ladd, John, 26, 210
Lagnado, Lucette, 47, 211
Lawrence, L.H., 183, 210
Lehman, Jeffrey S., 64, 211
Lelyveld, J., 187, 211
Leonhardt, David, 51, 211
Lerner, Melvin J., 22, 211
Levin, Henry M., 66, 211
Levin, Herman, 44, 207
Locke, John, 28, 82, 100, 145, 211
Longman, Phillip, 77, 157, 211
Luther, Martin, 190

Mahavira, 11
Mashaw, Jerry L., 77, 209
McLanahan, Sara, 62, 209
McVeigh, Timothy, 150
Merleau-Ponty, Maurice, 169, 211
Miles, Jack, 19, 211
Milgram, Stanley, 184-185, 188, 189, 211
Mill, John Stuart, 28, 35, 36, 200, 211
Miller, David, 108, 123, 131, 211
Mooney, Chris, 151, 211
Moore, Charles A., 10, 212
Moses, 1, 5, 6, 7, 13, 20, 172, 174, 175, 176
Muhammad, 172, 176, 177
Murray, Michael L., 89, 91, 211
Musto, David F., 45, 211

Name Index

Nanda, B.R., 37, 211
Nash, Gerald D., 207
Noah, 1, 3, 8, 176

Oliner, Pearl M., 193, 211
Oliner, Samuel P., 193, 211
Ontario Fair Tax Commission, 83, 84, 211
Opton, Edward M., Jr., 187, 211
Ottenberg, Perry, 187, 207

Paneloux, Father, 173
Parker, Hermione, 89, 211
Patterson, James T., 138, 212
Pear, Robert, 160, 212
Pechacek, Terry, 156
Pelton, Leroy H., 23, 30, 45, 72, 105, 116, 126, 128, 131, 134, 147, 163, 187, 194, 212
Peter, 15, 176
Pew Research Center, 138, 148, 212
The Physicians' Working Group for Single-Payer National Health Insurance, 161, 212
Picasso, Pablo, 78
Pius XII, Pope, 191
Posner, Richard, 63, 212
Potter, Will, 159, 212
Pritchard, James B., 10, 212
Pugach, Noel H., 207
Puit, Glenn, 114, 212
Purdum, Todd, 47, 83, 212

Radhakrishnan, Sarvepalli, 10, 212
Rawls, John, 28, 31, 38, 41, 99, 101, 102, 152, 153, 154, 212
Redl, Fritz, 187, 207
Rein, Harald, 89, 210
Rein, Martin, xi, 212
Reischauer, Robert D., 207
Rhys Williams, Lady Juliet, 89, 212
Riley, Governor Bob, 159
Roth, John K., 181, 184, 186, 190, 191, 212
Rousseau, Jean-Jacques, 28, 100, 101, 212
Rubenstein, Richard L., 173, 181, 184, 186, 190, 191, 192, 195, 212

Salmon, Jacqueline L., 46, 213
Samuel, 1
Sandefur, Gary D., 208, 209, 211
Sanford, Nevitt, 207, 211
Saul, King, 1, 103

Schieber, Sylvester J., 77, 212
Schindler, Oskar, 193, 194
Schmid, Randolph E., 118, 212
Schmidt, Peter, 81, 212
Schön, Donald A., xi, 212
Schopenhauer, Arthur, 28, 36, 53, 54, 55, 200, 213
Selingo, Jeffrey, 139, 213
The Sentencing Project, 162, 213
Seredi, Cardinal Justinian, 191
Sharp, Gene, 37, 213
Sheatsley, P.B., 138, 213
Shoven, John B., 77, 212
Shridharani, Krishnalal, 30, 34, 213
Sivard, Ruth Leger, 16, 213
Skinner, B.F., 171
Skocpol, Theda, 209, 213
Slemrod, Joel, 87, 213
Smart, Ninian, 10, 213
Smith, Adam, 53, 55, 213
Smith, Elizabeth H., 210
Smith, Ryan A., 69, 208
Social Security Administration, 157, 213
Staples, Brent, 111, 213
Starr, Paul, 69, 213
Stern, Jessica, 195, 213
Strauss, David A., 63, 64, 213
Sullivan, Roger J., 26, 213
Sun, Lena H., 46, 213
Sunstein, Cass R., 56, 213

Tec, Nechama, 193, 213
Thurow, Lester C., 141, 213
Tolstoy, Leo, x, 10, 20, 213
Tomasson, Richard F., 207

U.S. Bureau of the Census, 98, 213

Van Parijs, Philippe, 81, 213

Wagner, David, 122, 213
Weaver, R. Kent, 61, 64, 208
Webster's New World Dictionary, 36, 213
Weinberg, Daniel H., 208, 209, 211
Wells, John David, 144
White, Julie Ann, 56, 213
Wiener, Joshua M., 61, 64, 208
Woods, Ngaire, 211
Worth, Roland H., Jr., 9, 10, 12, 213

Zimbardo, Philip, 188, 209
Zimri, 4

Subject Index

abortion, 102, 125, 126
Acts, Book of, 15, 176
afterlife. *See* hereafter
Aid to Families with Dependent Children (AFDC), 61, 64, 94, 147
affirmative action policies, 17, 45, 67, 69, 102, 104-106, 108, 109, 114, 128, 129, 135, 139-140, 151; public opinion of, 69, 138-139, 149
aggregate reasoning, 60-64
ahimsa, 10, 11, 25, 29, 33, 36, 42, 194, 201, 202, 204
Al Qaeda, 133
animal treatment, 21, 54-55, 135

battered women's syndrome, 45, 116
Bible, ix-xi, 7, 8, 11-13, 15, 19, 22-24, 52, 104, 169, 174-177, 196, 197, 199. *See also* New Testament; Tanakh; Torah; *and under the specific titles of the books of the Bible*
black rage, 45, 46

capital punishment. *See* death penalty
causation: agents of, 116, 126, 156, 170, 190; and group differences, 67-69; motivational, 179, 188-189; obscuration of, 68-69
charity and sentiment, 46, 47, 122, 123, 127, 130
child welfare system, 72, 163
Church, the, 15, 16, 173, 190-191
civil disobedience, 30-31
civil rights movement, 39, 56, 137, 138
coercion and freedom. *See* freedom and coercion
community of unearned abundance, 81-83, 142-143
compensation, 3, 12, 22, 44, 46, 47, 50, 76, 79, 98, 102, 108, 109-115, 127, 134

compliance and complicity, 30, 33, 41, 62, 112, 125, 155, 183-191, 200, 203-205; of churches, 16, 190-191
constructive program, 36-38, 39, 41, 132
contract, social, 28, 38, 40-41, 99-103, 123, 142, 146, 152, 153, 175, 185, 202
Covenant, 174, 175, 202
criminal justice policy, 16, 18, 23, 45, 50, 115-117, 126-128, 162-163

Daniel, Book of, 172
death penalty, 3, 4, 17, 18, 20, 23, 32, 33, 38, 39, 45, 47, 102, 117, 125, 127, 128, 134, 135, 155, 199; public opinion of, 150-151
dehumanization, 187, 188
demogrant, 102
desert: for beliefs, 197; in the marketplace, 145, 152, 164; and merit, 108-109; and need, 49, 51-52, 74-75, 143, 146, 152, 153, 160, 161, 165; and noncooperation, 32-35; and nondiscrimination, 75-76, 81, 88, 98, 109, 122, 152; politics of, 137-142; principle of, 51-52, 101, 107, 108, 110, 111, 115, 117, 120, 121, 123, 137, 198. *See also* justice, individual-desert frame of; policies, desert-oriented
Deuteronomy, Book of, 1-4, 6, 7, 20, 21, 43, 175, 206
driver's license renewal, 63, 71, 106
drug prohibition laws, 39, 45, 68, 106, 116, 127, 162-163
drunk driving, 68-69

Ecclesiastes, Book of, 171
equality, 25, 28, 37, 59, 64, 66, 69, 73, 85, 96, 97, 103, 114-115, 123, 128, 135, 138, 151, 152, 163, 164

220 Frames of Justice

euthanasia, 125-126, 181, 186
Exodus, Book of, 1-6, 9, 15, 20, 21, 43, 54, 175
Ezekiel, Book of, 5

Five Books of Moses. *See* Torah
foreign policy, xi, 18, 41, 94, 129-135
formula of humanity. *See* humanity, formula of, Kant's
formula of universal law. *See* universal law, formula of, Kant's
freedom and coercion, 26-32, 33, 38, 39, 40, 42, 101, 127
functional desirability, 19-24, 154, 157-163

Galatians, Book of, 15
Genesis, Book of, 1, 3, 7, 8, 13, 175
genocide, 1-2, 16, 20, 115, 130, 169, 180, 181, 189, 201. *See also* Holocaust
God, x, 1-8, 11-15, 19-21, 23, 103, 191, 195, 196, 198, 200, 202-204; and desert, 170-174, 197, 199, 200; faith in, 169-177, 198; and the group frame, 173-175; and the hereafter, 14, 15, 172-173, 176, 177, 195, 197, 198, 203
group relevance, 65, 68, 78, 108

Hammurabi Code, 8, 9
health care policy, 17, 18, 22, 23, 40, 60, 95, 102, 104, 117-118, 123, 151, 153, 154-155, 160-164; public opinion of, 148-150, 159, 160
Hebrew Bible. *See* Tanakh
Hebrews, Book of, 15
hereafter, 14, 15, 172-173, 176, 177, 195, 197, 198, 203
Holocaust, x, 16, 24, 115, 174, 179, 183, 184, 186, 187, 189-191, 194, 196, 203, 205
homelessness, 40, 45, 93, 119-125, 128-129, 130, 143-145, 147, 154, 155, 158, 163, 164, 201, 203; public opinion of, 148, 159
human rights, 65, 67, 130, 132, 152
humanity, formula of, Kant's, 26, 53

incapacitation, 17, 115, 126, 127
Isaiah, Book of, 9
Israel(ites), 1, 4-6, 12-16, 18-21, 24, 103, 110, 112, 113, 173-176, 196

Israeli-Palestinian conflict, 16, 24, 134-135, 195

Jainism, 10, 11, 20, 25
Jeremiah, Book of, 5
Jew hatred, 15-16, 24, 179-182, 187-192
Jewish Bible. *See* Tanakh
Job, Book of, 4, 198
John, Book of, 9, 15, 172, 176
Joshua, Book of, 2
just-war doctrine, 104-105, 194
justice: as balance, 199, 204; biblical, 1-24; derivation of, 52-55; frames of, ix-xi, 11-12, 13-24, 99-103, 169, 177, 180, 188, 196, 199, 201, 204, 205; genesis of, xi, 12-14, 19; group frame of, ix, 1-9, 11-18, 20, 22, 24, 100-102, 114, 115, 133, 134, 140, 173, 174, 178, 182, 183, 189, 195-197, 199-201, 204, 205; individual, 1-9, 13, 14, 20, 21, 140, 141, 146, 177, 182, 183, 196; individual-desert frame of, ix, 3, 4, 8, 11-12, 14, 16-18, 22-24, 32-36, 38, 40, 41, 44, 51, 100-102, 107, 118, 122, 127, 133-135, 137, 140, 142, 145, 146, 150, 152, 155, 171-173, 175, 182, 183, 185, 192, 195-201, 204, 205; life-affirmation frame of, ix, 9-11, 12, 14, 18, 19, 22-24, 33, 36, 40, 41, 100-103, 107, 117-135, 146, 150, 151, 153, 154, 158, 159, 161, 164, 182, 183, 193, 198, 199, 201-205; passion for, 20, 55, 202, 204; procedural, 3, 13, 18, 23, 25, 73, 145; and religion, 196-200; sense of, ix, 7-9, 11-14, 19-24, 36, 52-55, 70, 100, 101, 117, 122, 134, 135, 137, 141, 146, 154, 165, 170, 174, 176, 177, 182, 183, 192, 195, 196, 198, 199, 202-205

Kings, First Book of, 4, 5; Second Book of, 19
Koran, ix-xi, 169, 172-177, 196-200

Leviticus, Book of, 2, 6, 10, 20, 21, 43, 52, 54, 146, 175
liberal philosophy, ix, 25-26, 28, 29, 31, 33, 38, 41, 59, 60, 67, 68, 71-73, 75, 78, 80-81, 85, 89, 96, 103, 106, 115, 152, 195; ambiguities of, 101-102; and constructive program, 37-38, 39;

Subject Index

as a moral philosophy, 73, 88, 94; Democratic, 138
life affirmation, x, 192, 193, 195; principle of, ix, 9-11, 18, 20, 21, 25, 32, 33, 36, 54, 99, 101, 106, 107, 113-114, 115, 117, 118, 122, 125-128, 131, 134, 151, 152, 178, 182, 193, 194, 200, 202, 205, 206; political strategies toward, 146, 151-165. *See also* justice, life-affirmation frame of; policies, life-affirmation-oriented
Luke, Book of, 9

Mahabharata, 10, 11
Matthew, Book of, 9, 14, 31, 33, 146, 172, 176
meaning, search for, 19, 169, 174, 202-204
means and ends, ix, 73, 106, 107, 173, 183, 191-192, 194, 198, 199, 201, 203, 205; principle of, 25-27, 29, 32, 38, 42, 53, 127
Medicaid, 118, 147, 154
Medicare, 17, 84, 91, 106, 118, 142, 149, 153, 154, 155, 160-163
mental defenses, 45-46, 50, 116
merit and desert, 108-109
Montgomery Bus Boycott, 30
Moses, Five Books of. *See* Torah
Mylai massacre, 183, 187

narrow reasoning, 47-52, 54, 56, 58, 106, 108, 139, 142, 143, 154, 156-157, 160; and sentiment, 47-52
Nazi Europe, 16, 191, 193, 196, 203
Nazi Germany, 112-113, 115, 120, 179-184, 186-194, 196
necessity, 19-21, 29, 42, 104, 108, 125, 131, 133-135, 158-160, 162, 177-178, 180-184, 186, 195, 204
need and desert, 49, 51-52, 74-75, 143, 146, 152, 153, 160, 161, 165
need and nondiscrimination, 56, 74, 75, 78, 88, 103, 107, 152, 158
New Testament, x, xi, 9, 12, 14, 172, 176, 177, 196, 198-200. *See also* Bible; *and under the specific titles of the books of the Bible*
noncooperation, 30-32, 39, 131, 132, 192, 194; and desert, 32-35
nondiscrimination, 25, 56, 64, 65, 67, 73, 75, 78, 82, 83, 85, 88, 89, 92, 98, 99, 102, 103, 107, 109, 115, 121-124, 128-132, 137, 140, 146, 151-153, 162, 164; and desert, 75-76, 81, 88, 98, 109, 122, 152; and group frame, 102; and need, 56, 74, 75, 78, 88, 103, 107, 152, 158; promotion of, 94-98, 130, 145, 206
nonviolence, philosophy of, ix, x, 20, 21, 25-26, 28-39, 41, 42, 125, 194, 205
Numbers, Book of, 5

Old Testament. *See* Tanakh
original position, Rawls', 28, 38, 41, 99, 101, 102, 103, 135, 154

Pentateuch. *See* Torah
policies: of compensation, 109-115; desert-oriented, 16-18, 23, 77-78, 80, 96, 103, 105, 107-117, 118, 135, 145, 150, 154, 181, 186; group-oriented, 16-18, 20, 22, 67, 69, 78, 102-111, 114, 121, 135, 137, 140, 141, 154, 191; and the Holocaust, 190, 191; life-affirmation-oriented, 18, 22-24, 39-40, 117-135, 150, 154, 164, 200, 203, 205, 206; and sentiment, 44-52, 55-58, 105-106, 108; and social science research, 59-72
policy frames, x, xi, 11-12, 18, 99, 157
power dynamic, 188, 199, 204
principle and sentiment, 43-58, 86, 105-106, 110, 122, 125, 137, 140, 174, 193, 198, 201, 202, 205
Proverbs, Book of, 10, 21, 175
Psalms, Book of, 9
public education, 66, 69, 95-96, 104, 105, 128, 129, 138, 141-144, 150, 152, 154, 159
public opinion research, 69-70, 138-140, 147-151, 153, 159, 164, 172, 183

reparation. *See* compensation
rescue and resistance, 191, 192-194, 196, 203, 205
restitution. *See* compensation
retribution and revenge, 15, 17, 23, 32-35, 39, 47, 115-117, 126, 127, 173, 180, 182, 194-195, 196, 197, 199, 200, 203, 204
Revelation, Book of, 14, 15, 172-173
Romans, Book of, 15

Samuel, First Book of, 1, 2; Second Book of, 2, 6
selection and exclusion, 175-177, 191, 196, 197, 199, 200, 204, 206; in Nazi Germany, 179-183, 186
self-made wealth, myth of, 142-146
self-preservation, 100, 170, 204
sentiment. *See* charity and sentiment; narrow reasoning, and sentiment; policies, and sentiment; principle and sentiment
September 11, 2001 attacks, 46-47, 110-112, 133, 150, 195
Sermon on the Mount, x, 9, 10, 16, 20, 25, 33, 36, 101, 191, 198
"sin" taxes, 45, 48, 83-84, 106, 141, 156-157, 159
slavery, 1, 21, 107; reparations for, 113-114
social contract. *See* contract, social
social dividend. *See* universal social dividend and taxation system
social engineering, 39, 41, 105, 106, 125, 158, 181
social policies. *See* policies
social science research, ix, 22, 48, 59-72, 106, 193
Social Security (OASDI), 17, 44, 50, 51, 63, 65, 76-81, 91, 92, 102, 104, 106, 110, 123, 124, 129, 140, 142-144, 150, 157, 158, 160, 162
Sodom and Gomorrah, x, 7, 8, 14
stereotypes, 17, 45, 48, 50, 51, 62, 64, 65, 67, 72, 78, 105, 108, 116, 119, 121, 143, 146, 150, 151, 169, 179, 180, 182, 187, 188; statistically valid, 62-65, 68, 78, 105, 116
suicide bombers, 194, 195, 201
Supplemental Security Income (SSI), 64, 65, 75, 91, 147, 157, 160

talion, law of, 3, 4, 8, 9, 11, 14, 17, 115, 117, 197
Talmud, 200

Tanakh, x, xi, 1, 2, 4, 9, 10, 12-15, 19, 21, 35, 172, 174, 177, 196, 197, 199, 200. *See also* Bible; Torah; *and under the specific titles of the books of the Bible*
tax breaks, 17-18, 45, 47, 51, 80, 83, 84, 91, 104, 106, 114-115, 129, 141, 157-158, 160, 161
taxation, 38-39, 44, 45, 48, 66, 76-77, 78, 81, 83, 95-96, 112, 128, 130, 140-141, 144, 147-150, 156-159, 161-162, 164; fairness in, 83-88, 89, 91-94, 98, 130, 151, 154, 158, 159; negative income, 87-88, 90, 141; progressive income, 83, 85, 87, 90, 91; proportional (flat) income, 86-87, 89, 90, 129; regressive income, 86
Temporary Assistance for Needy Families program (TANF), 17, 60-61, 64, 65, 75, 91, 105, 108, 125, 128, 147, 157, 160
Ten Commandments, 2, 4, 8, 13, 175
terrorism, 22, 46, 47, 110, 133, 134, 150, 194-196, 201, 205
Thessalonians, Book of, 15
Torah, 1, 4, 6, 8, 9, 20, 21, 35, 43, 44, 54, 92, 146, 175, 176, 196, 202. *See also* Bible; Tanakh; *and under the specific titles of the books of the Bible*
Tulsa Race Riot, 111-112

universal law, formula of, Kant's, 27, 28, 31-33, 38, 99, 102, 200
universal principle of right, Kant's, 26
universal social dividend and taxation system, 88-94, 102, 124, 125, 129-130, 160-162
urban survival syndrome, 46
utility, 23-24, 28, 41-42, 85, 101, 103, 104, 108, 118, 135, 191, 200, 202

vegetarianism, 22, 55

White Rose, 192-193, 194